to Marie
with love

Frank

Aug '86

Frank Arneil Walker, Emeritus Professor of the University of Strathclyde in Glasgow, Scotland, is an architect and architectural historian. He has written extensively in his academic field and is the author or co-author of some twenty books and numerous academic papers.

In 1959 he made his first visit to what was then Yugoslavia, travelling in the interior and along the Adriatic. Captivated by the scenery, architecture and not least the people of the Dalmatian coast, he has returned almost every year since. In 1991 he and his wife Jasna found a second home on the Croatian island of Korčula, fabled birth-place of that most celebrated of travellers, Marco Polo. There each year they spend the spring and autumn months. Passing lazy days, they

> "…eat, drink, sing, play, bathe, sleep, eat again,
> Or read, or wanton in the Muses' train."

Well, perhaps not sing.

BLACK ISLAND
Memories from the Adriatic

Frank Arneil Walker

BLACK ISLAND
Memories from the Adriatic

Vanguard Press

Kneeling by R.S. Thomas
Reproduced by kind permission of J.M. Dent, A division of The
Orion Publishing Group.

A CIP catalogue record for this title is
available from the British Library

ISBN 1 84386 288 3

*Vanguard Press is an imprint of
Pegasus Elliot MacKenzie Publishers Ltd.*
www.pegasuspublishers.com

First Published in 2006

**Vanguard Press
Sheraton House Castle Park
Cambridge England**

Printed & Bound in Great Britain

IN MEMORIAM

Marko Kalogjera
Katica Mirošević Batistić
Ivo Jeričević

ACKNOWLEDGEMENTS

It is more than a quarter of a century since I paused under the almond tree, checking my directions and catching my breath in the summer heat, before pushing open the gate onto the Batistić family terrace. We had come, my wife Jasna and children Davor and Dara, to spend our summer holiday in Lumbarda on the Adriatic island of Korčula. Since that first visit Jasna and I have returned every year but one, staying with the Batistić family until, with their help, we had found our own *vikendica*, extending our visits as the course of our working lives permitted so that at length we have been able to enjoy each year's spring and autumn on Korčula. For this undiminishing pleasure I want to thank Niko and Katica Batistić (Belo). We have known and loved four generations of their family, we have become friends of their friends, we have picked the Batistić grapes and drunk their wine, we have picked the Batistić olives and cooked with their wonderful oil, we have sat at their table and still do as regular and always warmly welcomed guests. Without the hospitality and enduring friendship of this family our lives would have been the poorer – and this book would never have been written.

The Batistić kindness passes from generation to generation. Niko and Katica's three children now have their own families and they too have welcomed us into their homes. My thanks to them: to Nikša and Jagoda in Lumbarda, Mirjana and Nebojša in Medvinjak and Vesna and Tomislav in Zagreb. Particular thanks to Nebojša for smoothing some paths through Korčula society and to Vesna for help with the translation of Goran Duka's verse in Chapter 5.

There are, of course, many more whose friendship and hospitality Jasna and I have been privileged to enjoy over the years – too many to be acknowledged by name here. But one or two must be mentioned. The Rajić family – Marjan, Dragica, Josip and not least Blaženka – our immediate neighbours, who as refugees from Bosnia have made a new home in Lumbarda; it may be true for some that 'good fences make good neighbours' but for us, on the contrary, it is a shared courtyard and open doors. In Prigradica, Jakša Kalogjera, 'Uncle Jakša', whose reminiscences drawn from a long life have held us in thrall; stories, now comic, now tragic. In Dubrovnik, in her narrow little house squeezed into the incredibly picturesque quarter of Brsalje, Marija Kralj, has so often been our gentle landlady when we passed through *en route* to Korčula. How many times we have enjoyed cake, coffee and conversation with her, hardly believing her eighty and more years, wishing but never daring to call her 'Aunt'.

I should like to express thanks to Goran Duka for permission to incorporate some lines from his text written for the pageant *Povratak Marka Pola* (The Return of Marko Polo) which is performed annually at the start of the summer season in Korčula and which forms the core theme of chapter 5. I am also indebted to Boris Marelić for the invitation to the party which is the subject of chapter 6. I trust he will excuse some of the liberties I have taken in describing this occasion. I have changed the names of most of the guests who attended this enjoyable event but, if there are those who think they recognize themselves, again I can only hope that they do so with pleasure. Thanks too to Tino and Davor who in their respective internet shops in Korčula were always helpful with computer problems.

I am immensely grateful to Margaret, Andrew's widow, and to Ian and Susan (these are not, of course, their real names but they know who they are) for permission to include in chapter 4 *verbatim* passages from the e-mails we shared at a time of great personal stress to them and their families. I count it is a measure of our long-standing love that they have so willingly allowed these words to appear.

Thanks to J.M. Dent, a division of The Orion Publishing Group for permission to include the poem 'Kneeling' by R.S.Thomas.

I am grateful to Pegasus Elliot Mackenzie Publishers Ltd. for reading and accepting my manuscript. Particular thanks to Max Bédar for his editorial co-operation and for the speed with which he and his colleagues worked to achieve publication. The photographs were taken by my wife, Jasna. The occasional sketches are my own. So, too, are any factual or textual errors.

This book was written intermittently over a period of many months, a fact which may be evident from the episodic nature of the text. It begins in arrival and ends in departure but there is no strictly sequential narrative in between. Instead, each chapter tells its own story. What pervades the telling – and what matters – is the place and the people, Korčula and the Korčulani. Time has passed, of course, and those events and encounters of which I have written are, as they must be, locked in that past. There is, too, a deceit in memory – though not so much, I hope, as to abuse the truth. What happens in the mind happens too. I think of some lines of T.S. Eliot –

'See, now they vanish,
The faces and the places, with the self which, as it could, loved them'

But then I remember – the words remain.

PRELUDE

To begin with a cliché. It is the banal wisdom of bar-stool philosophers, patronising uncles and Presbyterian ministers that 'life is a journey'. Not that everyone, of course, agrees on where we all might be going. Not that everyone cares. But for some, existence takes on a teleological cast: destination heaven – or hell. The journey becomes a kind of pilgrim's progress and life itself no more than a test bed for eternity or perhaps for a reincarnated second go. For others, there is only oblivion; no harps, no flames and certainly no question of changing trains. Fate issues its tickets to ride – single journey, non-transferable, mystery tour.

I have never quite been able to make up my mind about this. Is there a holy city terminus, a new Jerusalem at the end of the line, or will the train simply run off the rails and plunge into the abyss? Either way, whatever lies at journey's end, the getting there is all we can know. Cliché or not, life *is* a journey and it's the journey itself that matters. We may plan our itinerary, lodge credit where we can, be as circumspect as fate permits or we may simply seize the day for fear there will be no tomorrow. And I have to admit that whatever the equivocation of earlier years the older I become the more *carpe diem* seems like a good idea. It's not that I feel a desperate last-minute need to top up the credit balance (though, God knows, I should and I have certainly not given up on the gamble on eternity) but rather that, as the compartment empties, what's left of the journey seems more and more precious. Struggling to hold on to a present that is now as diminishing as it has always been elusive, I realise, like Stevenson, that 'I travel not to go anywhere, but to go. I travel for travel's sake.' The journey is the thing. 'The great affair is to move.' Time and tide…

Unlike Stevenson, we most of us travel not with a donkey but, so to say, with a doll – a Russian doll. Every life's journey has its own inner journeys. Yet it is a paradoxical truth that the signpost to these excursions through spiritual time and space may itself have been some emotionally orientating experience of travel made in the real world of minutes and miles. For me there have been two such journeys. Both were made on the threshold of manhood, both were shared with the woman I loved and still love, and both in their different ways have directed the course of my life.

I am an architect. Since the age of twelve it is what I have wanted to be. No doubt this had something to do with my father being a joiner or perhaps with the example of an older cousin who preceded me in studying and training for the profession. At any rate, I had few if any doubts and was confident enough in my own desire to persuade a classics-orientated headmaster that art should figure in my senior school curriculum. In due course I entered architecture school in Glasgow, fulfilled the five years of full-time study and did well enough to win a modest scholarship which offered me the prospect of several weeks private study abroad. Welcome as this good fortune was it was hardly the most defined of opportunities and I found it difficult to decide where to go. Finally, however, much against the traditional preference for classical Italy or Greece, I resolved to visit Czechoslovakia.

A number of factors influenced what was then certainly an unconventional decision. What kind of country was it, I wondered, which, despite its size and ill-perceived remoteness, had caused such moral embarrassment to us in Britain in the years preceding the Second World War? Lying at the heart of Europe, infinitely complex in its historical and cultural subtleties, that 'far-away country' exerted a peculiar attraction. There was, too, a certain appeal to the traveller's vanity. In 1960 there was a seductive *frisson* in going behind the Iron Curtain – gun-belted guards, machine-gun towers, darkened railway carriages; crossing the frontier, I was to discover, did indeed afford a macabre thrill. And there was a still more personal attraction: the girl with whom I planned to travel, Jasna (she was later to be my wife), had Czech forebears. Her father's family had originated in Bohemia, though he had been born and brought up in that part of the Austro-Hungarian empire that was to become part of Yugoslavia. But none of these factors would have been of much consequence had it not been for a more compelling architectural reason.

At college, a tutor, who was later to become my colleague and friend, spoke of Prague with infectious enthusiasm; it was, he said, a never-to-be-forgotten architectural experience. Memories converted him into an eloquent panegyrist, for as a German Jew fleeing Berlin he had lived for several years in Czechoslovakia during the 1930s and still saw the city in a mystical afterglow. I was persuaded – not least by his talk of an 'architectural experience'. Not that I was entirely sure what he meant by this phrase. Until then architecture had been for me a job, a profession, a career. What was this strange almost poetic advocacy with its promise of revelation? I felt myself the earnest believer always a little discomfited by talk of blinding Damascus road conversion. Disturbed, but captivated and curious, I found irresistibly attractive the idea that architecture, *pace* all considerations of utility and firmness, might, in its very perception, attain some quasi-religious justification. The thought that architecture could, as it were, be 'saved' by aesthetic grace alone invaded my imagination. If the streets of Prague offered this experience then I would go.

And so I made that journey.

The impact of the grey city, melancholy as it then was with Communist piety, was stunning. Time has dulled memory's diary but flashes of recollection still bring back the immanent delight of the place, walking through the cobbled shadows of Staroměstské náměstí or struggling up Nerudova in a delicious afternoon sweat. The senses mingle in the memory: the smells of dank crumbling stucco, of brown coal burning, the always menacing sight of black Tatras swooping past the kerb, the sharp taste of Chinese orange juice in some back-street *kavárna*, the sound of trams rattling through Malostranské náměstí. But it is the architecture that hits hardest. The very fabric of the city, woven over centuries, wraps itself around you. Vast tracts of the city stretching from the hectic activity of Wenceslas Square, through the Old Town, across the Vltava, and up the steep winding streets to the cool courtyards on Hradčany, remain almost exactly as they were two, even three, hundred years ago.

Shadowy streets and lanes, cut from the dense mass of stone and stucco, are voids full of palpable substance – urban space, eddying in medieval streams or lapping luxuriantly along the rolling mouldings of Jesuit churches, tangible and intoxicating. In this 'architectural experience' my feet ached and my young head swam as never before or since.

Day by day I made discoveries. The spires and vaults of Gothic; the mesmerizing elliptical geometries of Bohemian Baroque; exuberant Secessionist facades, alive with sculpture and colourful fresco; the few facetted gems of Czech Cubism; the ascetic aesthetic of Thirties Functionalism. All this was, however, subsumed in one grander discovery. For the first time I knew what architecture meant, I felt its power and knew I had chosen correctly. That journey to Prague had set the working itinerary for my own life's journey.

The year before, however, thinking little about architecture but a good deal about sun and sea, I had made another journey, one that was to prove scarcely less significant in its impact on my developing life. Again it was an adventure, again I travelled with Jasna, and again it took me to what was then discouragingly demonized as Eastern Europe. This time the journey was to a country then called Yugoslavia.

This trip too had its personal aspect. Jasna had been born in Zagreb and had spent the first few years of her life there only coming to Scotland at the end of the Second World War. Her Yugoslav father, entrapped in the ambiguous *demi-monde* of survival and resistance, had perished at the hands of the *Ustaša* fascist government, tried and executed for crimes against the state all in the space of twenty-four hours, leaving her Scottish mother alone with three young children. The family survived and when the war was over and Jasna's mother was presented with the option of repatriation all four travelled to a new life in the United Kingdom. Not for ten years were they able to return but as the Communist curtain drawn across Europe grew flimsier in the Balkan wings and Tito's Yugoslavia declared Jasna's father to be among those victims of fascism who had fallen during the war, Jasna and her mother revisited friends and relations in Zagreb. A few years later, intent on seeing more of her native country, Jasna made a second trip, this time with her older sister, Dubravka – and me. She had forgotten all but a few words of the language she had spoken in her early childhood. I knew nothing of Serbo-Croat. But Duba was still fluent; she would be our interpreter, act as our guide in Zagreb and guard Jasna's honour – chaperone and *cicerone*, we joked, deliberately rhyming the pronunciation.

The plan was ambitious. In a summer break limited by a tight budget and our respective commitments to work and study we hoped to spend time in each of the country's six republics. We managed five (though, to be truthful, Slovenia passed in a morning mist, dimly seen from the train) Not bad, nevertheless, in just under three weeks. More than enough to convince me that I must return. And return I did: for since then not a year has passed without a trip to the Adriatic. That first Balkan excursion was the beginning of an obsession, the first sign-post on a longer, lifetime's journey in Illyria.

We reached Zagreb by train after one of those better-to-be-forgotten, day-and-night, trans-European experiences which even the stoical optimism of youth would have found hard to bear had it not been for those moments of relief from the relentless monotony of economy class travel provided by an *ad hoc* compartment feast of bread, beer, salami and chocolate, or the unexpected conversation shared with a fellow traveller, or, best of all, the rare reprieve of sleep. In Zagreb, however, we found a bed, a big soft Biedermeier bed into which we sank, at once exhausted and excited, to dream of the unknown world that lay ahead of us.

We were in the home of Jasna's uncle and aunt. They made us welcome but it did not take me long to realise that life for them was not easy. Jasna's uncle Josip, *stric* Pepo, was too ill to work; for much of the day he lay on a couch, hollow-cheeked and grey, every now and then shaken by a racking cough. Her aunt, *teta* Zdenka, held things together, managing somehow to make ends meet – just – by the little money she earned from repairing nylon stockings. The house, too, like the family, had fallen on hard times: a once-smart detached villa not far from the centre of town, its red-tiled roof, unusually and impractically Italianate in the Zagreb climate, was in disrepair, the paintwork had not been touched for more than twenty years, the parquet floors squeaked with reproach, torn squares of newspaper served as toilet paper. In those difficult days a shortage of urban housing imposed shared occupancy on many and Jasna's relatives did not escape this humiliating invasion of privacy, though the old lady who lived in the room across the hall from the kitchen and kept very much to herself was accepted by the family with respect and friendship. Life in communist Yugoslavia after Tito's break from the Cominform might be lived with a measure of political independence or so-called 'non-aligned' freedom, but it was still a hard life. Not only were the consumer goods of the west largely unobtainable – and those that were, unaffordable – but many of those things we had always assumed to be the indispensable necessities of civilized life had had to be forsworn.

Yet we were welcomed with unstinted kindness. We were given that bed; thinking back, it must have been the biggest and best in the house. We were given a key and could come and go as we wished. *Teta* Zdenka made her special *štrudl od višnja*, cherry strudel, for us, rolling and stretching the pastry across the kitchen table until it was so thin that you could see the wood grain below; the rare real thing. We were family, of course. Or at least, Jasna and Duba were. But there was more to our welcome than kindred affection, or so it seemed to me. Perhaps it was my semi-detached role that led me to sense that besides kindness there was something else, something that I felt to be akin to gratefulness; it was as if we were being thanked for coming, for remembering and reinvigorating family ties. To be conscious of this, when I was not yet, strictly speaking, a member of the family, was an unmerited privilege. I knew myself to be indebted; I know it still. Perhaps, indeed, it was that heartfelt obligation, so keenly apprehended at the very outset of the journey, as much as the memorable moments that were yet to come, that was to bring me back again and again. I like to believe, too, that what I write now about these and later times is written with thanks.

We spent almost a week in Zagreb, the longest stop-over of the trip. There were friends and more relatives to be visited, and there were sights to be seen. Seventeen storeys above what was then known as Trg Republike, Republic Square, but has since reverted to its earlier name of Trg Bana Jelačić, from the rooftop terrace of the first, and at that time the only, high-rise office building in town (with some understandable pretension it was called *neboder*, skyscraper) we looked down on the spreading city. To the north, on rising ground, were Kaptol and Gornji Grad, the two contiguous, though for centuries administratively separate, settlements that form Zagreb's historic core; one flanked by towered walls and dominated by the Cathedral, the other, the Upper Town, a cluster of narrow cobbled streets gathered around the Church of St Mark. On flat land to the south lay the gridded streets of the late nineteenth century Lower Town – shops, apartment houses, parks, museums, theatres – and beyond that the rapidly developing districts of New Zagreb, spaciously laid out and boldly traversed east-west by the arrow-straight boulevards of socialist planning, Ulica proletarskih brigada, Proletarian Brigade Street, and Avenija bratstva i jedinstva, Brotherhood and Unity Avenue. Further off, glinting in the sunlight, the slow curve of the Sava river marked what was then the built-up extent of the city's southern expansion. We explored much of all this. We climbed up the steps to Dolac, the city's main open-air market, on through the candle-lit vault of Kamena vrata into the Old Town lanes and then, dropping in a funicular box-car to Tomićeva, back downhill again. On the tree-lined streets and squares of Donji Grad we wandered aimlessly from café to café. When we were too tired to walk any further or had to pay another visit to an aunt or friend of the family somewhere in the suburbs, we would take the tram, braving the inevitable crush with its gratuitous intimacies perfumed with cheap scent, garlic sausage and sweat.

Towards the end of our stay, accompanied by a friend of Jasna's sister, we escaped to the country. At Viktor's suggestion we set out to visit his mother who, with the help of a brother, worked a small farm a few hours distant from the city. The trip entailed a late-afternoon bus journey that took us deep into Zagorje, the hilly agricultural land that lies to the north of Zagreb and is the rural heartland of Catholic Croatia. By the time we arrived at our destination – or, rather, at the point beyond which there were no longer any roads suitable for cars let alone buses –

it was night. Now we walked, climbing for a time up through still woods into the moonlight before plunging down again along muddy paths through the valley mists. At length, tired but exhilarated by our trek, we reached a darkened cottage. Viktor's mother was roused – there were, of course, no telephones to warn her of our coming – introductions were made, paraffin lamps lit and within minutes we were sitting down to a late supper of chopped ham in sour cream with bread and beer. Soon, buried in goose-down quilts, we were deep in sleep.

I have only a dim recollection of the next morning's events. With a shudder of perverse pleasure I can recall washing and shaving in ice-cold water. I have no idea what we ate for breakfast nor whether it began, as I was later to discover it often did in rural Yugoslavia, with the more or less obligatory shot of *rakija*. I suppose we must have spent some time exploring the farm and its surroundings, though only some abrupt excursions into the privacy of the maize fields remain vivid – a memory that makes me think the day probably did start with brandy. Fortunately lunch proved easier to cope with than the ham, sour cream, beer and brandy of the previous twelve hours. Chicken soup followed by boiled chicken, potatoes and cabbage (all eaten from the same soup-plate) – wholesome and familiar enough, even if for Jasna the meal had been rendered rather problematically palatable since the very bird we were eating was the one Viktor's mother had only an hour or so earlier called to her by name before wringing the unsuspecting creature's neck. Lunch over, it was time to leave; not this time on foot but in the family's pony-and-trap. With Viktor's brother holding the reins with a straight-backed balanced assurance that eluded the rest of us thrown together and apart by the unpredictable jolting of the track, we lurched through the afternoon heat. Sometimes we could see for miles across rolling meadows, sometimes, despite our elevated position, tall fields of maize or sunflowers blocked our view. Every now and then we passed a cottage; some were silent, the peasant family at work somewhere in the fields, but at one we were offered a slice of freshly made pumpkin pie to eat on the journey. At length, after well over an hour, we arrived at the local railway halt whence by slow train, on slatted bench seats every bit as uncomfortable as the ride from the farm, we returned to Zagreb.

Next day we took a different train, our destination Belgrade. This was (or so I contrived to believe) Agatha Christie's 'Orient Express', it was Graham Greene's 'Stamboul Train', and though our journey would be over in a few hours, we imagined ourselves *en route* to the edge of the continent. We were travelling east, crawling through the endlessly flat fertile fields of Slavonia along the southern edge of Central Europe's Pannonian Plain. Time passed and in the miasma of heat the scenery remained unchanged. The compartment filled with the sweet conspiratorial smoke of Turkish tobacco. No-one talked. We had given up on conversation with our three travelling companions who, all male, moustached, black-eyed and inscrutably Balkan, their language and nationality a mystery, were evidently in some kind of protracted European transit. We read. We slept. Read again. Sometimes we simply stared out at the horizon sliding slowly past us. But each time when we looked up from our book or awoke suddenly or caught a fleeting reflection passing across the compartment window, we were at once aware that our fellow passengers were watching us. They returned our quick cautious smiles, clearly amused at our western inability to hold their gaze for more than a moment. I suppose that our clothes, the books we were reading and the few words that we did speak betrayed us as the real strangers on the train; like it or not, it was we not they who were different, we who attracted attention. But these unabashed stares were a new experience. Read at first as hostile and intrusive, they made one feel uneasy and vulnerable. But taken up as a challenge, as we later learned to do, they were no more than an exchange of honest curiosity. For now, however, trapped in our Anglo-Saxon reserve, we looked away, hiding in the wide open spaces of the landscape beyond the window. Not until we reached Belgrade and found ourselves struggling to make headway down a platform thronging with the obsessive chaos of arrival and departure did we realise that both timidity and self-consciousness had gone.

Of that first visit to Belgrade I remember little. Perhaps because we spent only two nights there (though the sight and sound of cockroaches scuttling under the duck-boards of the showers in the youth hostel where we stayed is vivid still), perhaps because we knew no-one and had no relatives or friends to welcome us and put us at our ease, perhaps because, although I have returned on a number of occasions since, I have never got to know the city in the way repeated visits have familiarised me with Zagreb; perhaps in the end it is the very passage of time which has, like the ubiquitous cyrillic script that adds its runic carapace to the Serbian language, raised a barrier to memory and understanding. Cyrillic, indeed, is perhaps the strongest memory: newspapers, magazines, posters, shop signs and neon signs, epigraphs and menus – all alien, intriguing, but impenetrable. Belgrade was exotic; it seemed more Slav.

From the walls of the Kalemegdan fortress, looking down on the confluence of the Sava and Danube rivers and the endless plain beyond, it was easy to sense the Serbs' frontier mentality, their ambivalent edginess. Here had been the border between Rome and the barbarian world. Here for centuries Orthodox Christianity had confronted the Ottoman Empire and the Islamic advance into Europe. And here, now, even allowing for the ideological windbreak that Titoism afforded, one could still feel the cold blast of totalitarian communism blowing from the east. Belgrade, literally 'the white city', blushed red. Were its ponderous red tramcars a political statement? The red flags and red stars on the rooftops certainly were. And so was the new red architecture which from the late 1940s had been appearing in the city. Downtown, the immensely wide concave front of the Dom Sindikata embraced Marx and Engels Square with sullen gravity. The same slow-curving facades, the same relentless repetition, the same symmetries shaped the Presidium Building in New Belgrade out across the river. Not by any means the most banal examples of Eastern Europe's addiction to Socialist Realism, but an architecture none the less sterile and cold.

Food, on the other hand, was hot. We ate daringly and well. After an innocent *čorba*, as nourishing as every Jewish mother's chicken soup, the palate would be attacked by a fiery bowl of *paprikaš* or a heaped platter of strongly spiced *čevapčići* straight from the grill. Counteracting this might be a cold beer or, better still, a glass of *ajran*, a deliciously cooling dilution of yoghurt available in one form or another east from Serbia as far as India.

And finally, of course, the sweet finish of honey-soaked *baklava*. Fortunately, in the gastronomic geography of the Balkans there are no borders. In Belgrade, Budapest and Istanbul are only a recipe away.

Macedonia, however, was a long night's journey to the south. Back in Belgrade station the concourse was littered with the human detritus of travel. Families, engulfed in luggage, arguing amongst themselves, sharing a makeshift meal or momentarily adrift on the restless surface of sleep. Backpackers packing and repacking, spreading their maps as if to be reassured that tomorrow, a day's travel on, they would reach a better, cleaner, more comfortable world. Gypsies begging; men legless or deformed, women desperate, the children dark angels of deceit. People queuing. People drinking. People going nowhere. Off-street vagrants looking for a night's sanctuary, glamourless prostitutes touting for the night's work, sellers of newspapers, sunflower seeds, flowers, all in search of the dinar – or, if they were lucky, the dollar. We picked our way carefully through these hazards, avoiding eye contact, aware again of our vulnerability. Only on the platform did things grow calmer and for a moment I had the impression that by passing through the ticket barrier we had crossed a frontier, exchanging anarchy for order. But the illusion was short-lived. Confusion over our ticket numbering entailing an incoherent dispute with the ticket collector and an understandably aggrieved Bulgarian couple forced to vacate what finally turned out to be our compartment, the realization that mineral water was the only sustenance available on board, and an exploratory, instantly constipating glance at the toilet facilities, restored cynicism. Too tired to undress, we tumbled into our couchette bunks. As the night train to Niš lumbered out of the darkened city I began to wonder just how 'Balkan' our journey might become.

At Niš, the train divided. While the *wagons-lits* of the Orient Express swung east to Sofia to arrive eventually at Istanbul, we continued south. Morning revealed a mountainous Macedonian landscape. I fancied myself in the land of Alexander and Aristotle – a delusion that did not last long. It was much more like Turkey: groves of poplars lining the river courses, the white shafts of minarets marking the villages. It may once have been Greek, 'the advanced line of defence', as Polybius called it, protecting first Hellenic and later Byzantine culture against invaders from the north. Much later, it had become Slav. But finally and for more than six hundred years this was a country overlaid by Ottoman rule. I had been reading some book or other, trying to make good my lack of local historical knowledge (it may have been Rebecca West's *Black Lamb and Grey Falcon,* a closely printed copy of which Jasna carried with her and into which I occasionally dipped and never exhausted) and now in the heart of the Balkans, on a slow train to Skopje, I began to apprehend some of those contradictions and complexities that bewitch the stranger, but have so often bedevilled relationships amongst the people who share these hills and valleys in this south-eastern corner of Europe. Beneath the then much vaunted 'brotherhood and unity' of communism lay the great divide separating Christianity and Islam, while deeper still were the ethnic schisms that have so repeatedly alienated the communities of Macedonian, Serb, Bulgar, Albanian, Turk, Greek, Vlach and Roma. I recall thinking how much this *macedoine* reflected in microcosm the diversity I had begun to see in my journey across Yugoslavia itself. I thought the mix rich, exciting and enviable, but fragile too. I had no idea then how tragic that added qualification would prove a generation later.

We found a hotel in Skopje, the first and the only such indulgence, if such it could be called, of our trip. Perhaps, after the experience of Belgrade, we were too afraid to go downmarket again. Not that we were able to rise to more than one star. The room was minimal – beds (two), chairs (two), table, table-lamp (not working), telephone (not used). The walls were damp. But we did have a bathroom all to ourselves and for two whole days, as we began to feel the cumulative effects of too much paprika, carbonated mineral water and rough red wine, this was a luxury. A tiny balcony overlooked a tree-shaded square surrounded by buildings of varied style and condition. New, brightly coloured shoe-box flats; some shabby shops and offices from the thirties; a bank, its decorative turn-of-the-century stucco-work stained and spalling; and, incongruously but picturesquely persistent, a handful of old Turkish houses with framed and plastered upper storeys pushed precariously forward on sagging timber struts; urban and rural side by side, clashes of scale and provenance that made Skopje, in the days before the 1963 earthquake changed everything, such a uniquely provincial regional capital. In the centre of the square, an explosion of scarlet Canna lilies burst with beauty in a plot of scythed grass that would have brought shame if not dismissal to any municipal gardener in Britain.

These contrasts, the mixture of old and new, of the Ottoman past and the Yugoslav present, pervaded Skopje. We soon realised that the legacy left by the Turks had not been – could not be – tidily sanitised in museums nor simply consigned to some atrophied 'safe house' where tourists sat on carpetted couches sipping rosewater. It was all around us, everywhere evident and integrated into the life of the city. There were ruins and monuments, of course, like the rebuilt ramparts of the ancient Kale fortress and the still-galleried courtyards of fifteenth and sixteenth century caravanserais. But when we crossed the Vardar river from the New to the Old Town it was on a bridge whose eleven stone arches had served the city for more than five hundred years. Visiting an art gallery we found ourselves under the thirteen domes of what had been the Daut Pasha baths. And when we passed the Mustafa Pasha mosque, constructed in the same year that Columbus had set sail for the Indies, we could see the faithful coming and going as they had done for centuries. Lost in the Old Town's crowded *čaršija*, we were bewitched by sights and smells that seemed to us as exotic and timeless as those we might have found in Istanbul, Kayseri or Konya. Stalls were heaped with peaches, apricots, apples, pears, oranges, lemons, and the weeping, blood-tinted flesh of cut water melons; there were mountains of nuts, every kind of vegetable. We tried to identify flavours and scents from the variegated palette of spices ranged in open sacks along the alleyways. Our bodies poured with sweat, our senses, assaulted by new delights at every step, almost ached with pleasure. Trapped by an enthusiastic carpet salesman who turned rug upon rug as if he were flicking through a swatch of upholstery fabrics, we felt the dust catch in our throats until glasses of sweet black tea appeared to slake our thirst and ease our escape.

We bought some sunflower seeds to nibble on. I tried *halva* only to spit it out on the cobbles; pistacchio ice cream soon took the dry sandy taste away. Noisy and colourful, the bazaar engulfed us, sucking us halfway to Asia.

But we had to travel west, not east. A journey through southern Kosovo into Montenegro and on to the Adriatic coast now lay ahead of us. We knew we should have to travel by bus but had no idea what this might entail – what the route might be, how long we should be on the road, how much it would cost. To be sure we would not starve, we stocked up in the market with bread, tomatoes, salami, cheese and water. At the bus station we purchased tickets, learned that it would take two days to reach Dubrovnik and were told to present ourselves the following morning at seven. Back in our hotel we tried to sleep.

Of all the journeys we made on that first grand tour through Yugoslavia, none was more scenically spectacular and none more physically draining than this transit to the sea. From the outset we realised it would be a rough ride. The bus was old, there was no air conditioning, the cushioning on the seats meagre and flaccid. We had been allocated places at the rear over the wheels, a misfortune which not only cramped our leg room but would dramatically worsen our travelling discomfort, especially on the rough mountain roads of Montenegro. But the sense of impending adventure, the scarcely believable thought that we were about to cross a remote corner of Europe where, so I supposed in my fevered imagination, warriors and poets still walked, overcame all misgivings. Settling in as best we could, we smiled at our travelling companions in neighbouring seats. They smiled back. There was something, however, in their expressions – a hint of rueful resignation lurking behind the warmth of their response – that made me think they knew what was coming.

In less than an hour we were back in Serbia or, to be more precise, in what was then known as the autonomous region of Kosovo-Metohija. The road ran west then north-west through hilly country – Prizren, Đakovica, Peć. Never much more than ten kilometres distant on our left, the high ridges of the Albanian border rose to more than two thousand metres. Passing through dusty villages, where white mosque or brick church affirmed the local religious allegiance, we grew increasingly aware how jealously nourished and distinctive were the two cultural traditions confronting each other in these frontier valleys. On the verandas of roadside cafes, groups of men sat in the shade: now Albanians in white wool skull-caps drinking tea or Jugocola; now Serbs raising their glasses of beer as we passed. At Peć, where the journey halted for a couple of hours in deference to the midday heat, the contrasts became even more marked. More men in skull-caps, Moslem women in baggy trousers and bolero jackets, a thickly bearded Orthodox priest gowned in black, young Serbian women in short skirts, their grandmothers in widow's black, a few straight-backed Montenegrin men recognizable by their height and the small embroidered tarbooshes they wore. But Slavs were in the minority; nearly two thirds of the population here were Albanians. The town itself looked Turkish. Houses, rubble-walled and austere at street level, white-washed upper storeys and window bays jettied and bracketted above, hidden courtyards with cool balconies within. The fifteenth century Bajrakli mosque. The market or *čaršija*, like Skopje, alive with vendors, carpet dealers, coppersmiths, goldsmiths, slipper makers, tailors, tanners, leather workers. And throughout the town, running water; streams to carry off the dirt and dust of the streets – and more! Bridging one of these open water-courses we found a public toilet: two or three barely enclosed timber cubicles through which ran a timber bar positioned for convenience more acrobatic than ergonomic. While Jasna kept a fastidious distance, Dubravka and I, by now beset by stomach pains and the clenching threat of diarrhoea, found precarious relief.

And yet, oriental as all this was, Peć was no less Serbian. Fourteen kilometres south of the town we had passed the road to Veliki Dečani, one of the great monasteries of Serbian Orthodoxy. But the bus had not stopped. Now, though limited by time and the explosive threat of unpredictable inner discomfort, we took the opportunity to visit the medieval monastery and churches of the Patriarchate of Peć. The complex lay in the lap of the mountains not far from the town: three churches, each with its characteristically Byzantine cupola, undulating eaves and round-arched openings of receding reveals, united as one architectural structure. Forming the axial core of this unique arrangement, the Church of the Apostles, built in the middle of the thirteenth century, had been sandwiched between the Church of St Demetrius, 1320, and the Church of the Virgin, 1330, their three domes thus set symmetrically in a triangular relationship, their naves fronted by a vast common narthex. Inside, frescoed walls and ceilings and gilded iconostases glowed with the enduring ardour of Orthodox faith; saints and angels, patriarchs of the church. We stood in the stillness catching in a moment of mystery the lingering scent of incense. Outside again in the blinding sun under the hillsides of the Rugova Gorge, the phalanx of stone buildings appeared as implacably Christian a fortress as any Crusader castle in Palestine.

It was into this gorge that our bus now took us, grating and growling through the gears as it negotiated bend after hair-raising hairpin bend. Climbing and tunneling our way up over the Čakor Pass we entered Montenegro. Despite the name, the mountains were not black but scarred an arid grey, the rivers coiling below us a brilliant copper sulphate blue. Somewhere, in what as much to most of our fellow passengers as to us seemed an inhospitably remote spot, the bus shuddered to a stop. Two young men struggled aboard. Without a word the driver handed each of them a sick-bag. Ten minutes later, as the journey became even more spectacular and dramatic, the bus swinging from side to side, rising and falling over crests and dips, teasing us on the gravel lip of precipices, the two were already vomiting. Evidently regulars, they coped calmly enough with their problem. Soon, however, they were not suffering alone.

At length, with the late afternoon sun casting dark shadows across the mountainsides, we began to descend less precipitously down the valley of the Lim river. Feeling ill and yet at the same time exhilarated by all the sights and impressions of the day, we arrived in Andrijevica.

I don't remember much about this little town. We spent the night there, all of us who were travelling on to the coast. I imagine the overnight stay must have been included in the fare from Skopje for with the due social economy of Communist necessity, the accommodation was shared – after a frugal meal we slept in two long dormitories, males in one, females in the other. I suppose we must have been housed in some kind of military camp or perhaps an expropriated monastery. At four in the morning a bell rang to wake us, not for matins, however, but to ready us for the road. At five, fortified by a wash in ice-cold water, a ham sandwich fit for a stevedore and a cup of strong black coffee, we continued our journey.

More precipitous meanderings. More spectacular mountain scenery. More sickness. Soon, however, the road became marginally less tortuous as the bus followed the course of the Morača river south. Even so, arrival in Titograd (Podgorica) failed to dispel the pangs of importunate discomfort built up over two days of travel on mountainous intestinal tracks; while Jasna felt able to explore in the hour or so we had in the town, Duba and I could do little but sit on a drystone wall, mind and body taut in preventative concentration. But there were no disasters and by the time we were back in the bus, whether as a result of the cumulative effect of the pills we had been taking or simply because mind and body had finally felt the need to relax, we found ourselves in remission able to enjoy the journey again, not least because we knew now that we were on the last lap.

Cetinje lay in a crater-like bowl girdled by fearful crags and ridges. There was not much to it but what little there was seemed perversely ennobled by its dramatic highland setting. Its few streets were short and straight, its buildings low in scale without flamboyance. Yet this was the village-city that for much of the nineteenth century and into the twentieth had been the capital of the fiercely independent mini-state of Montenegro. It was a capital 'on a doll's-house scale', as Lovett Edwards has described it, a city where the palaces of the government and the embassies of the great powers were no more than the kind of modest villa residences which in most European towns would have slipped undistinguished and unremarked into suburban anonymity. As we passed through in the early afternoon heat, its low stuccoed houses slept in the sun, dreaming perhaps of diplomatic intrigue and political pretension long gone. We disturbed little but the dust of memory.

The bus ground on across the mountains. At length, gears

whining over some lonely rise on the heights of Lovćen, we saw the sea. Far away to the south, out beyond a burnt coastal plain, the Adriatic shimmered in the haze. Mirage islands floated on the horizon. Another world.

Suddenly the road fell away to the north-west, a long slow descent of chicane and switch-back tumbling in precipitous drama to the Gulf of Kotor, the long fjord-like inlet that snakes deep into the Montenegrin mountains. Bend by bend, panorama after panorama, our dust-drenched bus negotiated the slopes, now crawling now careering, held from catastrophe by a low concatenation of ancient stone bollards marching from the summit to the sea in dizzily serpentine file. Down and down we drove until at length by the water's edge we drew to a halt under the battlemented walls of Kotor. Another stage of the journey completed, another pause.

Through the sixteenth century Sea Gate, behind the Venetian fortifications, we discovered a stifling labyrinth of shaded alleyways only barely cooler than the scorching quayside. Time for a brief stroll, a Turkish coffee and, decidedly for medicinal purposes, a small glass of *travarica*.

Back on board our bus we began to negotiate the sinuous, sea-level route round Boka Kotorska. Twisting and turning, the road held to the shore under vineyard-clad slopes that rose abruptly through wooded heights to the peaks above. Small towns passed, no more than villages yet with the architectural vestiges of civic dignity. Perast, still deep in the innermost reaches of the fjord but strategically located to command the approach through the narrows from the outer arm of the gulf; famous once for its shipbuilders and mariners, some of them navigators in the Venetian fleets, some trained for Peter the Great's navy, the town, empty in the afternoon heat, its houses tired, ill cared for and ruinous, seemed to have been deserted for centuries. Risan, no less tranquil; hard to imagine this ancient settlement the base from which the mysterious Illyrians had once confronted the might of Rome. And less than eight hundred metres off-shore, floating on the black glass of the gulf, the tiny islands of Sveti Djordje (St George) and Gospa od Škrpelja (Our Lady of the Stones), Benedictine abbey, baroque church and cypress trees mirrored in the stillness. At every picturesque bend of the road, fresh intimacies of water and stone; boats bobbing at jetties, green-shuttered houses blinking in the sunlight, pergola'd gardens clouded with oleander and bougainvillea. We could sense it: ahead lay the Mediterranean. Behind us now, the sublime fastnesses of Montenegro.

And so we reached the Adriatic. At Herceg Novi the road turned west to follow the sun. Then we were in Croatia again, at the southern tip of the long Dalmatian littoral. Mountains still towered above us on our right while somewhere to our left was the open sea. For now, however, it remained tantalisingly out of sight. Only when we had passed the airport at Čilipi did we see it below us, revealed in the glistening sweep of the bay of Cavtat. Green banks of pine punctuated with cypress rolled down to the shore and for a few moments we were entranced by this soft idyllic landscape. It seemed as if, seeing the sea after the bleak grandeur of our two days travel through Montenegro, we had at last reached journey's end. And, indeed, in all the years that were to come, it was to this coast that I would return again and again.

Soon, as the road wound higher around the coastal cliffs, we saw Dubrovnik. Far below us, its walls shadowed and the detail of its red-roofed mosaic of gridded streets darkened in the setting sun but still distinguishable, the city lay on the shimmering sea like a fairy-tale fortress. Minutes later, scarcely able to believe we were not trapped in some hallucinatory state brought on by the hours of aching confinement we had had to endure since leaving Skopje, we found ourselves standing beneath the city walls. But the moment was real. Crowds of people were strolling by. The pavement cafés were full. There were swallows swooping through the gathering twilight. Close to the Ploče Gate to the Old Town we found a room.

Was it the impact of the journey we had shared through the interior of Yugoslavia with its *pot pourri* of landscapes and cultures? Was it the memory of those last lazy days in Dubrovnik? Was it perhaps the slow self-indulgent savouring of all we had experienced, the dreamy remembering as we lay on the sun-warmed deck sailing north through the Dalmatian islands to Rijeka and the train home? It was all of these. The pattern of my life had been irrevocably shaped by these two weeks of Balkan travel. Every year after we would return, Jasna and I, spending longer and longer each time. Though it never lost the exotic intimations of its name, Zagreb became a familiar city. We visited Belgrade, Novi Sad, Sarajevo, Ljubljana. But it was Dalmatia we grew to love above all: the sun and the crystal-clean sea, grilled fish and tannin-rich red wine, the company of friends.

I have not here described those first few Dalmatian days we enjoyed more than a generation ago, nor the delights of the Adriatic sail that ended our first Balkan journey. But that has been deliberate. This has been a prelude. Such pleasures – and more, I hope – are in the pages that follow.

Frank Arneil Walker
31 January 2005

TO THE ISLAND

'And what should I do in Illyria?'

William Shakespeare
c.1600

The Aperitif Bar of the *Marko Polo* lies aft; high above the stern, it seems to float over the darkening quayside. Glasses in hand, Jasna and I lean on the rail looking out over the city. Now, at last, it begins. Four fast-driving days after leaving Scotland, we are finally here in the warm south waiting to steam into the Adriatic night. Below us the last cars roll off the Riva Boduli vanishing into the open maw of the ship. Up on the skyline of the Transadria Assurance building, six Secessionist storeys high, a thin line of red neon, more and more startlingly red in the ebbing light, records the temperature, 20 degrees Celsius, the date, 16.9, and the time, 19.39. The moments disappear with digital precision. To the west, in a watery glow over Mount Učka, the sun is beginning to set beyond Istria.

As we watched the rooftop clock with growing excitement, eager for that first slow shudder of the ship's engines that would tell us we were underway, down below us the Riva proper, accustomed to the comings and goings of countless ferries, went about its early evening business. Broad and straight, it ran at the water's edge past three projecting piers, stretching west for four hundred metres as far as Trg Žabica and the city bus station. Known once as the Via del Lido, now it belied the promise of that early name; what we were looking down on was no *lungomare*, no sand-blown boulevard, but a restlessly urban thoroughfare animated by the traffic and trafficking of the city. This was, after all, Rijeka, formerly Fiume (the words mean the same – river – though again the name is misleading for the Rječina river makes an unremarkable impact on the local townscape), a great Adriatic port since the time of the Austro-Hungarian *Ausgleich.*. Never the equal of Trieste whose direct connections with Vienna were established much earlier and made it the Empire's leading *entrepôt*, Fiume had none the less prospered, rail links with Zagreb and Budapest securing its mercantile future as an important outlet to the sea for much of Central Europe. Today, while Trieste languishes in haunted Italian isolation, somehow ineptly located, if aptly described by Jan Morris, 'on a fold in the map, hemmed-in, hole-in-corner', Rijeka enjoys a qualified prosperity as the chief port of Croatia.

The buildings fronting the Riva, cornices and eaves lines more or less level with our elevated gaze, reflected something of this history. Immediately across the quay from us, eight-storeys of classless Modernism, box-framed and finned with concrete mullions, a legacy from the Yugoslav seventies; upstreet, perhaps a century older, some *kaisergelb* Renaissance Revival, seventeen bays of government and municipal offices, five pedimented and balconied upper-windows at the centre; further to the west and grandest of all, the palatial headquarters of the Jadrolinija shipping line with its convex, copper-covered roofs and columned frontispiece, pompous testimony to the sea-borne wealth of the *fin-de-siècle* city. Below this extravagant and at times unlovely parade, the street was awash with cars. A thick tide of traffic moved slowly, save for momentary eddies of speed as lights changed or a slow-moving bus or lorry left a tempting gap to be filled. Along the quayside two parallel ranks of densely parked vehicles separated the busy street from the sea. Occasionally a lone car would pass under the raised red-and-white-banded barrier to crawl between the packed rows in search of a space. It felt good to be above all this knowing that for the next eighteen hours or so we should be free of driving. We clinked our glasses again, congratulating ourselves at our superior detachment.

And then, as if to confirm our smug amusement at the urban congestion we were about to leave behind, something totally unexpected happened. Far to our left down the quayside, out of the lengthening shadows falling across the Riva, came a large lumbering diesel locomotive. The realization dawned that the aisle separating the two long rows of parked cars served also as a riparian railway track. Cars and trains used the same harbourside route! Evidently some system of traffic lights determined their respective rights of way, though no less evidently this precaution must have been deemed not wholly reliable for, standing over the buffers at the front of the slowly advancing engine, was a small uniformed man waving a red flag to and fro with measured authority. However familiar and unremarkable this anachronistic performance was to the citizens of Rijeka, it captivated our fellow travellers on the *Marko Polo*; the shoreside rails were now crowded, alight with flashing cameras. The train rolled past below us, six silver-and-blue passenger coaches beginning their overnight journey to Zagreb. I thought of our cabin waiting below and did not envy them.

By now the sun was lower in the western sky. Emerging from a veil of cloud it cast a last buttery glow over the Riva. A final pallid blush and the day was gone. Café lights sparkled below us. On the hillsides the town woke to the night in diamond-dotted glitter. Necklaces of orange street lamps looped across the darkness. Under the awning of the bar behind us the lights came on splashing onto yellow table-covers and out over the green-painted steel of the open deck.

With three loud blasts of its siren the *Marko Polo* announced its departure to the town. Slowly the ship began to ease its way out from the Gradska Luka to the open sea. To starboard, one by one the Riva piers slipped past – spider-legged cranes, bleak warehouses, grain silos; on the port side, the rusting hulk of a huge floating dock lay moored to the long mole that protected the inner harbour. In a few moments we had rounded the last mainland light and were out in the black depths of the Kvarner Gulf. It was time for dinner.

The restaurant was not crowded. Although the tourist season, certainly for the southern Adriatic, stretches well into October, by mid September the ferries are already quieter. We found a window table easily. With food and wine ordered and little to look out on beyond the ruched surface of the sea glinting like shot silk in the ship's lights, we turned our attention to our fellow passengers. Looking round it was soon clear that, apart from one or two couples with young children and a few business men betrayed by dark suits, briefcases or sheaves of papers spread across their tables, the majority of those dining were, like us, decidedly middle-aged. Not for the first time I reminded myself that it is the fate of all who choose to travel in late summer or autumn to find themselves surrounded by those whose very lives are entering that same season. There they were: the bus party of overweight German oldies from the 'former East', casually though not smartly dressed, raucous over their beer; the self-absorbed, second-time-around lovers holding hands across the table, he excessively bronzed between close-cropped greying hair and loose-fitting cream pullover, she revealing tanned shoulders whose arousing colour must, I found myself thinking, continue below the thin fabric of her skimpy black silk top; and in the middle of the saloon, a tall, white-haired couple, erect, self-assured, remote and elegant in expensive designer-label clothes – surely Italians. The more I looked, the more intrigued I became. But such curiosity has its corollary. I began to feel a little ashamed at my inquisitive inferences and imaginings. Perhaps, I surmised, as if in expiation, perhaps we too were under the covert scrutiny of our fellow diners. What would they make of *us*? Would they guess our age, our relationship, our nationality?

It amounts to a point of honour with Jasna and me not to be identified as Brits since such recognition almost inevitably implies 'English'. With Jasna this resistance is as much a matter of asserting her paternal part-Croat, part-Czech inheritance as it is pride in her Scots mother. For me, *pravi Škot*, real Scot – as I am always keen to declare myself to Croatian friends – it is the recurring spur to break free from what I perceive to be an all-pervasive linguistic imperialism. I try to insist on my Scottishness, an attempt repeatedly doomed but defiantly repeated. Nor, for reasons more to do with a desire not to be taken for granted than any wartime hangover, were we keen to be taken for Germans. We had already rejected our waiter's '*Guten Abend*' with a mildly petulant '*Dobra Večer*', continuing in Croatian to explain that we were not German but Scots. Thus doubly endeared – or so we liked to think – by our ability to converse (if only at a basic level) in the language of the country and the romanticising response that regularly seems to greet our admission that we come from the north-western edge of Europe, we had won his favour. Instead of the dry *roulade* billed as dessert on the *table d'hôte* menu, *palačinke* with hot chocolate sauce and cold ice cream appeared on our table. Has this convivial *rapport* confused our imagined observers? Have they taken us for Croats? For a moment or two I enjoyed the thought that we might have carried off the masquerade – until it occurred to me that some at least must have noted our car with its GB plate and tell-tale right-hand drive waiting in the quayside queue at Rijeka. Perhaps, then, we are *émigrés* on a family visit? Pouring the last of our wine, I shared these musings with Jasna who takes the same traveller's pleasure in the gentle pretence. It was as if this fantasy of ambiguous identity, all the more potent for its confinement afloat in a context of limited time and space, like that of the country-house crime novel or the train-borne espionage thriller, imparted some added *frisson* to the sail as buoying as suntanned skin or fashionable clothes.

Up on deck again we find the exception to the middle-aged rule. Hunched together in the dark, a young back-packing couple are sharing a cigarette. She strokes his neck with an exquisite enviable tenderness. He places his hand on her inner thigh, softly, as if without deliberation. The ship throbs on through the night.

There is no-one serving in the Aperitif Bar. The tables are deserted, the open deck now wind-blown. Off duty, a white-shirted barman leans on the rail, staring into nothing. We do the same. The ship seems to be sailing in space; there is no horizon, no distinction visible between sea and sky, only a dense intensity of blackness pierced occasionally by the lone brilliance of a fisherman's lights. Time for bed.

Drugged by the wine we have drunk and the dull drone of the ship's engines, we slip into sleep, dreaming of our destination – Korčula. *En route* to Dubrovnik, the *Marko Polo* will call at Zadar, Split and Stari Grad and then, soon after noon tomorrow, she will reach our island. We have been making this journey to the southern Adriatic for twenty-five years now and always with the same yearning for sun and sea. At first we spent only a brief two or three weeks but latterly we came for longer periods stretching to six or seven weeks in spring, late summer or autumn. We found ourselves not so much on holiday – this was how I explained our extended absences to envious friends in Scotland – as living our life in another place, a place we had grown to love.

In 1991 we bought a tiny house in the village of Lumbarda. Not the best moment, since within a matter of months the whole country was engulfed in war. But we kept coming, flying at times to Split, at times to Dubrovnik, where we would find a local ferry, take a bus, or hire a car. The war came close. From October 1991 till almost the end of July the following year, the Yugoslav army, advancing from the south, laid siege to Dubrovnik, occupying the coast from the Montenegrin border as far north as Mali Ston at the armpit of the long Pelješac peninsula. This brought danger no more than an hour's drive from the short ferry crossing to Korčula. In Lumbarda we could hear the guns. But that was as near as it got. The sea saved Korčula as it did most of the many islands of the Adriatic. I listen to it now, that same sea, washing against the hull.

In recent years these islands and shores have been among the least visited of Europe's Mediterranean coastline. The break-up of Yugoslavia has had much to do with this for, while the worst internecine conflict of the 1990s was concentrated in the interior in Bosnia and Hercegovina and most of Dalmatia remained no more than putatively a war zone, few travellers were prepared to cope with the necessary inconvenience of *ad hoc* travel arrangements or lie on deserted beaches listening to the lugubrious drawl of NATO bombers heading for Kosovo. Peace has brought the tourists back – Slovenes, Czechs, Hungarians, Poles and Slovaks whose shared Habsburg past draws them south – but for many Europeans the Adriatic's eastern sea-board is again regarded as, at worst, a Balkan borderland best avoided or, at best, 'that strange, mysterious, almost unknown shore' it was for the pioneering travellers of earlier centuries. And this is a pity for it was those very travellers, many of them Brits sailing like us through the succession of island archipelagos scattered along the Dalmatian coast, who, as one of them, T.G.Jackson, author of the definitive three-volume on the architecture of *Dalmatia, the Quarnero and*

Istria (1887) wrote, 'were the first to make these countries and the monuments of art which they contain known to western Europeans'. Jackson may have been excessively chauvinistic in his claim but it is certainly the case that Brits were early on the Dalmatian scene. From the seventeenth century onwards the corpus of English-language travel literature and the evidence of architectural and archaeological study is impressive.

There were, of course, earlier visitors, many of them pilgrims travelling to and from the Holy Land. Among the more celebrated was the English king, Richard the Lionheart, who, returning from the Third Crusade in 1192, was shipwrecked off Dubrovnik where, by way of thanksgiving for his saved life, he donated money towards the building of the town's cathedral. Though recent research has largely discredited this legend and it now seems more than likely that Richard did, in fact, put in much further up the coast at Zadar, the association is still staunchly promoted in Dubrovnik. Exactly two hundred years later the future king Henry IV of England, Henry Bolingbroke, journeying to Jerusalem, visited the same two cities. But it was only with the appearance of a topographical account of a journey made in 1675 by the English baronet George Wheler and the French physician Jacob Spon, published first as *Voyage d'Italie, de Dalmatie, de Grèce et du Levant* (1678) and a few years later as *A Journey into Greece...* (1682), that the natural landscape, towns and architecture of the eastern Adriatic littoral began to be known. In the following century Richard Pococke in 1745 and Thomas Watkins in 1792 added their contributions to the literature of Adriatic travel, commenting on the religious situation and the nature of Venetian rule in Dalmatia, while Robert Adam, not without encountering difficulties with the Venetian authorities in Split during five weeks of architectural measurement and research, published his detailed and influential study of the *Ruins of the Palace of the Emperor Diocletian at Spalatro in Dalmatia* (1764). Finally, in the nineteenth century, with the publication of travelogues by Wilkinson (1848), Paton (1849), Neale (1861) and Freeman (1881), a fuller picture emerged. Freeman, an Oxford historian who had published a formidable history of architecture in 1849, journeyed to Dalmatia in 1875, 1877 and 1881, on the two latter occasions in the company of his future son-in-law, the archaeologist Arthur Evans. Together, as Evans remarked in his *Illyrian Letters* (1878), they devoted themselves to the study of 'the scenery of these countries, their antiquities, and even the folk-lore and domestic life of their peoples'. Yet despite this cumulative Victorian endeavour, including his own *Sketches from the Subject and Neighbour Lands of Venice*, Freeman felt bound to write that 'the best guide to those parts is still the account written by the Emperor Constantine Porphyrogenitus more than nine hundred years back'. Ultimately it was the Oxford architect, T.G.Jackson, who in 1887 published the study which, in its scholarly combination of historical background and architectural description and analysis, surpassed this revered Byzantine commentary.

Jackson's first landfall in Dalmatia was at Zadar. He knew of its foundation as a Roman colony in 78BC and was thrilled at the prospect of arriving at what, with all the cultural prejudice of classical orthodoxy, he considered to be 'the border lands of European civilization'. It was 1882. Full of nervous curiosity, he and his wife watched from the deck as their Austrian Lloyd's steamer moved slowly into port.

'...before we well knew we were there, we were entering the historic harbour... We saw nothing indeed of the mighty walls whose strength made the crusaders wonder at their own success, for they were long ago removed to make way for the more modern fortifications of the Venetian engineer Sanmichieli [*sic*]... Toward the harbour however the bastions and curtains of Sanmichieli remain standing, with a wide quay, at which the steamers are able to lie close to the shore in deep water.'

We, too, called at Zadar. We, too, saw nothing of the city's 'mighty walls' for, while Jackson had reached the town as the sun rose, it was the middle of the night when we tied up at the deep-water quay. For us, however, it was not, as it had been for Jackson, the first time. Years ago we had seen the sights that he described – the Renaissance Town Gate with its Lion of St Mark guarding the entry to the old town, the Franciscan Church, consecrated *c.*1280 and said to be the oldest Gothic church in Dalmatia, the Romanesque Cathedral of St Anastasia (Sveta Stosije), and the magnificent 'Old Croatian' Church of St

Donatius (Sveti Donat), built in the first years of the ninth century, a drumlike country cousin to San Vitale in Ravenna and the Carolingian chapel at Aachen. But not this time. While the *Marko Polo* loaded and unloaded its half-hour handful of midnight travellers, we slept on.

Hours later we woke to find ourselves approaching Split in a hazy dawn. By the time we had breakfasted the sun was up, as it had been for Jackson in Zadar a hundred and twenty years ago. So, too, were all our fellow passengers – or so it seemed – anxious not to miss the drama of arrival. As the ship began to reduce speed, close on our port side was Marjan hill, quilted in its green woods of Aleppo pines. Rounding the marina at Sustjepan Point, past a second forest of sail-free masts loose-rigged and glittering in the low early morning sunlight, we entered the great bay that forms the city's passenger port. It seemed to clutch at us, drawing us into an inner pool of activity already congested with the comings and goings of local island ferries. To our left, the yachts receded behind a long protective mole; to the right, the harbour breakwater quay passed by. Several vessels lay at their berths: cruise ships, ferries, a naval frigate, an immense floating dock. Ahead, the white palm-fronted city stretched out before us, orange roofs and fleeting sheets of mist layered under a suburban high-rise silhouette battlemented against the mountains. The ship seemed to pause as if allowing us time to relish the view and then, with a swing to starboard, began its cautious approach to the quay. It was 6 a.m.

The Jadrolinija time-table for the overnight ferry from Rijeka to Dubrovnik allows an hour in Split, a longer stop than that made at any of its other ports of call. This is usually more than adequate to deal with the frenetic roll-off roll-on exchange of cars, lorries and buses that invariably occurs, but it is scarcely enough to permit a casual stroll ashore. Passengers travelling further south must watch and wait. Their reward is a spectacle played out in three parallel acts.

Immediately below us the access ramp to the car-deck lay like an apron stage open to the quayside. An audience had gathered – anxious travellers, some unsure whether to return to their queuing cars and dare a determined dash for the ramp or wait to be directed to make their move, others already revving their engines impatient for their cue; a crowd of bus passengers, obliged to leave their coach and walk aboard, lingering to admire the skills of their driver as he negotiated the ramped portal into the ship; a handful of old men and boys, their fishing temporarily disturbed by the arrival of the *Marko Polo*, content for a while to enjoy again the whole familiar farce; some curious passers-by idly interested and amused. Vehicles manoeuvred for position, all semblance of ordered precedence abandoned. Deck-hands in white Jadrolinija T-shirts acted out their regular routine of exaggerated gestures and oath-laden imprecations. Poses were struck: fury, disdain, despair. Mutually contradictory cries of '*Naprijed*!', forward, and '*Rikverc*!', reverse, rang out, echoing through the car-deck cave. Ashen-faced drivers, hopelessly confused between the aggressive confidence of these conflicting commands and their own instinctive judgment, struggled to cope. Gears crunched. Bumpers bumped. Now and then sparks flew as a car bottomed out on the steel ramp. For the bystanders on the quay it was all gratuitous entertainment. And for us, too, watching from the deck above – though our innocent *Schadenfreude* was tempered by the knowledge that in a few hours time we should have to play *our* part in a re-run of this same chaotic comedy.

Perhaps it was this cocktail of pleasure mixed with a dash of guilt and apprehension that made me look away from the pantomime on the pier below. At any rate, momentarily distracted, I found my gaze drawn to a different scene. Upstage, out on the waters of the inner harbour, a second show was playing. One after another, a succession of small island ferries passed in and out of the port, advancing and retiring with all the practised precision of local folk dancers. These were the daily life-lines of Central Dalmatia linking Split with the island communities on Šolta, Brač, Hvar, Vis, Korčula and Lastovo. Like dancers, too, the vessels varied in appearance; some, conventionally maritime, slim and sleekly shaped, others a little gawky and graceless perhaps but solid and robust. Crossing the harbour, all moved slowly with an almost balletic circumspection, their white wakes cutting wide arcs in the water as if to trace some fleeting choreographic evidence of their course. It was a continuous performance. It would continue all day and every day, sustaining Dalmatian life.

Wrapped around all this like a low cyclorama was Split itself, its 'stage-curtain of distance' drawn out in a static *tableau* along the water's edge. The third and final act in our hour-long harbour drama, the city played its role in silence, its protagonist architecture. Not the quayside clamour of people, not the stately surge of shipping, but the still, stolid speech of ancient stone. Some of that four-hundred-metre-long wall of building on the *riva* had been there for seventeen hundred years – Diocletian's Palace, the creation of an absolute ruler who divided the governance of the Roman Empire then renounced all power to return to this Bay of Aspalathos where his Illyrian mother and father had lived as slaves. There it was across the harbour from us, the home of an emperor, built as a vast and luxurious retreat, sub-let over the centuries to become a medieval town, crudely assimilated within the angular bastions of a Venetian fortress, and still today densely inhabited. Its wide south façade, filling half the *riva,* bore the traces of the great *crypto-porticus* loggia where Diocletian would have walked in the shade, looking out over the palace's sea-gate to the bay. Vestiges of this classical colonnade – crumbling pillars carrying an intermittent cornice that here and there rose to form an arcuated accent – clung to the wall of housing like some parasitical *piano nobile*. Yet it was the housing itself that had colonized the palace, growing inside it to such effect that in time it had become the dominant element, the elevational remnants of late Roman splendour locked like phantom shards in a populated quarry. Faced with this symbiotic puzzle, Robert Adam had found his efforts to make a systematic record of the dimensions and detail of the palace fraught with problems: 'first from the numbers of modern houses built within the walls of the palace and even upon the old foundations; secondly from the inhabitants having pulled to pieces and utterly destroyed some parts of the antique work; and lastly from their having so blended the ancient and modern work together by repairs and alterations that it was not without great difficulty they could be distinguished'.

Yet even at a distance, some of the earliest architectural lineaments of this urban palimpsest could still be read. But far from all. Not, for example, the squatly towered south-eastern corner of the palace, obscured by the buildings of the old *lazzaretto* quay which pushed obliquely forward from the wings, stage left. Not the towers and walls buried back in the built-up city, nor the grand axial gateways that marked the entrances to the palace from the west, north and east. Not the constricted straight streets that led from the gates, axes of the four-square *castrum* plan that formed the hidden armature of Diocletian's design. Above all, not the imperial apartments, mausoleum, temples and peristyle court that lay at the heart of it all, squeezed by centuries of labyrinthine encroachment yet still, largely unimpaired in fabric and form, in the same grand grip of cruciform geometry. None of this could be seen, except perhaps the hip-tiled roof of Diocletian's octagonal mausoleum long since conscripted as the city's Cathedral, its transformation devoutly signposted by a tall campanile raised in superimposed Romanesque tiers. But it was all there, I knew, hidden behind the long *riva* wall.

I knew because we had been there often. The plunge from the pavement brilliance of the quayside into a vaulted gloom of dank Piranesi-like cellars and the sudden eruption back up into the open splendour of the palace peristyle; that first shock of entry came back to me. I remembered, too, the warm grey stone, crusty with age or keen and crisp in profile as if the Roman masons had only just departed. And the buildings. The dark domed void of the mausoleum, ringed by wonderfully carved cornices and friezes, its double tier of eight detached columns tightening the space around me like the tension rods of a drum. The ponderous, corniced-and-consoled portal exposed in the lost portico of the Temple of Jupiter. The maze of narrow streets, disorientating as Venice. And the time, years ago, when we lost our four-year-old son, Davor, in these crowded alleys; no more than a matter of five or ten minutes perhaps, but an age of panic.

Prompted by this stab of memory, I turned to look at my wife beside me. I wanted her to say something. Perhaps I needed some reassurance that that terrible despairing moment was buried in the past. She was silent, gazing out across the harbour at the city. I put my hand over hers, locking our fingers together. She looked at me and smiled. Was it no more than a routine response of affection, loving but perfunctory, or had she somehow sensed my mood?

'Do you remember drinking coffee in the peristyle?' she said, and then, returning her gaze to the distant *riva*, added, 'Like being on stage.'

I felt no surprise that our thoughts had followed the same track – it happens sometimes after years of marriage. At any rate, it was enough to dispel my momentary depression. I knew what she meant. It was one of the pleasures, perhaps the greatest of pleasures, Split had to offer – sitting in the sun of the peristyle court. And it was different; the experience was unique, far removed from that of the familiar streetside café where the passing shopper or tired tourist lingers in comfortable anonymity watching the world go by. Crowds passed by the peristyle, too, of course, emerging from dark lanes onto a small paved square two or three steps above the coffee-drinkers or up from the darker depths of the palace to cross through the court itself. But they were the watchers not the watched. It was us, I remember, innocent strangers, pausing to write a postcard and drink a *cappuccino*, who found ourselves the centre of attention, actors in our own thirty-minute theatre. On each side of the court, raised on stylobates that doubled as stepped seating for our audience, tall round-arched arcades lent classical dignity to the scene. To the south was the pedimented three-bay portico or *prothyron* that once led to the circular *vestibulum*; stage set, indeed, with its two Renaissance chapels inset in the outer bays, it has often served as backdrop to *plein air* opera. It could all have been too much – the attention of the crowd an embarrassment, the scale and *gravitas* of the architecture intimidating – but, in fact, the reverse was the case. A kind of unmalicious arrogance seized us. We sipped our coffee slowly, affecting a lofty self-esteem, and from behind our shades stared back at the throng, determined to revel in our fleeting moment in the sunlit limelight. Yes, it *was* like being on stage. And how strange it was, having just pictured ship, harbour and city in a *voyeur*'s lens, to have the relationship now so symmetrically reversed in that one remembered moment of urban exposure. I thought back to the previous evening in the restaurant and the sobering realization that my inquisitive speculations about others might be reflected, and not necessarily favourably, in theirs about me. I wondered, with some unease, if perhaps it is the deserved fate of every traveller to become the observer observed.

We left Split on time. Punctually at 7 a.m. the *Marko Polo* pulled out from the quayside. Three valedictory blasts of the ship's horn, an increase in speed and we were out of the harbour steaming south. A few yachts already under sail tacked out of danger. For a long time, the low profile of the city remained in view below the mountains. Then it was all but gone, a pale blur on the horizon as we sailed through the Splitska Vrata, the narrow sea gap between the islands of Šolta and Brač. Now, as we looked back from the deck rail trying to convince ourselves we could still pick out the white pencil shaft of the Cathedral belfry tower, the ship's wake fanned out in a slow gentle curve swept with froth like a Rococo arabesque. We were headed for Hvar.

The north-western coast of the island of Hvar is indented with many small inlets. From the rocky shore an undulating landscape, thick with *makija*, rolls back to the high east-west ridge that forms the backbone of the island for almost the entire sixty-eight kilometres of its length. A large gulf penetrates deeply inland leading us to the sheltered port of Stari Grad. The town is, as its name implies, an ancient settlement. Easy to see why the place should have proved attractive to both Greeks and Illyrians. Easy, too, to see why the Croatian word for the island, Hvar, should have come from the Greek, *pharos*, a name which, though lighthouses are common enough throughout the Adriatic, appears to be itself a corruption derived from the island of Paros in the Aegean Cyclades, the home of the original colonizers. Less easy to understand is the Italian name for the island, Lesina. Strangely, it seems that this may be connected with the Slavic *les,* meaning wood, though much of the forested land on Hvar has long ago been cleared leaving the hillsides, where they have not been laboriously tiered, walled and cultivated with vines and olives, matted with a dense evergreen scrubland of low pines, cistus, buckthorn, juniper, erica and laurel and perfumed with the pervasive scent of lavender.

As the shore on each side of the ship drew nearer and ahead we caught a first sight of a massive concrete jetty, I was reminded of similar sails up the long sea-loch of West Loch Tarbert in Scotland. Here, too, as on the Kintyre coast, the roll-on roll-off quay was constructed in rural, deep-water isolation. As the ship's engines began to growl in obedience to the demands of the approach, the little town of Stari Grad barely revealed itself in the distance, a church belfry tower nipped between low pine-clad promontories. The smell of the pines carried on the breeze. The quay was quiet: four cars and an antiquated lorry waiting to load, a few foot passengers, the usual enterprising landladies ready to accost any disembarking back-packers. A local bus waited to convey new arrivals to Stari Grad or Jelsa or Hvar town. A large tarmac-covered expanse of white-lined parking, interrupted at regular intervals by lamp standards and young, shaving-brush palm trees neatly planted in groups of three, extended back from the jetty to the *makija*. It seemed a lavish layout for the meagre attendance. I supposed that the tourist traffic of July and August must merit such provision and felt smugly glad to be travelling in autumn.

It took little more than twenty minutes to complete the exchange of vehicles and passengers. I watched the bus, no more than quarter full, climb up the bosky hillside and disappear from view. A brief shudder shook the ship as the car-ramp clanged back into position. Freed hawsers, splashing into the churning crevasse opening up between us and the quay, were hauled aboard. Below on the receding quayside, the young man and woman with whom we had shared an otherwise deserted deck late the previous night appeared engaged in protracted negotiation with one of the local landladies. Voices were lost in the noise of the ship's engines but her unperturbed shrugs were a sure sign she had set her final price. A re-united family were still embracing one another. Some children waved. Then the figures grew smaller, blurring into irrelevance. The ship wheeled round towards the open sea and the journey continued.

Brač was now on our right. Its hog-back profile, high and rugged, spilled into the Adriatic in a succession of tumbling ridges outlined in shadowed profile in the morning sun. Sailing west, we held close to the last long finger of Hvar until, reaching the low promontory of Pelegrin, we began to swing to port. A wide one-hundred-and-eighty-degree arc brought us into the Pakleni Kanal, the open channel of water that lies between Hvar and the Pakleni Otoci, the Hellish Islands, low, bare and seductive on the glistening sea. The damning name may be, as some claim, a corruption of the Croatian word, *paklina*, the pitch or resin used to caulk ship's timbers, but the more direct derivation from *pakleni*, hellish, has always been a much more attractive and more likely explanation for a place so sun-scorched and devoid of shade. The islands are parched and waterless and yet, like a stolen draught of Lethe in Hades, their intoxicating spell lures those who come to swim or sail into hours of languorous oblivion. Their votaries were all around us now. Some ardent and impetuous, power boats keening through the calm water; others, more practised habitués, prolonging the anticipation, taking their time, trailing a fishing line behind their purring outboard. A lazy flotilla of yachts limped along the channel struggling to find wind and energy. More flaccid sails appeared; a white cloud of dinghies flooding out from Hvar town.

Ten years or more ago we had called here at Hvar on the southern coast of the island rather than at Stari Grad, putting in to the long stone quay that runs along the eastern side of the harbour bay. It does not happen now, the loading and unloading of vehicles forbidden; but I could recall it well, the slow passage past hotels and lido, the intimacy of docking at the palm-shaded *riva* and how almost god-like it had seemed to look down through the trees on the affairs of the town. While the familiar sequence of events unfolded – the shock of the car-ramp's crash on stone, the clatter of the passenger stair flight lowered against the side of the ferry, each releasing and receiving its wash of travellers – Hvar's everyday life continued, no more than momentarily jostled by the sudden juxtaposition of ship and shore. There on the quay was the Post Office with its queues, there the local tourist bureau offering *sobe i izleti*, rooms and excursions, and there the canopied terrace of the Slavija Hotel, its early morning patrons drinking their *espresso* and reading their newspaper unperturbed by our incongruous intrusion. It seemed as if by leaning a little further over the rail and raising our voices we could mail our post cards, change money or order a glass of cool white wine. Now, however, remote and still, as if chastened by the frowning vigilance of its hilltop fortress, the town kept itself to itself and the Venetian buildings, struck golden in the morning sun, passed in the middle distance. Back in the inner harbour the arches of the Renaissance loggia, seven bays balustraded below and above, were sunk in shadowed reflection. Across town to the left, I picked out a tall elegant tower, almost Romanesque in style, the belfry of the ruinous Church of St Mark (Sveti Marko). Well to the right, another, rising in similar stages of diminishing round-arched colonettes; this the bell-tower of the Cathedral of St. Stephen (Sveti Stjepan), its nave and aisles hidden in the dense fabric of the town at the eastern end of its eponymous square. Then, a third campanile, round-arched again, marking the site of a Franciscan convent down on the rocky shore. All three belfries, built or rebuilt in the aftermath of the Turkish attack of 1571 and probably by the same hand, were much admired by the tireless Jackson for whom their 'tall slender round-headed lights, the columns doubled one behind the other, and the rosettes and discs in relief which decorate the wall space' merited 'a high place among works of their class and date'. Perhaps. I could not read the detail and saw the towers not so much as works of architecture but simply as landmarks in the townscape passing before us. In any event, all was soon gone. However tantalising, the prospect of the harbour bay permitted us by Jadrolinija was brief. In no more than a few minutes' time, town and citadel had slipped astern, lost to sight.

As the *Marko Polo* moved out into open water, we watched the steep coastline of Hvar ebb into the distance on our left. The height of the island's long spinal ridge grew less and less, receding east until there seemed no more than a low reef reaching out to the mainland below the grey peaks of the Biokovo range. Now we were in the wide Korčulanski Kanal. Ahead, already visible but hazily indistinct in the morning sunlight, lay Korčula itself.

I make a conscious effort to curb anticipation deciding, Odysseus-like, to resist for the moment the siren call of recognition. Closing my eyes to the view and the glare of the sun, I try instead to prolong the strange placeless pleasure of the open sea, as if by postponing all thoughts of landfall I might not only defer but deepen the final delight. I give myself up to reverie, drowning in that sense of expansive indeterminate dreaming which only the sea traveller feels. I surrender purpose and personality. The journey is taking me somewhere, but for the moment it is the going there, the joy of the journey itself, the endlessly hypnotic symmetry of sea and sky, that numbs desire. There is no need to arrive. The wide Adriatic horizon blurs in the gathering heat, Hvar, Vis and Korčula no more than nameless mirages. The ship sails on in a boundless nowhere. Adrift in these parenthetic moments I seem to float aimlessly in and out of time and place. No other journey is like this. Cramped in a plane's cabin, we count the hours and, lacking space, cannot escape our own presence. In the train we must confront our companions, compartmented together in polite dialogue, however dismal and desultory. But at sea the hours flow slowly and our life of timetabled urgency is on hold. We find the space to stand apart: alone at the edge, we watch from the rail, half-freed from ourselves in the observing of others until, turning to the waves again, we lose a last conceit in the amorphous immensity above, around and beneath us. I gaze at the empty horizon and sink into a delicious anonymity. Claudio Magris knew the truth, musing at the heart of Europe: perhaps even the distant promise of the ever-changing river, even a great river like the Danube, cannot liberate us from the familiar fields of our own self-serving self-assuring world and that 'to know how to be Nobody, like Ulysses… one needs the sea.'

Abruptly, I was roused from this abstracted state by a leap from the dark. Five hundred metres back beyond the whitening wake of the ship two dolphins erupted into the light. A twisting corkscrew thrust, a second's poise, and they were gone, crashing back into the deep. A gallery of spectators gathered quickly, cameras at the ready. But the thrill was short-lived. Here and there the glistening surface of the sea continued to break in sudden flashes of energy – a low lancing leap, the sudden sheen of an arching back, a fleeting fin. Eyes strained to follow but spray and splash were soon lost in the distant coruscating glitter.

A few watchers remained at the rail mesmerised by the moment and unwilling to believe the excitement could be over so quickly, but most returned to deckchair or lounger. The Aperitif Bar resumed its indolence. The sun grew warmer. A sense of patient contentment descended on the ship. Some read. I recognized the local papers and journals – *Slobodna Dalmacija, Jutarnji List, Globus, Nacional*. Seated on the deck, back propped against rucksack, a young Japanese girl was absorbed in the *Lonely Planet* guide. And there, unexpected and incongruous, was the garish cover of Irvine Welsh's *Porno*, its brash, tongue-teasing vulgarity all the more noticeable in the hands of a deeply lined sixty-or-so-year-old woman whose douce, not to say drab, appearance would otherwise have given little clue to any latent prurience. Some drank. *Espresso*, *cappuccino*, mineral water, a glass of Prošek. Some drank with serial dedication: two grey-haired Austrians, their lilting Viennese accents betraying them, were already on their third beer of the morning. Some slept.

An hour passed. I made some notes, Jasna brought her diary up to date, we shared a coffee. By now we could see the north coast of Korčula clearly to starboard. The lonely promontory light on Proizd lay behind us. A landscape of dark, green-backed hills stretched to the east. *Korkyra Melaina*, Black Korkyra, the Greeks had called the island, differentiating it from the barer Corfu to the south. Now on these northern slopes most of the pine forests had gone, replaced by the familiar Mediterranean *makija*, but from the deck of the *Marko Polo* Korčula still looked black, shadowed below the southern sun. We began to look for familiar landmarks. It was difficult to pick out Prigradica, one of only a few villages sited on the northern shore. Harder still to spot the tiny hamlet of Babina. Below some of the island's highest peaks, came a long stretch of barren coastline with neither settlement nor road. Then, as the ship drew closer to the island, we saw the bay of Račišće and knew we were within an hour of arrival.

By now there was land to port too – the western extremity of the long mountainous peninsula of Pelješac stretching back over sixty kilometres to the neck of land which connected it to the mainland at Ston. The channel narrowed. As we passed the navigation light on the small offshore island of Vela Kneza, it was down to little more than a kilometre. On Pelješac we could see the ochre scar of a road climbing north over the hills to the bay of Lovište where once we had eaten the most wonderful tiny *lignje*, grilled squid. To the east, heaving in gaunt grey folds of rock and scrub, sunlit ridges and shadowed valleys pushed up to the summit of Sveti Ilija (St Elias), cloud-capped in cotton-bud cumulus, at a height of more than 950 metres above the sea. Far higher than the wooded ranges on Korčula, it dominated the scene, throwing the orange-roofed ribbon of small settlements strung out along the coastline – Viganj, Kučište and Perna – into toytown relief. Barely visible on the gilded mountainside, two belfried chapels, no more than single-cell sanctuaries, clinging to the lower slopes immediately above the tree-line, seemed at once trivial and audacious, statements of a rude faith daring to propitiate elemental odds.

Sveti Ilija is majestic, Olympian even. Like a sleeping giant it slumbers in what might be taken for lofty indifference high above the small communities that cling to the shores of the Pelješki Kanal. Yet by its very presence it is complicit in everything that happens here. No-one on Korčula passes the day without some glance north at the summit and though they may say that they look to the mountain merely to forecast the day's weather, it is rather as if, awed by the blind perpetual gaze of nature, they feel this ritualistic need to acknowledge and perhaps placate the gods that walk in these high snake-ridden gullies. But the *Korčulani*, though respectful, are more than docile supplicants. Centuries ago, emboldened by the first stirrings of Renaissance culture carried south from Venice on the Adriatic currents, they raised their own mountain. Founded on the much-indented north-east coastline of the island, Korčula town is a man-made hill of superimposed stone gables and tiled roofs from which the *tempietto*-topped belfry tower of the island's Cathedral of St Mark (Sveti Marko) emerges like a spiritual lighthouse. The compact little town, once itself an island but long connected to the mainland of Korčula by a built-up isthmus, juts out into the channel, a handsome if impertinent David to the Goliath on Pelješac; architecture assailing nature.

We lean out over the starboard rail straining to catch a clearer glimpse of the old town. And there it is, perhaps two kilometres away in the hazy distance, bathed in sunlight like a tiny hill-town in Istria or Tuscany, not perched above green, cypress-pegged slopes, but, as it seems, stone afloat on the water. We pass the bay of Žrnovska Banja, the houses of the coastal hamlet indistinct but the line of the road winding uphill through the *makija* to Žrnovo clear enough. Approaching the narrow creek of Strećica bay we begin to distinguish a succession of large villas half-hidden among the trees that shade the shore road; there are balustraded balconies, steep flights of steps leading up from the rocks, small boats and dinghies idling at the jetties. This is the start of Korčula's 'West End'. On a blunt promontory thick with trees, the restored sixteenth-century masonry of the Dominican monastery of St Nicholas (Sveti Nikola), simple in form and texture, catches sculptural drama in the steep shadows cast by the noonday sun. Walls and roofs gather in prismatic clarity around the church tower, a simpler and less elevated version of the Cathedral belfry we can already see more clearly on the hilltop ahead.

The deck is busy now for this is one of the great views of the Adriatic: rugged grey mountains vanishing into the distance of Pelješac, green slopes, a blue infinity of the sea, and Korčula, launched out on the channel like a floating fortress. It is clear that for many travelling on the *Marko Polo* all this is new, the beauty of the scene startling and memorable. For us it is familiar, just as memorable and no less beautiful, our absorption not in the new but in renewal, in the reassuring discovery that things are still as they were, like coming home. Stretching from the monastery to the old town, we see again the sweep of the nineteenth-century *riva*, peppered with small boats and small cars; there, on an uncomfortably low wooden bench, I often sketched. Behind a parade of palm trees, some tall, some small, the narrow houses pack together, gable-to-gable, three-, four-, and five-storeys high. There, stepping down into a small semi-basement shop, we might buy flowers for a friend's table. On the wooded hill, more houses. There I remember dinners with Ivo and Lejla, looking out from their balcony across the channel to Sveti Ilija on Pelješac. And, on the skyline, barely visible above the trees, the low remnants of Fort Wellington (Forteca), built by the British in 1813; there one April we picked wild flowers, carrying them home to a jam jar. At the end of the *riva,* three flag-flying flagpoles on the circular Trg

Pomirenja, the Place of Reconciliation, mark the isthmus hingeing the newer town to the old.

The western face of the old town narrows in perspective as the ship pulls nearer. Some of the walls have gone but the perimeter course of the Venetian fortifications is still evident. From the swelling stone drum of the Prince's Great Tower, with its higher, thinner companion, the Prince's Small Tower, still ruffed with stone brattishing, the line follows the low arcaded façade of the customs offices to the Sea Gate Tower. Then come the curving flights of the staircase that leads up into the old town, the Renaissance loggia, recognizable under its hipped tiled roof, and, below palms, the quiet white-tabled terrace of Hotel Korčula. Finally, at the end of the western quay, two more massive masonry drums, the Bokar Tower and the Zakrjan Tower, both ringed with arched machicolation. Now, as we pass these two towers, sailing in deep water no more than fifty yards from the town, the eastern side of the old town begins to reveal itself. Here, the great walls survive intact wrapping themselves round the town in a high buttressing girdle. A pine-shaded promenade, thus splendidly elevated, softens the transition from the austere horizontality of the walls to the vertical complexity of gables and balconies piled up below the Cathedral. People are strolling or lunching under the trees. A few ignore us – I imagine they are locals going about their business accustomed to the event or disdainful tourists feigning seasoned indifference – but most stare out, beguiled by the proximity of the ship and the prospect of quayside theatre. The *Marko Polo* sounds its siren. More heads turn. We gaze back, a last look before diving to the car-deck. Under the sights of the cannon that sit, gargoyle-like, on the cut-down Tower of All Saints at the end of the town wall, the ship comes to a stop and begins its slow reverse approach to the eastern quay.

THE VILLAGE

'Lumbarda is completely different... they take life quietly and, in some indefinable way, they have an air about them of quiet satisfaction, perhaps emanating from the fact that they have been "established" for at least 2,500 years.'

Celia Irving
1988

Lumbarda. A quiet village straggling round the succession of small bays bitten into the eastern extremity of Korčula. A village of villages – and vineyards. To all appearances a Croatian village. Yet the name has an Italian ring to it. And this even more so in the past. A document surviving from the late fourteenth century tells of the demand made by the ruling Venetian Doge that the bishop of Korčula should instruct repairs to the little monastery Church of St John (Sveti Ivan) at 'Lombardo'. Could there have been some connection between this Lumbarda / Lombardo and the wide fertile plain of Lombardy far to the north beyond Venice? Might some homesick *émigré* serving in Korčula as a functionary of the Most Serene Republic have built a summer house for himself here, a medieval *vikendica* where, like his contemporary Petrarch, he could 'enjoy the pleasures of light, air, and spacious walks and fine prospects'? Or perhaps there was more to it than recreation or cultured leisure. Might it have been mendicant friars who established themselves here *extra muros* in rural seclusion, as others did on the nearby island of Badija? Yet the name is all that prompts speculation. There is nothing in the island landscape to evoke memories of the flat marshy basin of the Po. Nor, in contrast to Korčula itself or almost any of the towns of the eastern Adriatic littoral, is there much in the village to recall Italianate models, certainly not of such antiquity.

Indeed, in medieval times the very existence of any kind of viable urban or semi-urban community on these open shores seems highly doubtful. Only ports like the town of Korčula, deliberately fortified by their Venetian rulers, could expect to remain safe from the attacks of the Turks or the random incursions by those pirates who regularly plundered the whole length of the coastline. On the islands, most villages developed inland, well hidden from the sea, while on the mainland the country population held to the high slopes where they could be sure of advance warning of any sea-borne danger. Lumbarda's location, exposed at the low eastern end of the island, would have been hopelessly vulnerable.

On the other hand, seen from the sea, that same location with its sheltered bays and fertile gentle slopes must always have seemed an attractive place to put ashore. Around 630 AD, roughly two centuries before the Venetians first attempted to conquer Korčula and eight before the republic's final uninterrupted period of pre-Napoleonic rule, the Croats had arrived from the Neretva valley. They stayed. Before them had come the Avars; and before them, the Romans who, after twice subduing the resistance of the mysterious Illyrian tribes – the second subjugation by the Emperor Octavian in 35 BC being particularly brutal – had ruled the island for five hundred years until the fall of the Empire in 476 AD. A millennium or so earlier, probably sometime in the sixth century BC, Greek families from the island of Vis (Issa) had established communities near what is now the port of Vela Luka in the west and at Lumbarda on the eastern tip of the island. Those were distant, more mythic days when, as Freya Stark writes of another shore in the eastern Mediterranean, 'Boats could set out with their rowers and find a headland and build a city and stay'. A broken stone tablet from the fourth century BC, discovered in 1877 and now in a Zagreb museum, is inscribed with details of the Greeks' colonial foundation, solid proof of the Lumbarda settlement, lapidary and literary. They, too, it appears, were prey to piratical attacks and took the steps necessary to protect themselves: the psephitic epigraph records that 'The founders agreed and the people decided that those who first took the land and walled the town get special sites for building inside the fortified town...' But, though some slight archaeological evidence of classical occupation has been uncovered, no traces of any ancient defensive walls have yet been found at Lumbarda.

None of this is in our minds as we head for the village driving south-east out from Korčula town – except perhaps the thought that *we* are the invaders now. The sun is up and the Renault's hood down. It is the height of the day. The road is quiet and on the rare straight stretch beyond the little hilltop Church of St. Anthony (Sveti Antun), perched in Mayan-like elevation at the head of its long staircase ascent, it is, briefly, tempting to speed. But speed has little to commend it here; much better to hasten slowly. There is, after all, a harmless arrogance to be savoured in open-top driving, even if no-one is watching. Moreover – and, in the pleasant early autumn heat, this is the greater pleasure – there are the sights, sounds and smells of the open road. So we take our time, enjoying again the familiar landscape.

As the road begins to twist and turn in a succession of gentle curves, the hillside on our right rises through olives and pines to the upland fields of Gornje Blato. To the left, a few metres below road level, lies Donje Blato, tidy vineyards and random cultivated plots spreading in a flat blanket of patchwork greens to the bushy ridge that hides the island's eastern shore. I remember a walk Jasna and I made there trying to make directional sense of the paths that cross the *polje*, hoping some might lead to the coast but finding ourselves helplessly lost in thickets of bramble and briar. Goats are grazing in the distance. Here and there a lone figure is at work, digging, pruning or simply checking the vines to see how many weeks remain before the first picking. Small birds flutter through the roadside trees, their song caught up in the rush of the car's slipstream. The scent of myrtle and pine comes in gusts.

We round a bend, climb up a gentle incline and see Javić, the most outlying and the youngest of Lumbarda's clustering hamlets. Stone walls and terra cotta tiled roofs huddle together on the low rise like sheep gathered on a hillside and there, guarding the flock, is the little two-bay church of the shepherd saint, Saint Spiridion (Sveti Spiridion), spiking the skyline with its distinctive one-arch-over-two, three-bell bellcote. Cresting the slope, we begin to see more of the village and then, suddenly, we are at the water's edge – Račišće bay. There are houses along both sides of the inlet: a tree-shaded track runs below terraced villas to end at a small jetty from which it is less than a hundred-metre row to the quarry islet of Vrnik; the other shore, more open, affects an air of rustic seaside ease before petering out on the rocky promontory of Koludrt. But Račišće passes quickly. The sight and the subtly slight smell of the sea are, to mix sensation with sensory metaphor, no more than a foretaste.

Inland again and there are fewer houses. To the south, vines, olives and some small cultivated fields. To the north, below the wooded hill of Koludrt where the stone tablet telling of the Greek settlement was found, we pass the village's handball court. At the roadside two plinth-posed obelisks flank some steps leading up to the balustraded grotto of the Virgin of Lourdes (Gospa Lurdska). Then, in an embrace of powdered bushes, comes a stonemason's yard and, as the sea sparkles into view again, the church and cemetery of St John (Sveti Ivan). The building and the graves that surround it are no older than the last years of the nineteenth century but the site is ancient – this is the place of worship mentioned by the Doge half a millennium earlier – and the church itself perhaps the most revered of all in Lumbarda. Sveti Ivan stands close to the shore: all who enter the village must pass by, as must all those, in car or coffin, who leave.

A narrow road, almost at water level, branches left round the end of the bay and then in a bold reverse curve climbs to the villas hidden in the trees on Koludrt. To our right, a concreted track runs up through neat plots planted with flowers and vegetables to older simpler houses at Kosovo. We keep to the main road, continuing east along the shore. Out on the water, low green-backed islands sail on the hazy horizon – they have strange Slavic names; Vrnik and Gubavac, Sutvara and Bisače, and further out, floating under the grey heights of the Pelješac peninsula, Stupa, Majsan and Gojak. The name of the village bay is simpler and more readily understandable – Prvi Žal, First Bay – though for anyone driving east (and this is the only road approach to Lumbarda) this is the *second* in the sequence of inlets that shape the shore around the village. First comes Račišće, then Prvi Žal, then, round the headland of Mala Glavica, the little bay of Tatinja, and finally, over the hilltop hamlet of Vela Glavica, the wide strand of Bilin Žal stretching away to the wooded hill of Ražnjić beyond which on a low promontory of bleached rocks, the easternmost tip of Korčula, a lonely light blinks its warning. But whatever topographical ambiguity attaches to the name Prvi Žal, the historical precedence of the place is immediately clear. Harbour and marina are here. Minimarket, butcher, cafés, restaurant and hotel. Children play and swim in the sandy shallows. All the communal activity of Lumbarda life occurs along the wide sweep of water from Sveti Ivan to the harbour mole on the opposite, eastern side of the bay – part village street, part promenade, part pier.

For a moment or two the sea disappears from view, briefly hidden by some waterside dwellings on our left. The row includes the local primary school, a structure scarcely less residential in appearance save for its tiny playground and, on the wall, three commemorative stone tablets; one, dated 1925, in millennial remembrance of the Croat king Tomislav, a second recording the date of the foundation of the village music society, Narodna Glazba Lumbarda, in 1929, and the third, appropriately enough honouring a much-loved teacher, 'raised by his former pupils of the Lumbarda Club, Oakland, California' in 1931. Across the street the houses of Žabnjak cluster haphazardly. Most are two-storeyed, built in local stone with gabled or half-hipped roofs. There is little in the way of ornament; windows have margins of dressed stone, there are some cornices, a few of the larger older houses have projecting consoles to carry fig-drying shelves. We glide through this short 'village street', careful to avoid the occasional car or motor-bike tractor-trailer parked on the narrow roadway and conscious, as in any rural community, that we are probably already under inspection. Exposed in our very visible, wrong-handed car, we try to look neither ostentatious nor apologetic, a little uneasy to be making such a conspicuous entrance but glad at the same time to imagine eyes behind the shutters and think ourselves already recognized. After twenty-five years, we are not strangers here. But we are not locals either. Each time we come we need a wave or smile or a shout of '*stigli ste!*', you've arrived!, to reassure us. Now, as always, our return is marked by this confusion of emotions, our exhilaration at arriving at last on familiar ground intense, yet muted by the respect of the incomer, as if, revisiting the house of one's birth, one stood on the threshold, excited by memories of the past but deferential, too, and just a little unsure of what might lie behind that once familial door.

The sea reappears. Shaded under bowing pine trees bent over the shore is the anguished bronze statue of the village war memorial, a naked male figure thrown back in wounded grief, the pose extravagant and rhetorical, teetering on the edge of homo-erotic mawkishness. The 'promenade' begins; less than a hundred metres of concrete, a painted bench or two looking out on the bay; on the landward side of the road, a minimarket, two small cafés and a pizza parlour retire discreetly behind terrace or forecourt. The houses of Vela Postrana begin to spread out along the contours of the hillside above. Ahead, facing the eastern side of the bay is the village hotel. It, too, has a terrace, wide, marble-paved and planted with a forest of tall trees – pine, holm oak, palm, tamarisk and eucalyptus. Begun in the late 1940s as a *Dom Kulture*, a communal Cultural Centre for the village, it was built with all the liberating enthusiasm and stolid aesthetic caution of Yugoslav communism. Fortunately, perhaps, lack of money to spend on gratuitous architectural detail, the admirably precise skills of the local stonecutters and, not least, the thick green screen of trees that for fifty years has cast its lengthening evening shadows over the façade, each in its different way has saved the building from the dull classical pretensions of Socialist Realism so familiar in so many contemporary urban incarnations. For twenty years this was Lumbarda's town hall. Then in 1968, a year after the community, sensing an easing in political conformity and with it the scent of commercial opportunity, had decided to form an organisation to promote village tourism, it was adapted and extended as a hotel. Local meetings, film shows, dances and wedding receptions were still held, the post office continued to operate and the village brass band, Narodna Glazba Lumbarda, went on practising, but now there was a bar, a restaurant and a three-storey block of balconied bedrooms full of strangers. For the next twenty years tourists filled the terrace every summer evening; paying guests of the village eating, drinking and dancing into the night. Then came the nineties war. The terrace was deserted, tables and chairs went into storage, a few locals drank what seemed an almost furtive beer watching the latest news of the conflict in Konavle or Kosovo flickering grimly on the small television screen mounted high in the corner of the bar. I can remember watching too in those deserted days: half in thrall to the hypnotic despair of it all, half dazzled and puzzled by the unsullied beauty of the setting sun blushing over Koludrt across the bay, wholly confused in an ironic melancholy, or, on a rainy day, when events conspired in depressing pathetic fallacy, numbed and saddened, my spirit flat as the half-drunk beer on the table before me.

The war is over but not much has changed. The hotel is still blighted and sad. Today there are a few tables on the terrace, all corralled close to the glazed front of the bar, but few patrons. A group of four men, in loosened ties and crisp shirt sleeves, have finished lunch and are beginning business. A middle-aged couple are bent over spaghetti. Behind its glass the long unattended bar-counter looks like some gargantuan ship model marooned in a museum case, irrelevant and ignored. Up on the flagpole in front of the trees, the Croatian flag stirs limply.

Much of the village lies beyond the hotel. A road branches left passing in front of the terrace under a line of low palms, spiked parasols planted to shade the quayside. This brief, rudimentary *riva* leads to a marina, not large but busy with yachts of varying size and condition ranked along its pontoon walkways. A long breakwater angles out into the bay. On its seaward side a wedge of shingle beach slips imperceptibly into water that is at first golden, then lime green, turquoise and deep dark blue. The black asphalted surface of the road, clinging to the water's edge half a metre or so above a shoreline of jagged mustard-coloured rocks, continues round the headland below the houses on Mala Glavica hill, curving first one way then the other as it embraces the little bay of Tatinja. Here there is a sandy beach and good swimming and, drenched in oleander blossom, a small café-restaurant where we have eaten mountains of *sitne ribe*, whitebait, washed down with Grk, the distinctively tangy white wine for which Lumbarda is renowned. A harbour shelters the boats of local fishermen and on a second breakwater nets are drying. On the slopes above, some of the oldest houses in the village sleep among olive groves and pines. This is the hamlet of Vela Glavica dominated on its hilltop site by the Parish Church of St Roch (Sveti Roko). Dedicated when the parish was first founded in 1561, the building was radically reconstructed in 1909 – three-aisled in plan and clearstorey-lit – to become the principal place of worship in Lumbarda. In front of its stepped gable façade, hidden from view by a dense clump of trees, is a small stone-paved square. Here villagers linger after mass to gossip and strangers, tired from their climb to visit the church, pause for breath, glad to find the low enclosing wall provided with built-in benching. At the apex of the facade a three-bell bellcote rises above the trees. Higher still is the church's stone belltower. Begun in 1967, it was only finally completed with money from Lumbarda *émigrés* around the world in 1996. Tucked against the chancel, its tall elegant form dominates the skyline like a golden obelisk garlanded with shadow at its triple-arched belfry.

The Tatinja road ends at the harbour pier where an ancient cobbled track leads up into the heart of Vela Glavica. Back at the hotel the main road continues east. It has less than a kilometre to go for the end of the island is not far distant. A gradual incline leads up under a canopy of mulberry trees and out into the vineyards. The sandy earth is a warm burnt sienna colour, the vines lined across flat or gently rolling fields, a continent away from the steep slaty slopes of the Rhine or Mosel. To the left, a road runs up to Vela Glavica and Sveti Roko. On the right, more tracks cut through the vineyards to the houses of Vela Postrana and Mala Postrana, ranged along the contours. We know one well, the home of our oldest Korčula friends Niko and Katica Batistić, a wide, two-storeyed dwelling with a tiled jerkinhead roof. The old house's pebble-paved terrace faces north, half hidden by a venerable almond tree and pergolas of vine and kiwi fruit.

The road runs on through the green and gold vines until it reaches the little chapel of the Holy Cross (Sveti Križ). Raised on an outcrop of rock in the midst of the vineyards, its small columned loggia gives welcome shade. Here at harvest time the grapes are weighed before despatch to the winery, the results of each family's labour religiously recorded in the shadow of the church. At Sveti Križ tracks diverge. One path winds south to the sands at Pržina bay, another north to the shore at Bilin Žal. A third runs on across the low isthmus, not more than four hundred metres wide, that links these two beaches. In the middle of this narrow cultivated neck of land, not far beyond the church, the central track passes an enigmatic ruined tower. It is three storeys high, its plan more or less square, barely a room, and though the architectural detail is minimal and the masonry scarcely distinguishable from recent building it is said to date from Roman times. The interior is void though the dome over the uppermost chamber survives; neatly constructed of small stones it rests on squinches at the four corners. A short stretch of walling not far from the tower constructed of small square stones laid in a diamond pattern lends some credence to an antique provenance but whether the simple structure is, as has been suggested by some, a watch-tower associated with the prison-camp set up by Diocletian to house Christians condemned to labour in the quarries on the nearby island of Vrnik, is at best no more than speculative. An equally reasonable inference might be that it was built as a look-out post intended to warn of attack from pirates or other enemies since, from its elevated platform, it would have been possible to scan the sea horizons both to the north and the south. Not many people pass this way: one or two local families tending their grapes or olives, a few nudists looking for a deserted cove, a lonely walker headed for the wooded hill at the island's eastern extremity.

It is tempting to renew our acquaintance with all this, to drive round the shore to Tatinja or out through the vineyards to Sveti Križ. But the listless village flag is as far as we go. Opposite the hotel we pull up at the *Caffé Mot*. Behind its low terrace wall the tables are deserted too. But the sun is sparkling on glass and chrome. The girl who serves us smiles; happy enough to be roused from the enervating inertia of the early afternoon heat, she brings us two Istra bitters. She is as slim and straight-backed as I remember her from our last visit. Does she recognize us, or is she amused by my out-of-practice Croatian? Perhaps both. At any rate, it is our first smile! Jasna and I exchange a glance. We sip our purply-cool drinks and gaze out on the quiet bay. We are here.

The *Caffé Mot* is new – well, relatively new. Twenty-five years ago when we first arrived in the village there was no café on the site, only a shuttered timber shed. This was the local *slastičarna*; hundreds like it were to be found along the entire coastline of communist Yugoslavia from Koper in the north to Kotor in the south. These shops, often no more than *ad hoc* temporary structures, all of them run it seemed by small dark Bosnians or Albanians, sold soft drinks, wonderful ice cream and even more wonderful sweetmeats – *baklava, burek, kadaif, halva, urmašice*, and many others whose names I never learned but whose gritty, frequently honey-drenched flavours seemed deliciously decadent. If there were seats you could drink sweet black coffee, equally delicious and equally gritty until the grains were washed away with a mouthful of the water from the glass that was always provided as an accompaniment. I remember how exotic all this was, how strange to hear Turkish behind the counter and how we – or more often our two young children, recalling the bare linguistic achievement of a five-month stay in Ankara a year or two before – would dare a grateful *çok teşekkür ederim* to the proprietor serving us, just to see his smile broaden. But the break-up of Yugoslavia wiped the smile from the faces of these warm people. No longer at ease in a then ultra-catholic Croatia, they shut shop and returned to their families in Bosnia or Kosovo; to what fate, who knows? In their place, literally in the same place (with what compensation, who knows), a new post-war generation of cafés appeared. These were glossier, modish and altogether more sophisticated. Anxious to prove their European credentials they served beer, wine and spirits, both domestic and imported; you could drink *espresso, cappuccino, machiatto* and every other kind of Italian coffee invention; ice cream came in a dozen different flavours; the cake shelf was packed with *štrudl, kremšnite* or *torte*. You might still order a *turska kava* and, perhaps, a portion of *baklava* but, in some places, you risked a strange look. The new cafés were smart and clean; a little too smugly perhaps, they wanted no reminder of their Balkan past. *Caffé Mot* was one such.

It was not large. A dozen small circular tables, each with four chrome tube chairs, filled the terrace. Here you could sit for hours watching the world and the day go by. Inside, behind plate glass, three or four more tables were provided with comfortable upholstered rattan furniture. Here you could enjoy some privacy out of the sun or the occasional wind and rain, or simply escape the neighbourly inquisition of passers-by. There was a neat L-shaped bar with its Italian coffee-making machine and open trays of flavoured ice cream. Ranged behind were most of the drinks any well-travelled European tourist might want as well as their less familiar, less expensive and only marginally less authentic local variants. A few promotional panels hinted at some elusive international glamour, incongruous but harmless – Cinzano, Cointreau, Johnny Walker. Fixed to a fascia above the bar's glittering cornice-rack of inverted glasses, was a small plastic plaque, a little out of tone with the rest of the décor, the kind of *kitsch* garage forecourts deal in. It read in perfect bad-language English, 'Don't drink water – fish fuck in it'. Amusing, if unexpectedly vulgar, but scarcely shocking, the recommendation was rendered oddly inoffensive, doubly diminished indeed, by its announcement here in a foreign tongue and, for those who did in fact understand the injunction, by its attractive alliterative punch.

Besides drawing tourists, the place soon became something of a local mecca (the word's unsolicited overtones, bearing in mind the Bosnian tragedy, ring with irony). Situated at the centre of the village, its location could hardly have been more propitious as a meeting place. Each Sunday afternoon the same all-male group played cards at the same three tables, throwing down their winners with a bravado that seemed as much a defiant gesture against the onset of age and the creeping infirmities of advancing years as it was intemperate delight in the mere victory of the moment. On Saturday evenings unattached young men ensconced themselves in a corner of the terrace drinking beer and shots of *lozovača* until, drunk and noisy but never unruly, they began to sing in a rough barber-shop harmony that offended no-one. Every afternoon of the week, around four or five o'clock, the young mothers of the village, some scarcely out of school, brought their babies. The girls smoked and drank Coke or tonic water while their children played on the terrace beside them or across the road at the water's edge. Every so often there would be a wail of petulance as an ice cream fell onto the sand, to be followed seconds later by a shriek from a mother alarmed to see her unhappy child about to cross back over the road. As for us, we often found ourselves spectators at these filial antics, having stopped for a coffee on our way back from the beach. There we sat for an hour or so till mothers and children had all gone home and the sun began to butter the bay with its late afternoon light.

And now we are sitting here once more. There are no card players, no revellers, not even a tourist or two waiting for an early bus back to Korčula. We are too soon for happy families hour. But the quietness is soothing and there is a selfish proprietorial pleasure in having the place to ourselves. Reflection sets in.

'Why are we here?' I fail to realise either the abruptness or the hackneyed philosophical immensity of my question until the words are out.

'What do you mean "Why are we here?"' Jasna – surprised, angry even, at the intrusion on her own private day-dream.

'No, I don't mean why are we here, not where did we come from, or where are we going, not all that. Not the meaning of life. Just… why are we here? Here, now, in *Caffé Mot*.' I think I know the answer but keep talking before Jasna can contradict or reassure me, 'We could have taken the side road at Račišće and parked just above the house. More convenient.'

'We're near enough here.'

It's true. A concrete path, only a garden's width away from the café, leads uphill to meet that road from Račišće. It's barely wide enough, however, for a small car. Not that this stops the proprietor of the shop which abuts the path on the other side, our neighbour Ivica, the village butcher, or his wife, Merica, or, more likely, one of his several sons, from gunning their battered Opel up between the verges to an abrupt halt where the path constricts between two gables, one of which, conveniently enough, is their house. But it stops us.

'Yes, but why do we do this – drive all the way in? We always seem to do it when we arrive.'

Jasna thinks for a moment, persuaded that the question merits an answer. 'I suppose,' she begins, then pauses. 'I suppose we want to see the sea, feel we're really in the village, that we've arrived again.'

'Not much happening.'

'Makes it all the more special, as if the village is ours alone.'

That's true too. And that's part of the answer – alone on the terrace of *Caffé Mot*, we can imagine Lumbarda is, indeed, somehow, ours. Perhaps it's having come here regularly for so many years. Perhaps it's because we have never been semi-detached visitors packaged in hotels but from the beginning lived *en famille* or later in a place of our own. Perhaps it goes deeper and has something to do with Jasna's own family roots. Perhaps it's because we speak, or try to speak, the language. Perhaps coming here all through the war has strengthened the bond we feel with the village. But it is, of course, the traveller's conceit to presume that places visited are places possessed. He comes, he sees, and, with his passing presence, fancies he conquers the strangeness of it all, conscripting each port of call to the imperium of personal experience. What was unknown becomes known, colonized, at least in part. And it is *his*, the traveller's secret place, his discovery, his vanity. Jealously guarded and seldom shared, its exoticism is hoarded and cultivated in the memory to be reported, if at all, with a devious combination of diffidence and teasing mystique calculated to underscore possession and leave the envious tantalised. I plead guilty. It *is* worthy of envy, the simple life here in Lumbarda. Back home in dismal November days when a rarely lit fire and a second bottle hold depression at bay around the dinner table, I want friends to know what pleasure the months we spend here bring us and yet, in the telling, I often catch my tongue, reining back the detail, afraid to reveal too much, reluctant to relinquish the lien that fortune has given us on this special place. Worse still, in Lumbarda itself, in the deserted village of the 1990s, when the tourists vanished and the bombers flew high over Korčula locked on a bearing for Kosovo and it was not just the early afternoon terrace of the *Caffé Mot* that we had to ourselves but, day-long and undisturbed, almost every beach and bay on the island, how we would preen our pretence to solitary possession. Selfish and ill tuned as it was to the pain of the place, that was, I had to admit, how we sometimes felt. The memory is an embarrassment; it irks my conscience. Perhaps it is as well that a Slovenian-registered combi has drawn up onto the concrete of the promenade across the road and is discharging its tumbling cargo of dogs and children in our direction. Our acquisitive fancies justly violated, we pay our bill and leave.

We reverse the car in front of the hotel and head back west. Reaching Račišće we make an acute turn back to our left away from the sea. The narrow asphalted road twists and bends up through the olives, squeezing between old close-gabled dwellings, then on past newer, half-built, balconied houses set back behind gardens full of ripening tomatoes, aubergines and peppers. We pass a joiner's shed barricaded with sawn logs and miscellaneous lumber, masons' yards stacked with cladding and paving slabs, columns and urns, a blacksmith's workshop and, on the hillside to our right, sitting incongruously high and dry in what looks like a minor quarry or the excavation for the basement of a very large house, the timber skeleton of a half-constructed fishing boat. At length we come to a small parking place built up from the hillside below where a retaining wall supports the broadening of the road. Nosing forward, we park alongside an immobilised Yugo, careful to stop short of the unprotected edge. The village lies below us, Koludrt to the left, the hamlet hills of Mala Glavica and Vela Glavica to the right, and the sea, no more than a hundred metres distant downhill, where Prvi Žal widens out to the north-east. Out across the channel the size and disposition of the off-shore islands become clearer, the ridge-riven profiles of Pelješac more majestic.

Below us is a grassy yard carpeted with late wild flowers, the tiny garth of the Church of St Bartholomew (Sveti Bartul). Built in coursed blocks of local limestone, the church is small like most of the village's places of worship, little more than a modest room with a sanctuary recess backing onto the lane to the east. At most, perhaps thirty people can cram into its barrel-vaulted cell, though on the rare saint's day occasions when mass is celebrated here priests and people spill out into the yard. There are no windows, only a single quatrefoil light over the round-arched doorway in the west gable. Rising at the gable apex is a disproportionately tall bellcote; it, too, is round-arched. Beside the doorway, a stone stoup hollowed out for holy water projects from the wall. It is difficult to tell how old this simple unprepossessing building might be. Inside, a tiny timber balcony survives with indistinct painted images of the evangelists on four crudely framed panels that may be from the sixteenth century. The structure itself, rude and astylar, could almost be Romanesque in origin, though the barrel vaults to church and sanctuary are almost imperceptibly pointed. No-one seems able to give a reliable date. Nor, until recent years, did anyone seem to care about the church's condition. Now, however, there are bright terra cotta tiles on the roof, the stonework has been pointed again and a new rope falls from the bellcote. For us, living just across the lane, listening to the chanted Hail Marys of local women on a warm evening, the church has always seemed like an old friend watching over us. For our neighbour the butcher, too, no doubt, for the emblem of the apostle-saint is (recondite coincidence) a flesher's knife.

Piece by piece we unload the luggage, stacking it beside the car – cases, bags of various sorts, two new duvets, a weighty, forty-year-old food mixer that once belonged to my mother, a laundry basket, books. There's a drone of bees in the afternoon air. A chain-saw whines somewhere on the hill above. It's hot.

'*Eh! Stigli ste?*' It's our neighbour, Roko, on the balcony above his garage. The voice is disembodied for a moment or two and then his head appears above the geraniums. He is not tall but robustly built, barrel chest in a striped tee-shirt, thick arms, thick white hair. '*Dobro došli!*'

'*Da. Hvala. Došli smo trajektom, iz Rijeke.*' I shout back a thank-you for his welcome, explaining that we have travelled by the ferry from Rijeka.

'*Fino*'.

'*Kako ste*?' A polite 'How are you?'

'*Pa dobro. Nema problema.*' He shrugs his shoulders; he's fine. Then with a wave and a friendly '*Vidimo se, Bog*' – 'See you, bye' – he disappears indoors.

It's enough. Dalmatians are no more effusive than Scots, a character trait that for us has always seemed to establish a kind of bond. Social conventions are observed politely, if perhaps, measured by more urbane standards, a little gracelessly. I like that. Honesty. Caution. Friendship doesn't come cheap. I doubt if Roko would consider us his friends – not yet, at any rate. But there is respect. And this second recognition, with its added welcome, makes me feel good; the luggage seems lighter.

The steps down to the head of the path climbing up from *Caffé Mot* are sticky with seed-soaked fruit spilled from a spiny pomegranate tree growing beside the church. Here, on the upper, steeper stretch of the incline, the lane is at its narrowest: on one side, Sveti Bartul; on the other, a stone wall, increasing in height with the fall of the ground, links the gables of three houses that lie in parallel down the falling contours. The first of the three dwellings, entered from the high road just beyond where we have parked, has lain unfinished for well over a decade – we know it as Ana-Marija's house, after the thin, dark-haired woman who comes every now and then from Zagreb but never stays long. Its rough concrete walls are still unrendered, windows and shutters unpainted, a second storey has yet to be constructed. To the north a makeshift terrace overlooks a small overgrown garden thick with orange trees and the sinuous contortions of an ancient fig. The second house, shaded from the sun by Ana-Marija's trees, is ours; a simple, single-storey, stone-built dwelling, perhaps a hundred years old. The third, lower down the hill, is the butcher's: older and grander, the stone margins of its cusped Gothic windows set off against white-rendered walls, it is one of only a handful of houses in the village still redolent of the patrician patronage of wealthy *Korčulani*.

Our house is small but private. From the lane, little is revealed: the boundary wall with its white-painted doorway, the woodwork shrinking at the joints; the gable, its gaunt, heavily pointed stone relieved only by some roughly dressed blocks at the quoins and a small shuttered window placed centrally in the attic triangle; the roof, still with its original tiles, not tart and orange like the recently repaired war-damaged roofs of Dubrovnik but bleached by age to a warm texture of tawny browns, beiges and greys like the mottled plumage of young seagulls. Behind the door is an intimate yard, no more than two metres broad but stretching back beyond the house. Trailed overhead on a cat's cradle of wire and rope, a clambering vine gives shade. To the right, a stone retaining wall holds back the earth of Ana-Marija's garden. Rosemary and pelargoniums tumble through the insecure masonry under a green canopy of overhanging branches – orange, fig, and the sharp armorial spray of palm fronds. To the left, the rubble-built wall of the house is dappled in afternoon sunlight.

The cottage is divided. Our part, gable to the lane, is the smaller of two dwellings housed within the walls: a minimal entrance hall, shower bathroom and a single all-purpose room below, an attic bedroom tucked in the roof space above, a winding timber stair. When we bought it in March 1991 – or to be more accurate, when Jasna, taking advantage of her dual nationality, made the purchase (for at that time it was still impossible for foreigners to own property) – we were full of excitement at the prospect of owning our own second home and, though we had been regular visitors to Yugoslavia for over thirty years and knew something of the regional unease that had been festering in the protracted political fall-out from Tito's death in 1980, we had no reason to expect the imminent break-up of the country nor could we dream of the horrors the rest of the decade would bring. Our Lumbarda friends, Niko and Katica Batistić, in whose family home we had for many years spent the two or three weeks of our annual holiday and who knew how much we loved the village and how keen we were to buy a place of our own, had found a number of properties for us to look at. The decision was not difficult. Although it was small, the cottage we chose had all we needed – and more: it was unpretentious in form, built in the traditional way and located near the centre of the village. Moreover, it had been recently renovated; the owner, an engineer from Split had fitted it out as a holiday home, a *vikendica*, but now wanted to realise his capital to buy some land nearer home on the island of Brač. The floor was tiled, the walls plastered or lined in pine, there were new kitchen fitments; we would have little to do. So the price was agreed and paid – the wad of German marks passed in an envelope to the lawyer in Zagreb – and we moved in. Within a few months war had broken out.

Undaunted or simply foolhardy, we resolved to keep coming to Lumbarda. We flattered ourselves that this was because we wanted to show solidarity with Niko and Katica and our other friends on the island, but perhaps the real reason was much less honourable. Living up to our national stereotype – *škrti Škoti*, mean Scots, is the half-humorous, half-serious Croatian phrase – we were determined not to lose out on our investment. But if this were so, we could at least console ourselves with the conviction that money was not the reason. What we could not bear to lose was Lumbarda itself. It was inconceivable to imagine our life without its annual Adriatic adventure. So we came – and not just for a brief two- or three-week visit but, now that we had our own place in the sun and could begin to enjoy the opportunities for prolonged leisure that are the entitlement of a certain age, we came twice in the year, each time for several weeks' stay on the island. It meant some circumspect travel arrangements. Sometimes the overnight ferry from Rijeka was the only safe route south. Sometimes it was possible to fly, changing planes in Zagreb for Split. Then there would be a three-hour sail to Vela Luka on Korčula followed by an hour-long bus journey from one end of the island to the other. Later, once the airport at Čilipi had been repaired, we could fly to Dubrovnik, hire a car and reach Korčula over the short ferry crossing from Orebić on the Pelješac peninsula. These journeys were memorable: the coastal steamers crowded with bereft refugees, women, children and old men driven into hapless flight from their homes in Bosnia, their belongings crammed into battered cases and plastic bags; the saloon of the Vela Luka ferry fogged with the cigarette smoke of teenage soldiers, limbless victims of the conflict headed for hospital recuperation; hymn-singing Irish pilgrims filling the plane to Split *en route* to Međugorije to pray for peace within earshot of the guns; convoys of UNPROFOR jeeps and lorries down from Mostar in search of 'rest and recreation', slowing and disrupting the flow of traffic on the *magistrala* with all the indifference of an invading army. And when, scarcely believing we were so close to the war and yet so far from danger, we found ourselves at last in Lumbarda, how strange and ambivalent it felt to play the dual role of resident and visitor, to share in the village's morning obsession with newspaper and radio, fearful to learn of the latest destruction or atrocity, and yet, only a few hours later, alone on a deserted beach, to think ourselves castaways in some forgotten paradise.

It was not, however, only the village beaches or the terrace and bedrooms of the local hotel that lacked people; all through the war the other half (more like two-thirds) of our cottage remained empty. Indeed, it had been abandoned for many years. This had a certain advantage since it meant that we had the shaded courtyard to ourselves and did not need to share access to or from the lane with a neighbour. Though far from critical, it had been a factor in our decision to buy. On the other hand, the progressive dereliction of the rest of the property, both house and yard, did nothing for the amenity or value of our new holiday home. (One minor consequence was the occasional presence of mice. We found their droppings, heard their nocturnal scratchings in the roof, but, apart from the discovery of the dessicated skeletal remains of a single specimen which had probably expired decades before our arrival, we neither saw nor caught one. Traps, pellets and poison produced nothing. Even the local remedy of glue – applied to thin cardboard to which the luckless scampering rodent would adhere and, stuck in agonising immobility, expire – failed to succeed.) We thought of buying the rest of the building, imagining the possibilities that added accommodation might bring and how, when the war was over, friends and family might be persuaded to share our love of Lumbarda. But the owner, old Šime, something of a local patriarch well into his eighties, had no intention of selling. He had, he said, many grandsons, one of whom might some day need a home of his own.

But then things changed. Workmen appeared. The empty rooms were renovated, drains for a new kitchen and bathroom were laid, windows glazed, paint applied; for a few weeks clouds of dust billowed through the yard. There was, however, no sign of a grandson. Nor had Šime sold to some other interested party, though by this time, with the war over and the restrictive laws on foreign ownership relaxed by the new Croatian government, enterprising house-in-the-sun-hunters were already beginning to sense the potential of the Adriatic property market. Instead, our neighbours turned out to be a Bosnian Croat family, uprooted and displaced by the fortunes of war – Marjan Rajić, Dragica his wife, their teenage son Josip and eight-year-old adopted daughter Blaženka. Marjan himself did most of the work, digging, tiling or plastering through the heat of the day. Time after time he would apologise to us for the disturbance. We felt embarrassed by his concern and politeness, by the daily contrast between his physical labour and our self-indulgent leisure, but most of all by his family's longing for a home. Remembering the scenes of refugee despair we had encountered on our travels and the many more we had seen on television, we could not but think Šime's gesture admirable. How or why the deal had been done we never discovered, though we learned later that no sale had been made and no right of tenure granted; Marjan and his family might make all the improvements they wished but, no more secure than an over-ripe fig, their tenancy hung on a grandfather's whim. And Šime knew, as shrewd as he was generous, that for a family forced to make a new life for themselves, this chance coincidence of need and opportunity was too good to pass over.

At first we viewed the prospect of close neighbours with some alarm. This, too, like the gradual post-war return of tourists to Lumbarda, was a threat to our possessive fancy. Not only must we tolerate others intruding on beaches we had thought our own, now we should have to surrender the very privacy of the cottage yard. We needn't have worried. The house had never looked better, thanks to Marjan's efforts. If it rained while we were out of the village, Dragica would save the washing drying on the line slung under the orange trees. Josip kept his CD volume down. Blaženka was a delight, calling on us for help with homework or, convulsed in giggling, drawing beards and spectacles on the politicians, celebrities and soccer stars pictured in our daily copy of *Jutarnji List*.

We learned nothing of the family's previous life nor of their flight from Bosnia, and we didn't ask. But one day, when we were sitting in the yard showing photographs of our grand-daughter to Blaženka, Dragica brought the family album to the table. We sensed something of significance in this gesture. The album was worn and dog-eared, but precious, like a well-read Bible. Its pictures told us a story, a story no different perhaps from those told by the million and a half other displaced victims of the fomented hatred of the Bosnian wars – except that this was our neighbours' story. There was nothing extraordinary about the views of their home town of Zenica – except that now many of the houses and churches were in ruins. Their home looked cosy but unremarkable – except that now another family lived there. The faces of friends and relatives were like those caught in countless other family groups – except that now many were gone. Unable to find words, we listened as Dragica turned the pages explaining who was who. This brother had been killed in action. Another maimed. These two cousins had disappeared. And these were Blaženka's parents, both gone. The tone was matter-of-fact, the hurt, if not overcome, somehow suppressed. How was it possible, we asked ourselves, that through such trauma, experiences that seemed to us so irrefragably brutalising to human sensibilty, how could it be that this calm forbearance should prevail? Now, throughout our stay, as if sanctified by these confidences, our neighbours' every act of kindness acquired in our eyes an added dignity. And when each time we left Lumbarda to set out on the long journey home to Scotland and the whole family would appear to wish us '*sretan put*', loading us with fruit, wine and olive oil, we marvelled again. We had made good friends. Our house was safe. And the mice had gone.

Busy unpacking, we hear a knock at our open door. It's Blaženka. She is dressed in a simple short-sleeved dress, pale white cotton patterned with flecks of red and green. Her brown hair is drawn back and held in a poppy red bow. In her clasped hands she is cradling a tiny hamster, Miško.

'*Dobro došli, teta. Dobro došli, dundo*'. Her dark eyes are shining.

It's our third welcome to the village.

AT THE BATISTIĆ TABLE

'All happy families resemble each other'

Leo Tolstoy
1877

Each arrival at our house in Lumbarda follows the same routine. We unlock the door, throw back the shutters (one window downstairs, the other upstairs), switch on the electrics, open the water valve in the lane, unpack the bedding from the plastic containers that have protected pillows, sheets and blankets from mice and mites over the last few months, make up the beds tucked under the timber-lined camceils, empty our bags, hang up our crushed clothes, assemble the plastic table and unfold the chairs that turn the courtyard into an extra room, and only then, running with sweat, do we take a shower. Once refreshed and changed, we call on our neighbours Marjan and Dragica. Greetings and kisses are exchanged, gifts given. Blaženka hugs us with delight. Later, left alone, we sit quietly in the yard. Still tense with the cumulative expectations of travel, we try to relax, to live in the moment. And slowly, like the suffusing glow of the *rakija* we have just drunk, a childlike sense of incredulous amazement, disbelief at our good fortune to be once again here, fills us with joy.

There is, however, one further pleasure. We must visit the Batistić family. To arrive in Lumbarda without calling on our oldest friends would be unpardonable. To make that call now, however, in the heat of the afternoon when they, like almost everyone else in the village, have escaped to post-prandial dreams in the cool stillness of a darkened room, would be just as unthinkable. There is time. Time for us to rest and recover from the journey. Time for us to discover again the pleasures of indolence.

79

After a while we seek some shade. It's warm in our attic bedroom, a languorous disarming warmth. In an exquisite lethargy we slip into intimacy and sleep.

The sun was already low in the west as we passed the hotel. Long shadows leant ahead of us lancing through the carpet of lace cast below the mulberry trees. Once out beyond the green canopy we turned right. Asphalt to concrete. A gradual incline between low stone walls, the lane narrowed as it rose, barely wide enough for the driver of a *fico* or *deux chevaux* to negotiate, let alone open even one of his doors, in safety. Fifty metres or so ahead the path passed between the gables of two large houses, narrowed further, then rose steeply in an abrupt ascent to meet the high road above the vineyards. Beside us a familiar plot stretched up to the older of the two houses. How many times, when our children were young and we spent our precious summer fortnight with the Batistić family, had we walked up this path beside the garden: four of us, hot but content, trudging back from Bilin Žal or Pržina beach in the late afternoon, or Jasna and I alone late at night, counting glowworms on the wall or stars in the sky, and more than a little drunk. Things had changed of course. We had all got older – Jasna and I, Niko and Katica, the children. A generation had passed; another was growing up. Even the old house was no longer quite the same, now extended from the far gable in a two-storey, self-contained dwelling built for Niko's son Nikša, his wife Jagoda and their three boys. But the garden was as it had always been, the rich coffee-brown earth as productive as ever: ridges of potatoes, straggling tomatoes, swelling peppers and aubergines, carrots, beetroot, lettuces, and those two staple vegetables of every Dalmatian table, Swiss chard or *blitva*, and the broad bean plants endearingly known as *bob*. And there was Katica. Her back towards us, a wicker basket on her arm, she was picking lemons from the trees on the far side of the garden.

'Eh! Gospođo! Jeste-li dobro?'

Katica turned. Puzzled for a moment, she was soon smiling, at once glad to see us and, I guessed, amused by the mock formality of my call. I had played the fool a little, addressing her as 'Madam' or 'Mrs' (though in translation neither word sounds quite right) and enquiring after her health or wellbeing in the over-polite second person plural. She pushed a loose strand of hair off her forehead with the back of her hand. Now she was laughing.

'*Dobro došli.*' Welcome. She waved, pointing up to the house by way of invitation.

On the terrace, kisses. No aseptic head-bobbing but the warm meeting of cheeks and lips. Hugs, too, though Katica, conscious she had been working in the garden, made a fuss of holding her hands apart, embracing us with wrists and forearms only. Neither tall nor small, in blue shirt, jeans and trainers, she looked as she always did, younger than her years – more mid forties than late fifties. The sleeves of her shirt were rolled up to the elbows, her trousers muddied with earth at the knees. Not for the first time I fancied there was something of the unreconstructed tom-boy about her, as if, despite being the woman of the house and already a grandmother several times over, she was determined neither to take herself too seriously nor to grow old too soon or too gracefully. It was not that she was careless in dress, simply that she liked to be at ease in what she wore with no concern to play up her femininity or impress. If this casualness was assumed with a certain mischievous confidence it was more that of the schoolgirl than the hoyden. Away from the village, as I knew from times we had been together – Niko, Katica, Jasna and I – on visits to Blato or Zagreb and, indeed, on one memorable occasion when our holiday paths had crossed in Sydney, Australia, she would transform herself into a smart and sophisticated woman, silk scarf at her neck, suit elegantly tailored to her figure, her choice of half-height heels judged to perfection. In Lumbarda, however, where everyone knew everyone, where there were vineyards and olive groves to be tended, a garden to be cared for, housework to be done, family and guests to be fed, she dressed as she pleased. It was this freedom to be herself that kept her young.

She fussed around us asking questions, not waiting for answers, urging us to sit down then preventing us from doing so until she had produced cushions for the stone seats set into the low wall that divided the terrace from the garden. Had we just arrived? How was the journey? How long would we stay this time? We struggled to recover our dormant Croatian, the sudden speed of Katica's interrogation like a wake-up call, our responses inarticulate as early morning thoughts.

From inside the house Niko appeared, smiling. He must have seen us coming up the lane or heard us talking with Katica on the terrace. He was carrying a tray with four glasses and a large jug of iced water. These he placed on the stone table by the doorway, then turned to greet us. Embraces. More kisses. All the mutual flattery of renewed acquaintance. How well you look! You haven't aged at all. What's the secret? And then, as if perhaps to answer the question – or was it simply to draw a halt to this conversational foreplay – he put his forefinger to his lips, raised his eyebrows in a knowing look and disappeared back into the house, re-emerging almost immediately with a bottle of red wine in his grasp. The bottle was unlabelled. It had no cork. I knew what this meant. I knew that he had just drawn the wine from what still remained of the thousand or so litres the family's vineyards had yielded last autumn and I knew, too, that before the evening was over this would not be the only bottle we would drink. Was this the secret, the elixir? Why not? Certainly Jasna and I had long ago convinced ourselves of the health-giving properties of Niko's wine. Last year, indeed, we had joined the family picking the grapes, we had hauled our plastic crates laden with bunches of the ripe fruit along the vineyard lanes, we had helped load the lorry, and then in the late afternoon heat had ambled back to the Batistić home, tired but happy, sucking our purple-stained fingers with thoughts of the real thing. And here, in the kitchen yard behind the house, we had watched Niko, his son Nikša and son-in-law Nebojša, make the wine; no barefoot trampling, of course, for machines did the work of separating stalks and skins and pressing the juices, but still two or three hours of hard physical work until the huge concrete vat was full. I remembered the first taste of the new wine at the end of the day, sweet and tongue-tip-tingling.

Now that same wine was mature. We were being invited to drink it. Damson-dark, tannin-rich, it waited in the glass.

'*Živjeli*', said Niko, wishing us good health and long life.

'*Živjeli*' we replied.

And, in truth, I meant it for as the four of us sat together in the half-light of the evening, sipping the wine, relaxed and glad to be united once more, it had not taken me long to realise that for all his hospitable good spirits Niko was not at his best. His black hair was still as black – a piece of genetic good fortune which, as it always did when we met up again, momentarily irked me, my own hair, once every bit as dark, having long since turned to grey. His face, never lined, had grown a little heavier around the chin and jowls; but hadn't mine also? It was his movements – carrying the tray, pouring the wine, adjusting his sitting position – all unnaturally studied and evidently not without pain, that betrayed something more sinister than our common legacy of age. Though she tried to conceal it, I could sense Katica's awareness of her husband's discomfort. But the sensibilities of friendship work both ways; Niko had already read my thoughts. It was arthritis, he explained, confessional and matter-of-fact at the same time. *Poliartritis* the doctors called it. In all the joints. Annoying but not virulent – not yet, he might have added, but didn't. The aches and pains were intermittent, he said, preferring that word to the more negative 'recurrent' he might have chosen. Perhaps it was the way he spoke a little more slowly than usual, perhaps it was my anxious sympathy, perhaps it was the wine, but I was following his explanation without too much difficulty. Phrase by phrase, word by word, the language was beginning to come back.

'Maybe it's just as well we don't live in *your* climate. At least here the summer dryness and the sun seem to help. Maybe the wine too', he laughed, pouring us a second glass, but topping up his own only half-drunk glass with water from the jug.

I had noticed and admired this temperance before and had put it down to innate good sense, that very Mediterranean ability to measure one's drinking through the day with respect and control – that and the wisdom of the good host, always ready to share a sociable glass with his guests but careful to remain sober. Now I felt there might be more to Niko's abstemiousness. Did he perhaps regard the anodyne relief that alcohol might offer as a temptation to be avoided? More likely his caution was practical rather than moral, a dietary embargo imposed by his doctor.

'How was the summer in Scotland this year? Rain?'

The question, deceptively banal, carried a subtle compulsion. Enough! Not wanting us – and still less himself – to become preoccupied with his ailments, Niko had turned the conversation around. We were finished with talk of health. Now it was to be the weather, as much a matter of common concern here as at home, though here the daily preoccupation was more often with the degree of heat and the direction of the wind than the likelihood of more or less rain. I recognized the signal and replied that no, in fact the summer back home had been unusually warm, maybe not by Adriatic standards but, with the temperature often in the mid twenties and clear skies for three or four days at a time, exceptional for us in Scotland. It was, I said, the kind of weather that helped confirm us in our decision to spend spring and autumn in Lumbarda and the rest of the year at home. Summers in Korčula could be too enervating.

Too hot and too dry, agreed Katica. Like this past summer: too hot to sleep at nights; so dry the garden had had to be watered regularly through July and August. More importantly, the vines and olives had suffered. This year's grape harvest would still be good quality but the quantity would be down on previous years. It was too early to predict with any certainty how the olives would mature but things didn't look good. It seemed that even here there were times when rain could become an obsession.

As we talked it had grown darker. The air was still soft and warm. A scent of rosemary drifted from the garden. I seemed to catch music floating up from somewhere in the village, coming and going in gentle, scarcely audible sighs. One – two, three. One – two, three. Imperceptibly we slipped into the gloom gathering under the terrace pergola, our voices quieter, disembodied. In the anonymity of darkness, while the conversation idled in pleasantries, I slid into dreams. My eyes closed, doubling the delight. One – two, three. One – two, three. I felt myself afloat on the warm wine of friendship, borne on a wave of unconjured grace. For a moment I was alone, aglow with consciousness. It was as if, deep beneath the eddying trivialities of speech, I had heard unspoken in the closeness of friends some benediction meant only for me. I sensed the touch of life, remembered moonlit waters off the coast of Coll, saw my seven-year-old grand-daughter smile.

The moment passed. Katica rose explaining she must see to dinner. Disappearing into the house, she switched on the terrace light. A tangled canopy of vine and kiwi fruit appeared over our heads. A blanched *guster*, suddenly illuminated on the door lintel, scuttled into the leaves. Niko, Jasna and I, no less surprised by the light, shuffled guiltily in our seats concealing a yawn or two as we tried to assume a more attentive position. Niko poured more wine; we stayed his hand, thinking it wise to follow his example and add some water. As before, he did the same – only more so. Another light flashed across the foot of the garden. Headlamps. More visitors.

It was Mirjana, Niko and Katica's older daughter, and her husband Nebojša. Was this a chance visit? Or had they known we would be here? Perhaps Niko, to whom as usual we had telephoned the date of our arrival in Lumbarda, had invited them, guessing we should be almost certain to call that very day. Perhaps they themselves had made a point of asking when we were expected to be sure of seeing us. I liked to think so, for although Mirjana was in her late thirties and Nebojša past forty – not much older than our own children – we had always felt close to them, comfortable in their company, never aware, on our part at least, of any generational barrier. This could be presumption of course, I thought, succumbing to cynicism, but somehow, as we greeted one another in a happy confusion of kisses, surprised smiles and laughter, I found that possibility hard to believe.

Mirjana, in black jeans and a white sleeveless top whiter than white against her tanned skin, sat beside her father. She laid her hand on his forearm. They exchanged a brief complicit look, he smiling at the touch. They had the same brown eyes, the same dark hair, and yet it seemed to me that there was about the daughter more of her mother than her father. Taller and thinner than Katica, the slimness of her figure served to emphasise a similar, barely latent boyishness. Her hair, silky on the brow, was short, razor cut at the temples and neck. Her clothes, simple but stylishly ambivalent, added to the androgynous allure. Was this calculated? It was hard to know. On the one hand, there seemed to be some genetic legacy at work. But Mirjana was an intelligent woman, the proprietor of a small but successful fashion boutique in Korčula, she must know the tricks of her trade. All in all it was difficult not to imagine an altogether feminine guile behind the *gamine* innocence. I found myself wondering if it had been one or the other or the combination of the two that had captivated Nebojša. They looked happy together. Now, as always. She slight and slender, sexually intriguing; he strong, broad-shouldered and broad-chested from years of swimming, masculine. His physical presence was calm and assured, sculptural even. His hair, already thin and greying, had been cropped close to his scalp emphasising the perfect form of his skull. The head glistened with perspiration and, absurdly, I found myself thinking of sunlight on marble. By contrast, stubble shadowed his chin, his forearms were matted black, and a thicket of grey hairs sprouted around the neck of his tee-shirt. But there were no rings, no gold chains or bracelets, no medallions and no Rolex, the lack of these Levantine trinkets a measure of the man. Nebojša was at ease with himself, he did not need the reassurance of such affectation. As he shook hands, his grip was firm but without the false vigour of the exaggerated grasp. When he took the bottle to pour us the last of the wine, went to replenish it and returned with two more glasses, I did not see arrogance or impertinence but rather the good manners of a son-in-law who knew himself loved in the Batistić family.

We spoke of our children. Mirjana apologised that neither Roko nor Marija had been able to come tonight. They were teenagers now, though only just, and rapidly developing a social life of their own. Roko had gone fishing for octopus, though he hadn't said with whom – a strong indication, thought Nebojša, that there might be a girlfriend on the scene. Marija had a mandolin lesson in Korčula. Her teacher was enthusiastic about her playing and had recommended she should enrol in the Music School in Dubrovnik where her talent could be nurtured. But Marija was not keen, fearful it would mean breaking with all her friends on the island. Moreover, said Mirjana, neither she nor Nebojša had thought thirteen an age to leave home. I suspected, however, that Marija's parents' motives were more possessive than protective and I did not blame them – and said so; it was a view Jasna and I would certainly have shared had we been faced with a similar dilemma. I recalled the time years ago when we sent our fifteen-year-old daughter Dara on a six-week language course to Zagreb; seeing her vanish beyond the departure gate at the airport had been heart-breaking enough. Now Dara was in her early thirties, a mother twice over.

'Two children? A new baby? Maja and...?'

'Robert. Eight months now. Baby's the wrong word. A boy from day one.'

'And Davor?' asked Mirjana who had always liked our son.

'Still just the one, Ross. But Carol is pregnant again... November', Jasna added, anticipating the obvious question.

'Something to look forward to.'

'Yes. We're here till the end of October so we should be back in time.' And although we had only just arrived in Lumbarda and had six or seven weeks to go before we had to leave, the thought of that special family occasion made far-away Scotland seem suddenly and unexpectedly attractive.

I surprised myself by feeling a little ashamed at this premature fancy. But then, why should I? Wasn't this just another twist in the here-and-there dialectic that now ruled our lives. For months we had been longing for the sea and sun of Korčula, looking forward to renewing friendships. Yet, no sooner arrived, I was thinking of home. I knew that it would not be the last time I felt like this, that there would be more of these moments, occasional but recurring, and that eight weeks or so from now as we prepared to set out on the journey north across Europe I would be smelling fallen leaves and wood smoke, thinking of frosty nights and the possibility of snow. 'Home thoughts from abroad' alternating with dreams of 'the warm south'. This was, after all, the pattern of life we had chosen and grown to love. Summer in Scotland, autumn on Korčula. Winter in Scotland, spring on Korčula. But, as I sipped Niko's wine and contemplated becoming a grandfather again, I had to admit that this seasonal sequence was not without its irony, the immediacy of one enjoyable experience of time and place regularly compromised by a just as pleasurable anticipation of the next. However much this cyclical change of scene – with all the intoxication of travel that went with it – seemed to defer the depressing onset of old age, perhaps we had in fact only succeeded in speeding up the passage of precious time.

Katica's re-appearance cut short these sombre reflections. She stood on the threshold, arms on hips.

'*Večera je gotova.*' Dinner was ready.

We rose and followed her indoors, stepping from the terrace directly into the family's main public room, a large space as deep as the house and perhaps twice that width in length. At each end doors led to smaller rooms; bedrooms, bathroom, kitchen. The ceiling was panelled in dark-stained wood, the floor tiled, with a scatter of rugs and kilims. A number of paintings and drawings, mostly local landscapes, hung on white walls. Among them, framed on the wall to our right, was the Batistić family tree, its eponymous graphic representation showing every new member of the family as a fresh leaf on his or her relevant branch. Easy chairs and a sofa were grouped in a corner. A mahogany *kredenc* took up most of the wall opposite us. A winding timber stair rose to its right. Years ago when we first came to Lumbarda and stayed as a family in Niko and Katica's house, we would climb its squeaky treads with care trying not to disturb our sleeping children or our fellow guests. In the centre of the room was a long table at which ten high-backed dining chairs were placed with immaculate precision, four on each side, one at each end. Here we used to eat breakfast – salami, bread and cheese, and an egg fresh from the hens at the foot of the garden. Now, however, the table was not set for a meal. This evening we were to eat outside.

Diagonally opposite the door entering from the terrace a similar, two-leaf, partly glazed door led us into the yard. Though not broad, like the terrace it ran along the full length of the house. Timber-boarded gates gave access to the lane at one end; at the other, a luxuriant green gloom of paint-potted plants. There were shiny rubber plants, pittosporum, yucca and dagger-toothed fronds of palms arching over dark recesses. Pale oleanders blushed in the shadows. Rooted below the flagstones a venerable bougainvillea climbed up around a first-floor balcony and into the night. A single-storey structure running parallel to the rear of the house contained the summer kitchen, larder, wine cellar, tool store and workshop. Along its wall, I noticed tassles of tiny scarlet tomatoes strung like garlic had been hung out to dry. But it was the long dinner table, brightly illuminated by two bare bulbs hanging on cables slung between the house and the summer kitchen, that drew all eyes.

The white plates shone against the blue gingham tablecloth. Glasses sparkled. Cutlery gleamed. As Niko lit the candles, the decanters of red and white wine caught the light in reflected flashes, crimson-lake and gold. I counted the places set. Seven... eight... nine... But we were only six.

'Frank! Jasna! Evo mene! Here I am!'

Jagoda. She had appeared making a mock-dramatic entrance through the fly curtain that hung from the lintel of the summer kitchen doorway. Cupped in her hands was a large bowl full of chopped tomatoes and sliced onions which, with oblatory exaggeration, she placed on the table before embracing us and greeting her sister- and brother-in-law with a kiss. She was smaller than Mirjana and though her brown hair was cut in similar boyish style she was more elfin, more feminine in manner. I supposed that while we were on the terrace she must have been with Katica preparing the meal we were about to eat. Jagoda was, after all, a splendid cook. That was what had brought her to the village.

Twenty years ago she had left home in the mountains of rural Hercegovina to look for work on the tourist-rich coast. In Lumbarda she found employment as cook in a local *konoba* or taverna. There she caught the eye of Nikša Batistić, Niko and Katica's son. Within a year they had married. Welcomed into the relatively prosperous Batistić household with its annual influx of regular international guests, life for Jagoda had been transformed. As the family's only daughter-in-law, she became a willing and indispensable support to Katica around the house, helping with the cleaning, washing, and, of course, the cooking. She began to pick up some German, Italian and English, chatted sociably with the guests. Her very appearance changed: with a new and fashionable hairstyle, proper care for her teeth, simple but smart clothes, she became more glamorous. Best of all she gave birth to the next generation – three sons to carry the Batistić family name. But life had its sadness too, for in these years the war had come and, though it had all but by-passed the islands, it had ravaged Bosnia and Hercegovina. Jagoda's father had been killed. He had never been a combatant but, in the ubiquitous madness of the conflict that raged just across the mountains from Dalmatia, abjuring the bitter prejudices of one side or the other or both brought no security. A stray bullet had been enough. For all that, his death had been as hard to bear for Jagoda, her sister and mother, as it would have been had he been killed in action or murdered in the barbarous terror of ethnic cleansing. And perhaps, I suddenly guessed, surprised at the thought, perhaps its random pointlessness had made it all the more tragic, all the more painful to those who loved him; neither hero nor brutalized victim, his death swept up in the maelstrom of horror, unjustified by any kind of morality or logic. Nor did the knowledge that Jagoda's story was only one of thousands, that even here on the islands where, though the war came no closer than the distant sound of shellfire, scarcely a family had failed to experience some loss, make it any the less poignant. It was ten years now. The war was over. As best they could, Jagoda's mother and sister continued to farm in the same village in Hercegovina. The three Batistić boys were growing up. A better future? A different, wiser generation? Who could tell? Meanwhile, everyone looked forward, if only with a cautious, world-weary hope.

'But where's Nikša?' asked Jasna, sliding along the bench on the house side of the table. Nebojša, Mirjana and I followed, four of us in line, Niko waiting until we were seated before he took the chair at the head of the table.

'Band practice tonight. Didn't you hear them from the terrace?' So I hadn't imagined it, I *had* heard music. 'Frano goes too. They'll join us later.'

'And Ivan and Ante?'

'Both in bed. Maybe not asleep, but they soon will be. You'll see them another time.'

A pity not to see all three together. Well, we would have to wait. Another day; a pleasure in prospect, for they were always fun to be with. Nikša and Jagoda had brought their children up well; they were respectful and well mannered but at the same time full of energy and spirit as boys should be. As infants they had all been alike to me, chubby and round-faced with those half-closed-to-the-sun eyes that seem to give Mediterranean babies a fleeting, almost eastern look, but now each was old enough to have developed his own particular character and charm. Frano, the eldest, already thirteen, who wanted so much to be like his father and drive a lorry. No-one doubted he would stay in Lumbarda, marry locally, live in the family home, work the family vineyards and olive groves just as Niksa had done succeeding his father and Niko his. Ivan, the clever one, who didn't say much but drew like a dream. He would surely leave the island to make his way in the wider world – doctor, lawyer, writer, perhaps even priest. And Ante, the youngest, always the joker, full of mischief; not yet at school – it was impossible to guess what he would do. For that too, we would have to wait.

Katica emerged from the kitchen. Discarding an apron, she joined Jagoda, already seated opposite us. Together they urged us to eat.

'*Dobar tek.*'

We hardly needed the encouragement, Jasna and I; light-headed from the cumulative effects of a night and morning of travel, a day largely without food and now an evening begun with what might yet prove to have been too much wine, discretion made hunger the better part of social valour. We had to eat. A look at the table and a moment's instinctive reticence not to be first to begin was quickly dispelled. The great bowl of tomatoes which Jagoda had placed with liturgical care, almost as if in offering to the *Lares*, had only completed the spread of salads laid out as starters. There was much to tempt the appetite. A silver platter thick with folds of lean *pršut* garnished with olives, tiny gherkins and crumbling white cheese took pride of place. Beside it, salt-pickled fillets of anchovies, arranged to form the shape of a fish, swam in a sea of oil and vinegar. Layered in concentric rings were slivers of cucumber all but submerged under a paprika-dusted quilt of *kiselo vrhnje*, sour cream, and garlic. There was a wide shallow bowl of lettuce and other mixed greens, *zelena salata,* and another, edged with slices of lemon and hard-boiled eggs and heaped with thin brown-green spikes which, I learned from Katica, were the stalks of wild asparagus. We filled our plates; something of everything.

The saltiness of the ham and fish made us drink more. Mostly mineral water now, though the red wine mixing with the powdery cheese and *pršut* suffused in the mouth with a faint but delicious sweetness. I tried the asparagus but found it bitter. 'A special taste', Nebojša said, knowingly, helping himself to more with a smile that half-suggested he would be glad to take my share too. But the cucumber was good, not unlike the Greek *tsatziki*, with an added nip from the generous coating of paprika. The tomatoes were as always wonderful; rough, even ugly, in shape, varying in colour, but, sharpened by the onions, beautiful to the taste. And with it all, thick chunks of fresh bread.

Then came the soup. The salads cleared, Katica set an open tureen in the middle of the table with a flourish of the same ritualistic hyperbole that Jagoda had shown. Steam billowed into the night. The smell of fish and garlic was irresistibly appetising. Katica's performance – an exaggerated bow as she placed the large bowl, arms thrown wide apart before the final curtsey – had been done tongue-in-cheek, light-heartedly, but it struck me that, though conscious intention might be – indeed, almost certainly was – lacking, none the less something significant passed, dimly apprehended in the action. I resorted to analogy. A meal shared among special friends, was this not a rite meriting celebration in the observance? I looked again at the table with its careful geometry, opposed place settings balanced around an axis of symmetry that centred on Niko, *pater familias*, high priest. Had the invitation to eat been a call to worship, the ritual presentation of the food a sacrifice on the altar of hospitality? And if these thoughts were themselves pompous were they not pompous in the same way and for the same reason that the theatrical posturings of Jagoda and Katica had been: intuitively or innocently, both concealed something compelling yet impossible to express satisfactorily. Or so it seemed, as I struggled to make some sense of my feelings. More than a little frustrated by an inability to resolve these fanciful excursions, I consoled myself with the thought that there were limits, and these days limitations too, to religious metaphor. Perhaps all that was to be said was that a meal like this – the food and drink, the words, looks, and touches exchanged among old friends – was a kind of communion. But I did not dare to say it.

My confused attempts to articulate the strange sense of the sacramental that had come over me remained unspoken. Beyond the courtesy of some complimentary remarks about the food, I could not find the words that might have conveyed how I had begun to feel. To those around the table I must have appeared unusually tongue-tied, even allowing for my first-day Croatian. I said little or nothing. But while Jasna and Katica pursued a discussion about Dalmatian and Scottish soups, their similarities and differences (the latter largely boiling down, so to say, to the density of vegetables involved) and Nebojša was encouraging Niko to speculate on the prospects for the grape harvest, now only a few weeks away, I continued to marvel at the way in which this simple act of eating and drinking together – a pleasure we had been privileged to enjoy in the Batistić home over so many years – seemed not only to confirm but also to sanctify our mutual affection. Perhaps 'marvel' is the wrong word for there is nothing remarkable in finding friendship in a shared meal. Had I offered this far-from-perceptive insight to the conversation it would, I supposed, have been regarded as every bit as trivial as talk of soup or grapes – and possibly a good deal more vacuous. On the other hand, there was something more, something of the Emmaus road, in all this; the realization that things are not merely what they may appear to be, a feeling that the mundane might somehow be sacred too. Perhaps it is travel, being on a journey or in an unfamiliar place, that intensifies this awareness, turning the ordinary into the sanctified and at the same time transforming us, albeit no more than occasionally, into celebrants or – to use a word less euphonious but more familiar in our low-church Scotland – communicants. Rare as these moments of revelation are, from time to time they do occur and the traveller must count himself fortunate to experience them. I felt myself duly favoured.

Forgetting my manners (or was it simply a measure of how much at ease I felt at this back-yard table) I stretched for the decanter and poured myself a glass of wine. I drank a secret self-congratulatory toast, still preoccupied with my own thoughts. What was it, I wondered, that so often made dinner with the Batistić family affect me in this way? I counted the possibilities. The bonds of a friendship drawn closer over many years. The good food and drink. The narcotic spell of tiredness and alcohol. The calm warmth of the evening. Whatever the reason, or reasons, nowhere but at the Batistić table had I experienced quite the same trance-like peace of mind, as if at once shriven and elated. Over the years there had, of course, been other intimations of that special contentment: up on the *makija*, looking south out across the sea to invisible Italy; down on the rose-bathed shore at Pržina in the darkening moments before sunset; in our own attic bed after love-making; but most often, it seemed, around a table shared with friends or with each other. Lingering on this last image I began now to think of other meals in other Lumbarda places.

Not far from our cottage, no more than a ten-minute walk along the high road that runs back towards Račišće bay, is a small restaurant named *Zure*. You might easily miss it. It sits anonymous among the houses of Vela Postrana, hidden behind walls which the uninformed passer-by assumes conceal no more than a small secret garden. And, indeed, this is in part the case. The restaurant is small, half courtyard, half room, no more than five or six wooden tables, their varnished surfaces shining brightly under the few judiciously placed lights; the space is introverted, intimate and (or so I have sometimes imagined catching some clandestine exchange of affection in the corner) conveniently private; and, since to reach the tables you must duck through the branches of fig and orange trees that grow from large terra cotta pots and gaps in the paving, there is a sense of eating in the green warmth of a conservatory.

The owner is a Batistić. Bari (the name is short for Bartul, that is Bartholomew, the name of the saint whose tiny church lies across the lane from our cottage) is a cousin of Niko's. Not the only one by any means, a fact of village life which necessitates some means of distinguishing amongst those families bearing the same surname. The method devised is the nickname. Niko's is *Belo* – Nikola Batistić *Belo* – a tag which possibly derives for some reason from the Slav root for 'white' but which I have always liked to think had a rather more flattering Italianate source. Bari's branch of the family uses the agnomen *Zure*, a word which, if it ever had any semantic connotation, can only have been related to the verb meaning 'to stare'. Whatever the origin, it makes an eye-catching name for a restaurant.

We visit *Zure*'s from time to time. Unlike other eating places in Lumbarda it stays open all year round. It cannot do much business through the winter and even in autumn and spring when we are in the village, particularly in April or October, it is quiet. There is always a welcoming glass for us – *lozovača s rogaćem*, a local brandy softened and sweetened by carob pods and served as frequently before a meal as after – over which we chat with Bari and his German wife Sylvia. Often we arrive after dinner just to drink some wine and eat some cheese. Since most menus, including *Zure*'s, advertise cheese as a starter, this is regarded as somewhat odd, although for us it is always odder to find when the bill comes that our single plate of cheese, at most a dozen hard thin triangles, has cost more than twice the price to be paid for the half-litre of the house red we have consumed. But the wine, which is excellent, is remarkably cheap; so no-one is being overcharged. It is simply that coming from a country where cheese is plentiful and wine, though readily available, still something of an imported luxury, we cannot help but find the relative cost of such things here as anything other than bizarre.

When we do come to eat, and if we remember to choose the right table, we like to watch our fish, drenched in olive oil and garlic, as it grills over the charcoal. On one occasion, the cook, taking care to fan the embers but talkative too, surprised us with an unexpected traveller's tale. Evidently he had once served in the merchant navy – a career, we told him, as common for the islanders on the west coast of Scotland as it was for Dalmatians. Strangely, his ship had, in fact, sailed in Scottish waters calling at Greenock and Leith and had even put in at Invergordon on the Cromarty Firth. Intrigued, we asked what his impressions of Scotland had been and how his experiences there compared with life in Dalmatia. He told us, however, that he had never been ashore and could speak only of misty hills and grey, rain-lashed towns. It was not a conversation we pursued.

Bari, like his father, is a fisherman and sea-food the speciality of the house. Even without seeing the menu, no first-time visitor would be in any doubt. Across the rear wall of the restaurant a giant octopus is depicted, its tentacles sinuously elongated over the whole surface. This image is neither painting nor sculpture; the wall is covered in a texture of small sea-smoothed pebbles, cream for the background, grey for the creature itself. Two orange stones highlight its eyes; a slightly disturbing yet benign stare. Has this some eponymous significance? I have never felt able to ask.

The menu confirms that octopus is available. So, too, are squid, shrimps and mussels. Fish is simply billed as 'fish', details dependent on the previous night's catch. But Bari will bring a platter laden with what he has. With experience you may judge which type and how much to order. Without it, you must defer to his proposal. Our knowledge is limited. There may be times when we recognize a certain fish, gauge its size against our appetites and make a decision; more often we readily trust to our host. And this is particularly true on those occasions when, a week or so before it is time for us to set out on the drive north, we entertain our friends.

These nights are memorable. And now I remembered one in particular. It was April, a Thursday evening. *Zure*'s was quiet. Two tables had been pushed together to make a square at which eight of us sat, two on each side: Niko and Katica, Mirjana and Nebojša, Nebojša's parents Ivo and Lejla at whose home in Korčula we had enjoyed lunch earlier that month, and Jasna and I. We had let Bari decide the meal. First, *hobotnica*, octopus: a cold salad, the pale pink flesh perfectly tender and finely chopped with onion, garlic, olives and basil; and with the salad a warm *buzara*, a savoury stew of the same diced octopus with added tomatoes, garlic and white wine. Then the fish – and only the fish! Four scarlet, dragon-boned *škrpinje*, eight small, mauve-tinted *trilje*; grouper and mullet. No rich sauces or pretentious garnishes, just the grilled fish burnished with an olive oil so full of taste that the last dregs are avidly soaked up with the bread so stringently held here to be an indispensable accompaniment to the main course – and only the main course –

of any meal. (I recall a Serbian friend from Vojvodina warning me that 'only peasants eat bread with soup'). As vegetables, a combination of *blitva* and potatoes. We ate with relish. The wine flowed. And when dishes and plates had been cleared away and we were drinking a last small glass of Bari's carob-flavoured brandy, it was as if the world outside had shrunk to insignificance and we alone were left, drawn together around the table by the meal we had shared. The octopus on the wall stared back at me, its gaze steady, content with an observer's complicity in our pleasure. As we walked home in the black night I could still see its soft orange eyes.

Some evenings we find our way to *Feral*, another of our favourite places to eat and drink in Lumbarda. If there is no moon, the walk around the shore road below Mala Glavica needs care. To one side a high wall holds back the hillside, while on the other, somewhere in the darkness less than a metre below us, is the sea. Far out in the distance the lights of Orebić reveal the coastline of Pelješac across the channel, but in the blackness at our feet road and sea begin to vanish in alarming ambiguity. For several minutes it is difficult to tell where one ends and the other begins. We keep close to the wall, dragging our fingers along the rough stones for reassurance. Once round the promontory and into Tatinja bay the way ahead becomes clearer. Up on Vela Glavica the belltower of Sveti Roko is floodlit, golden against the night. Scattered lights glimmer in the windows of the village houses clustered below. We see our destination, bright at the water's edge, spilling silver over the bay. It's well named – *Feral*, lantern.

Well located too. Almost secretive, close to an attractive little harbour used by local fishermen and no more than a few paces across the shoreside road from the thin crescent of sand that rims the bay and makes Tatinja an agreeable spot for a quiet swim, it is rarely crowded yet never seems short of custom. Here the road goes no further than the harbour breakwater so that, as much for those who have walked round the coastal road from the village only to find themselves at a dead-end or, like us, have made the discovery long before and have come simply to linger or perhaps continue their walk around the shore rocks to Bilin Žal, *Feral* is the perfect spot to pause for a cool beer or Coke. The views across the bay past Koludrt to the green islands of Vrnik and Badija and across the channel to the high shadowed massif of Sveti Ilija are magnificent.

A small place, it makes the most of its narrow site, squeezing two levels into the hillside behind a lacy screen of oleanders; café bistro below, restaurant on the open terrace above. A straight flight of stone steps runs back into the hill linking the two. If the evening is cool we sit below; more often we eat on the terrace. The view disappears in darkness but the café lamps dance below us on the rippling water. Out at sea an occasional light glints: a yacht ending its day's sail late; a fisherman beginning the night's work.

Unlike Bari at *Zure*, *Feral*'s owner is no fisherman – but he *is* a Batistić. Ivica Batistić! Or, to give him the nickname which distinguishes him and his family – Ivica Batistić *Fidulić*. Like *Zure*, however, the restaurant is a family-run affair. Ivica's wife does the cooking in the spotless little kitchen open to the rear of the restaurant terrace. His three sons work shifts at the bar and tables, coping valiantly with the inconvenience of stairs and dumb waiter. Ivica himself will often be there supervising things.

I remembered one warm October night, years ago when we first came to *Feral*. The season was drawing to a close and we and a young German couple were the only people dining that evening. It was an evening when, in truth, there was little to supervise and Ivica and two or three of his friends had gathered around one of the tables to share a few beers. A guitar was produced and the songs began. Four men, in careless unselfconscious harmony. Ivica's wife, attractively casual in black tee-shirt and jeans, her blonde hair tied in a pony-tail under a white baseball cap, joined them, her cooking in the kitchen completed for the night. She did not sing but, sitting close to her husband, leant back in her chair, hands clasped behind her head, eyes closed, content simply to drift with the music, smiling now and then at some memory cued by the melody or lyric of a favourite song. We, too, sleepy after the huge meal of *sitne ribe*, whitebait, we had eaten and the wine we had drunk – a bottle of the local white Grk bearing the family's own *Fide*s label – slipped into Dalmatian dreams. From time to time we would recognize a familiar snatch of tune or phrase – *moje galebe , , , moja Dalmacija* – our evident pleasure delighting Ivica and his friends. While for our young neighbours, seated somewhat apart at the edge of the terrace, the music cast a spell that seemed to intensify their isolation in a kind of exalted self obsession, it drew us into new friendships. We exchanged smiles, laughed, tried to sing. An extra half-litre of wine appeared on our table. We exchanged toasts. The guitarist launched into *Auld Lang Syne*, not at all a sign that the evening was over but a gesture of our acceptance into the party. We should, I suppose, have responded by singing some Scots songs but clung to our timidity realising with shame how, though we might have managed a melody or two, we should almost certainly have failed on the words. But neither reticence nor forgetfulness mattered. We were welcome at this Batistić table too.

At length, however, it was time to go. The Germans had already gone, rapt in each other's gaze. The two on-duty waiter sons had vanished into the night on a moped. The guitarist had laid his instrument down, though not his glass for Ivica and his friends were still drinking. But the lights had been put out in the kitchen. We paid our bill, said our goodbyes and climbed down the stairs to the sea's edge. Half-way home, rounding Mala Glavica, we heard the soft tenor sound of singing floating on the water from *Feral*.

Perhaps it was the thought of that walk around the shore. A last few lights lighting not just the night but memory too. Behind us, *Feral* 's lamps dimmed. Ahead, the low glimmer of the village houses. On the long marina mole the regular red glow of warning. And out across Prvi Žal a single light flashed high over the trees on Koludrt – *Bebić*'s restaurant, another of our favourite places to eat in Lumbarda.

You can see that light from *Feral* just as you can see the splash of *Feral*'s lights from *Bebić*. The two restaurants face each other across almost a kilometre of open water, each at the end of a finger of road bent around the bay on opposite sides of the village. But while *Feral* sits down on the eastern shore, the road to *Bebić* twists up through the small west-end suburb of summer villas built in the woods on Koludrt hill. Larger than either *Feral* or *Zure*, but no less a family venture, *Bebić*'s place has become a rather grand establishment, at least by Lumbarda standards: a generous restaurant space with floor-to-ceiling glazing opening on splendid views east and south across the sea to the dramatic coastline of Pelješac and the mountains beyond; marble terraces planted with thick white banks of yellow-eyed marguerites, car parking tucked below into the hillside; and the three-storeyed *Villa Vesna* with balconied apartments and rooms to rent. But it wasn't always so.

Fifteen years ago when it first became possible to eat at *Bebić* there was little of all this here. A stand of pines had been cleared and a series of levels cut from the hillside. Some stone walls had taken shape and tables were laid out under a tiled timber roof. There was a kitchen and the dusty beginnings of a house, one of several then under construction on Koludrt. Not many visitors to the village realised that a new restaurant was in business and soon, when war broke out in Croatia putting an end to the tourist trade and much else in life, it seemed as if the Bebić family enterprise was doomed. We kept coming to Lumbarda through these difficult times but found it all but impossible to 'eat out'. A café or two remained open, perhaps a restaurant in one of the hotels in Korčula town. No-one was doing much business. At *Bebić*, too, when we climbed the steps, crossed the terrace and climbed the steps again to reach the restaurant, hoping selfishly to find business as usual, there were no guests. Yet still there was a welcome; we were greeted warmly, fussed over, invited to share the family's dinner. We became friends – with Bebić himself, his wife Vesna who did, and still does, all the cooking, and their three children, Marino, Maruška and Nevena.

The shock and setback of war with its protracted aftermath of lean years might have brought their investment to ruin but sometime in the early 1990s – it must have been soon after hostilities ended and the more adventurous traveller began to return to the Adriatic – chance intervened. Someone, perhaps commissioned, perhaps not, called at the restaurant, enjoyed the food and hospitality and was captivated by the place's *ambijent*; enjoyed it all enough to write a recommendation for *Bebić* in the first edition of the *Lonely Planet Guide* to Croatia. Nothing could have been better calculated to ensure the family's economic salvation. It worked wonders. The tourists began to appear; not many at first, but each year more and more. It meant hard work. By October, at the end of each season, everyone was tired. Vesna, in particular, always thin, had grown strained and haggard. But the money had flowed in, the restaurant was glazed, the terraces were paved, the apartments were completed, and the family's two daughters had been married.

The family's success did not, of course, pass unremarked in the village. On the one hand, the attraction of the restaurant brought visitors with money to spend in Lumbarda; island-hopping backpackers, families in search of a meal after a day on the sands at Bilin Žal or Pržina, yachtsmen at anchor locally or in the marina in Korčula. On the other, Bebić (even Vesna and the children use only his surname) was not from the island. He had come to Korčula from the mainland, from the Neretva valley, and this, for all the fierce Croat pride of that border region, made him different. No-one resented the family's good fortune; indeed, Bebić's endeavour was admired and the spin-off benefits it had brought to the village generally if tacitly acknowledged. But, as in any small community, perhaps especially an island community, the settler and stranger are aware always of living on the elusive margins of acceptance. The very location of the restaurant, uphill at the dead end of a road on the edge of the village, seemed somehow to suggest a measure of social as much as geographical separation. As seasonal incomers ourselves, marked out by our meagre linguistic abilities and with none of the accumulated credit that Bebić could call on, except perhaps the fact that we had at least kept faith with the place through the war years, we sometimes sensed this same distancing – a correctness in conversation, a cautiousness in relationships, the subtle inhibition in politeness. It was only natural, of course, and no doubt as much a matter of shrewd deference as a negative reaction triggered in social defence. When I thought of the English white-settler invasion of the Western Isles of Scotland and our own bitter grumbling at this latter-day colonisation, I realised just how indulgent and accepting the *Korčulani* could be. The island knew it needed its guests. As for us, regular if intermittent guests, perhaps it was some shared understanding of what it means to be an outsider that brought us that bit closer to Bebić and his family, just as it did to our neighbours Marjan and Dragica. Yet perhaps – and here paradox drew me back to reality – perhaps it was the very absence of this in and around Niko and Katica's table that made our friendship with them and their family so special.

Katica and Jagoda had cleared the soup plates from the table, the impressive tureen too. A huge casserole dish piled to the rim with *svinjski kotleti*, pork chops, had been brought from the kitchen. Beside it, a platter heaped with *čevapčići*, grilled fingers of minced meat. There was a steaming stew of vegetables – chopped peppers, aubergines, tomatoes and onions. A salad of beetroot. The tureen had returned, filled with a mountain of mashed potatoes on which butter was melting like golden lava. A bowl filled with chopped bread was passed round.

Suddenly, before anyone could make a start on this feast, a staccato salvo of sound exploded in the yard. A trumpet – abrupt, hortatory! A bugle-call grace filling the momentary gap between the desire and the decision to eat. It was Frano, the instrument at his lips, standing in the doorway. Behind him, Nikša appeared, as much a part of the mischief as his son. They were both laughing.

We recovered from the shock, laughed too. Jagoda scolded her two men with some half-hearted reproach; Nikola frowned unconvincingly; Katica grinned. I got up to greet Nikša who stretched his hands out, palms towards me, halting my move to disturb the seating arrangements.

'*Sjedi se, sjedi se*. Sit, sit, he said, stretching across the busy table to shake hands first with Jasna and then me. Frano returned our wave with a broad smile.

We began to eat. Nine friends. Three generations. The dishes passed from hand to hand. One family. And we were part of it again.

The author on an early trip to Korčula

Lumbarda from the vineyards with
Sveti Ilija on Pelješac in the background

The little Church of St Peter, Lumbarda

At the Batistić table

Korčula from the east

The cemetery at Blato

Siesta

Arrival

Blaženka with Miško

'Uncle' Jakša

WAITING @ TINO'S

*'One trait most islands share is anticipation of things to come:
even the smallest looks forward to the next boat, to the news it
will bring, to some scene, some event. Islanders have more time
for waiting than others; waiting marks their time.'*

Predrag Matvejević
1987

A shower of dappled light falling through the rosemary that
spills over the wall from Ana-Marija's garden marbles the white
plastic table-top. It's mid morning, breakfast is over and I'm
enjoying the sun, surprised and thrilled as always to be living
life *al fresco*. The sounds of the village drift over the wall: a
strimmer rasping through the grass below the olive trees, dogs
barking, cocks crowing, a mother remonstrating with her child,
the fierce macho acceleration of a motor bike. But it's peaceful
here in the yard; Marjan has long ago gone to work, Blaženka is
at school, Dragica is at work in her kitchen. Beside me Jasna is
reading one of the dozen or so books we have brought with us.

On the table are the day's newspaper and a broken-backed
copy of Drvodelić's Croatian-English dictionary. I'm trying to
do some translation. It has become a daily hour-long habit,
though 'duty' would be a better word since it has always seemed
to me that setting up home in another country, even an
intermittent home such as ours is, brings with it the obligation to
use, or try to use, the local language. Perhaps this is a
consequence of a Calvinist conscience, or perhaps it's prompted
by that ready ability to acknowledge and defer to other cultures
that is the up-side of the Scottish inferiority complex; it might
even be a matter of good manners. More likely it's simple
necessity. Unlike the time-sharing, golfing ghettos of the
Algarve or the Costa del Sol there are no *émigré* English-

speaking enclaves on the Dalmatian islands – not yet at any rate. Almost no-one drinks gin and tonic. *The Times* is unobtainable. Cricket may be played on that other Korkyra to the south, Corfu, but not here on Korkyra Melaina; no whites on black Korčula. Maintaining the often patronising pretence of 'England with sunshine' is not an option; the foreign resident on Korčula is still something of a curiosity, free to capitalise on what may be perceived to be his or her eccentricity but ill advised to play the aloof colonial. It's certainly true that most people – most younger people at any rate – speak English and for this we have often been grateful. On the other hand, to exchange a greeting, ask after a neighbour's health or converse across the counter in Croatian is to be granted a wider smile and the reassuring sense that, though one will always be an incomer, doors are opening. So I scan the collage of headlines splashed across the front page of *Jutarnji List*, ring the words I don't know in ink and turn to the dictionary.

The news this morning is dominated by one of those bursts of protracted soul-searching and face-saving that have gripped the country in the aftermath of war. Up to a point, the current coalition government, considerably more liberal and social democratic than the right-wing administration who prosecuted what is always referred to as the homeland war and never the civil war, has co-operated with the demands of the International Court of Justice in The Hague. But there are difficulties. War crimes are still being denied. A leading general has refused to submit himself to the court. My morning's vocabulary is beginning to read like a legal dossier: words like 'chief prosecutor', 'principal witness', 'arrested and detained', and so on, are scribbled across the page. I realise, of course, that none of this is likely to find much application in the life of a village like Lumbarda where crime is virtually unknown, but since it is my self-enforced, self-denying ritual always to deal first with the headlines (and to succumb to any infraction of this practice would somehow seem like disrespect), I persevere. In any case, this most recent development in the uneasy relationship between Zagreb and The Hague will, in all probability, run for several days, if not months, during which time the legalistic language will become increasingly familiar and the words lodge more and more comfortably in the brain. This is part of the logic of my daily routine; this and the superstitious conviction that were I to break the habit some linguistic block might ensue, rather as the housewives of Kőnigsberg might have feared catastrophe had they not been able to check their clocks against the metronomic regularity with which Herr Professor Kant took his daily walk across the city's bridges.

The task fulfilled, however, the front page defaced by circles, arrows and illegible notes, I feel free to address more parochial matters. Finding the three or four pages always devoted to news and features about Dalmatia, I wonder whether to read a piece on the quality of the wine harvest expected later in the year on Pelješac and Korčula, or another on the relatively unknown tourist attractions of Lastovo, an island further out in the Adriatic, visible from Korčula but for long commandeered as a Yugoslav naval base and for that reason inaccessible to foreigners. Then a third report catches my eye. It describes the opening of a new public toilet in Dubrovnik controversially incorporated into the old town by the Zagreb architect Nenad Fabijanić. Not the most engaging of subjects it might seem but I know Nenad, I know the exquisite precision of his work and I know too the furore which this particular design has stirred up, first over the years it took to win approval for the project and again, more recently, over the many slow months of building. Condemned, ironically almost as much for the cost of its high quality materials as for its daring intrusion close to the city's magnificent fortified walls – a location deemed sacrosanct by most *Dubrovčani* – its provocative history is already the stuff of legend. For me what Nenad had envisaged was both beautiful and brave. Glad to see the work finally realised, I settle down to read the article. Besides, as I know from the sometimes desperate exigencies of personal experience, augmenting my lavatorial vocabulary could well turn out to be a decidedly practical bonus.

I have barely mastered the first paragraph – a task which reveals the words for 'sewage' and 'urinal' (the latter, *pisoar,* rather disappointingly a transliteration from the French) – when Jasna interrupts me.

'We should check for news at Tino's. There might be

107

something from Susan or Andrew.'

She's right. I had forgotten. How easy, sitting here in the morning sunshine preoccupied in idle self-righteous self-improvement, to forget how different the days must be for our friends in Scotland. Susan, only just recovering from an operation for breast cancer, wracked with worry as she waits to see her consultant, convinced she would hear the worst about the treatment régime proposed, and Ian, her husband, opening up his heart to us in a stream of confessional e-mails. Andrew, with oesophagus cancer, keeping us regularly informed with clinically precise accounts of each stage of his treatment, betraying his intense determination to beat the disease with every matter-of-fact sentence. And still, battling with his demons, he finds the time to ask how *we* are! Ian, too. All we can do is keep in touch, wondering if this electronic friendship is enough, caught between a wish to soften the seriousness of it all with a few confident platitudes of good will and a deeper desire to find more honest words to face the fears we share. It's twenty years since Sue and Ian came to live round the corner from us back home in Scotland, more than twice that since we were at school with Andrew and Margaret. Now, only three days since we were last in Korčula typing in Tino's computer shop words we hoped were neither too sentimental nor too emotionally tepid, trying again to get right what it is so easy to get wrong, now again I realise just how easily and quickly the cares of others slip from the mind. A half-hour's concern reading their e-mails to us. A surge of love when we write back. Later perhaps, a perfunctory prayer. Not much; it seems a limp sum reward for all those years of shared affection. But then, as always, guilt works its redemptive magic; chastened by conscience I get up from the table. Nenad's toilet can wait. I make a mental note to pay it a visit next time we're in Dubrovnik, close Drvodelić and wonder where the car keys are.

But Jasna is not quite ready to go. 'What day is it today?' she asks. It is a question that speaks volumes for the extent to which after several spring weeks in Lumbarda we are already adrift in dreamy dislocation.

'It's Monday', I reply, puzzled. 'Why?'

'That's what I thought. The boat comes in today, doesn't

it? In fact, don't both of them call?' She means the Jadrolinija ferries; one *en route* north from Dubrovnik, the other arriving at Korčula after the overnight sail from Rijeka. One or the other – it might be the *Liburnija* or the *Marko Polo* – call regularly, more or less on alternate days, but for some reason their arrivals coincide within an hour of each other on a Monday. Since this occurs in the middle of the day, between noon and one o'clock, it is a major event for everyone in Korčula.

It's always a good reason for going into town. Besides, since today is warm, I might sketch a bit. I think of Susan and Ian again and the prospect of sitting in the sun drawing or watching the ships come and go with all the attendant entertainment of arrival and departure seems suddenly unpardonably self-indulgent. So, too, the habitual *cappuccino* and *krafna*, foamy coffee and jam-filled doughnut, still warm from the baker's. For a brief moment I suspect my priorities. Temptation? Obligation? Lustration? But this introspection is just as self-indulgent. I cut it short.

'Right. Anything we need to get when we're in Korčula?'

Jasna considers. Her brow creases a little, not unattractively. 'I could do with olive oil and we could get more Pošip, I suppose.' Though we usually drink the dark red wine of the island, bottles of which filled from the cask have been put on our table (and no less regularly replenished) by our friends Niko and Katica Batistić for more years than we deserve, we sometimes choose white and this we get from a small shop in Korčula where the growers from the vineyards of Čara and Smokvica sell their wine from the barrel. Pošip is the best of the whites. 'Can you find some empty bottles to take?' Jasna asks.

I find two in the kitchen. Back in the yard I catch the scent of perfume freshly sprayed on wrists and neck. Jasna has cleared the table and has the car keys already in her hand. I put the bottles down and go back indoors to find my sketchbook.

It takes less than half an hour to reach Korčula. The drive along the rather grandly named Lumbarajska cesta, properly asphalted but no more than a pleasant country road, is familiar. It's the only road and we've driven it often. We know the corners to watch, where the occasional oncoming car or biker is liable to appear suddenly in the middle of the road. But there is little traffic. Here and there an old Renault 4 (it sometimes seems as if more of these survive on Korčula than anywhere else in Europe) has been drawn up on the verge, the driver nowhere to be seen but certainly at work somewhere in the fields nearby. We pass a cyclist or two, some elderly tourists, red-faced and red-legged, walking the five or six kilometres from their hotel in Korčula to Lumbarda, though not perhaps back again, and an old woman clad in widow's black, hunched under a back-breaking burden of leafy branches, fodder for the two or three sheep she has closeted in some tumbledown outhouse. Everywhere there are wild flowers in abundance: banked clouds of yellow wort scarlet-starred with poppies. It is as if we are adrift on a Monet canvas; nature imitating art imitating nature. Past Sveti Antun, the little church high on its hill above a green waterfall of centuries-old cypresses, we reach Dubrovačka cesta, the main road that connects Korčula with Dominče and the ferry crossing to Orebić on the Pelješac peninsula. We turn towards the town and begin a slow gentle climb around Hober hill. Through the trees sunlight glints on the gravestones in the Cemetery of St Luke.

It's a bright, peaceful place this cemetery, but full to overflowing to such an extent that some of the old graveyard walls have been breached and an area of *makija* freshly cleared. New plots are under construction, and not for the first time. Until the early years of the nineteenth century Korčula's dead were buried in the island's churches. It was the British, installed on Korčula from 1813 until 1815, when the Congress of Vienna determined that all Dalmatia – Napoleon's Illyria – should be given to Austria, who forbade this practice. Thereafter, graveyards began to appear all over the island. Set apart in the woods above what was then still a very small but wholly urban community, as tightly ordered by social convention as it was spatially still largely constrained within its old fortified walls, Korčula's cemetery was opened in 1830, its tombs reserved to the town's principal families and religious brotherhoods. The original plan was square and the layout carefully regularised, as if the timeless rigours of geometry might somehow redeem organic decay. A chapel dedicated to the Holy Cross was erected in the 1850s but, shortly after the cemetery had been extended to the west in 1895-97, this was replaced by the little octagonal Church of St Luke. Through the trees we catch a glimpse of its sharp arrow-headed bellcote and orange-tiled roof, barely rising higher than some of the grander patrician tombs.

Past the cemetery the trees clear and we see Korčula town itself. Like many another coastal settlement, it straggles along the contours, tiled roofs among the pines and palms. But the old oval town guarding the channel below Sveti Ilija is different. It floats out from the land, composed and compact, islanded, it almost seems, on the shimmering water. Not a city set on a hill but a city-hill, a lived-in cairn of prismatic golden-grey stone dappled with the orange lichen of tiled roofs. At the summit, the cathedral's sunlit belfry shines white against the jade-dark coastal woods on Pelješac. It could be Tuscany or Istria were it not that this hill-town is not borne on the land; there are no cypresses, no striated vineyards raked across a tumbling hillside, no verdant meadows rolling down from fortified walls. Instead, stone meets sea, Korčula's foothills drowned in the deepening blues of the Adriatic. It is not, of course, unique in Dalmatia this phenomenon of the sea-girt town. To the north, memorably located off the main coastal road between Split and Šibenik,

Primošten sits out on open water. Five centuries ago it was an island settled by Croats fleeing from the Turks in Bosnia. A drawbridge was built (thus the name, from *primostiti*, to bridge over) and later a narrow silted isthmus formed linking the village to the mainland. To the south, on the Montenegrin coast, between Budva and Petrovac, is the off-shore rock of Sveti Stefan. It, too, settled as a safe house from the Turks, dates largely from the sixteenth century, though one of its three small churches is older. Little more than a hamlet of clustered fishermen's cottages, it is a spectacular sight, moored to the shore by a slender causeway. The old village of Primošten remains haphazardly rural on its hill, while the few dwellings on Sveti Stefan have coalesced into a single exclusive hotel. Korčula by contrast is decidedly urban, not large in area but grand in its conception, at once a floating fortress and a planned town, spatially ordered and socially urbane. Only Dubrovnik, it too begun as an island enclave, is more sophisticated in its beauty.

But there is more than beauty. Perhaps, indeed, beauty is simply the gathered attribute of time. Did the builders of these walls and towers deal in the picturesque? Or were they more concerned about the Turks on the horizon? Viewed from the hill as we descend, Korčula's strategic significance is clear. A highly visible point of orientation on the navigational route close to the mainland (as we know well from our own arrivals and departures) it commands all sea traffic through the sheltered Pelješac channel. From earliest times the site must have attracted considerably more than passing interest from Greeks, Illyrians and Romans and, later still, Croats, and it is difficult to imagine the little island hill, or the promontory it became, without some kind of permanent presence. But that such settlement had acquired any kind of *urban* form during the classical period is unlikely. Nor is the frequently made suggestion that the Slavic town mentioned in the tenth century writings of Constantine Porphyrogenitus is to be identified with present-day Korčula, altogether convincing. An alternative and perhaps more probable possibility, recently argued, is that, in adverting to 'Korčula', the Byzantine Emperor had in mind the long-established settlement at Blato further west in the interior of the island. Whether and wherever 'a fully-formed town' was in existence as early as the tenth century or not, it is certain that by the thirteenth century the name 'Korčula' (Curzola) applied not only to the island as a whole but also more specifically to the maritime location we are looking down on now. It was then that Marsilio Zorzi, whose family ruled on Korčula 'as feudatories of the Serene Republic' from 1129 intermittently until the middle of the fourteenth century, authorised a building programme intended to create a town fit to serve as the centre of government on the island. The sea-going Venetians built the fortified promontory port between 1254 and 1256 and by 1301, when a bishop arrived, the town had become a centre of both political and ecclesiastical administration, a status which, it has been suggested, entailed the local community's adoption of the island name. This, it seems, happened on the island of Hvar where Dimos became Hvar town while the former Hvar, appropriately enough, assumed the name Stari Grad (Old Town). Ivo Protić in his study *Župa Blata*, (The Parish of Blato), concludes that with the creation of the Venetian Korčula, the town hitherto known by the name of the island, Korčula, (that is to say the town referred to by Constantine Porphyrogenitus) became first Stari Grad and only later, to distinguish it from the place of the same name on Hvar, Blatta or Blato.

What's in a name? A good deal, it has to be said, here in Croatia where the post-war predilection for those linguistic forms that most emphatically distinguish the grammar and vocabulary of Croatian from those of its sister-tongue Serbian (even prime-time television has had a regular slot on usage and abusage) is a latter-day echo of that earlier struggle for identity fought for centuries between *Latini et Sclavi* in Dalmatia. It sometimes seems as true today as it was when T.G. Jackson first made the observation well over a hundred years ago that the traveller in Dalmatia 'has to be on his guard how he accepts the conclusions of a Latin or a Croat writer in a country where the politics of creed and race run so high'.

But for the moment, we feel ourselves above all this – literally, certainly; metaphorically... perhaps. The view from the hill down over the sunlit town is enough; nuances of speech or nomenclature can be dismissed. Korčula is Curzola is Korkyra. We drive on into the picture postcard.

The road ricochets down the hillside in a short series of reflected curves and, as I negotiate the bends in low gear, I suddenly think of another serpentine dropping into Rothesay on the Scottish island of Bute. An unexpected image to call to mind and a fleeting likeness that had never occurred to me before. Yet not so odd. The delaying twists in the route, the tilted views of the harbour, the hills and firth beyond. But it is not solely this physical similarity that gives the comparison its close-to-home edge as the fact that the islands of Bute and Korčula have been, unlikely as it may seem, twinned one with the other. The link rests on the personal bond established between Tito and the Argyll grandee Sir Fitzroy Maclean. Maclean, flown into war-torn Yugoslavia as Churchill's envoy with instructions to advise on the relative military strength and potential of the Communist partisans and royalist Četniks, chose the former. It was the beginning of a lifelong relationship between two men whose politics could hardly have been more contradictory yet who responded to each other's charismatic personality with mutual respect and friendship. Permitted – uniquely – to purchase a house in Korčula town long before the collapse of Communist power, Sir Fitzroy and his family endeared themselves to the *Korčulani* as regular visitors over the years. Ironically, perhaps their friendship and help was never more warmly felt than through the difficult years when Croatia was being reborn in the final disintegration of Tito's Yugoslavia and Sir Fitzroy was nearing the end of his life. Strange now to imagine all those exchange visits of local councillors, hotel waiters and others that once took place between the two communities. Stranger still to think of Tanja who made such a trip, married a local boy, left the sun and sea of Korčula for love and now serves behind the bar in the Creggans Inn on Loch Fyne, a short walk along the water's edge from the Maclean mansion, Strachur House.

We take the last bend and in a final downhill moment the wide-angle view from the hill flattens into close-up. Gone the all-but-aerial panorama of seascape, islands and island town, that big picture so often conscripted for card, calendar or framed remembrance on some northern desk. We are in the town now, though not within the old walls. It's still picture postcard country but fractured, quartered into familiar 'wish you were here' scenes: a yacht, jib sail raised, leaving the marina; small boats and water taxis bobbing at the jetties; white benches under palm trees; shuttered windows; tall narrow-fronted houses packed together along the *riva*, their balustraded balconies busy with potted plants and pink-purple falls of oleander and bougainvillea; and everywhere walls and walkways of grey-golden Dalmatian stone.

There are people in the picture too, filling the foreground. A fisherman is teasing out nets tangled from the night's work; another, bathed in sweat, bends over a temperamental inboard engine; still another, wrists on hips, stands easy in his boat swaying with the slow surge of the sea, his gaze fixed on some distant thought. Housewives, laden with the morning's shopping, are thinking of the lunch they have to prepare as they wait for the bus that will take them back uphill to Žrnovo or out to Lumbarda along the road we have come. Beneath the trees, infants are asleep in their push-chairs, their grandmothers, warm in the shade, still and watchful as the cats at their feet. A white-clad cook takes time out from his kitchen to enjoy a smoke. Old men are strolling or sitting, smoking too perhaps, watching certainly, saying little. Some younger men, jackets thrown cape-like over shoulders, stop to talk, greeting one another with a slapped handshake, forearms high and vertical, then kisses on each cheek. Most have a file or briefcase in hand and try to look purposeful. Among them is the local priest, disturbingly handsome and elegant in black; for him no file but a smart leather shoulder bag. Is it Gucci? A personal indulgence? But perhaps it contains the elements of the sacrament, the gifts of God stylishly packaged for a bedridden believer? For the moment, however, no-one is doing business, commercial or sacramental. White-shirted arms erupt in conversation, there is much gesticulation, a good deal of friendly touching. But the talk is no more than an excuse, a chance to linger and look. For the women of Korčula are everywhere, young and not-so-young, straight-backed, dress- and breast-conscious, with a cat-walk walk that turns heads. I try to keep my eyes on the road.

The town is awash with people. Most are locals going about their everyday affairs. There are tourists too, of course, who have bought into this island world for a week or two.

Strolling between hotel meals, they cope with the sun, helplessly
conspicuous in dress and demeanour: a few languid, dark-haired
Italians, cool behind their shades, eyeing up the motor bikes for
hire at 'Marko Polo Tours'; a French group, hot but scent-
drenched, earnestly and enviously attentive to their officious
parasol-wielding *cicerone*; some Japanese, corded with cameras
and photographic bondage; middle-aged Brits, culturally
indifferent and undemonstrative but betrayed none the less by
shrinking politeness and pallid skin; and beach-hungry
Germans, confident, by contrast, in their too-good-to-be-true
toffee-coloured tans. No less exposed in our open-topped car,
we must drive with care, not in the hope of concealing *our*
nationality (with a steering wheel on the right, a GB plate at the
rear and a St Andrew's cross sticker as prominently displayed as
we can make it, we are, on the contrary, keen to make clear our
Scots identity) but because, as we turn away from the eastern
quay and up onto the humped isthmus that links the new town to
the old, all the conventional territorial distinctions between
vehicle and pedestrian vanish. Kerbs disappear. The road, laid
over the low neck of land that separates the east and west bays,
is a hard pavement of marble, the stone worn and burnished
ochre-gold like the Stradun in Dubrovnik. There is nothing here,
however, outside the walls of the old town to match Ragusan
rigour; this is a younger part of the town, begun towards the end
of the eighteenth century, unplanned, *ad hoc*, but full of casual
intimacy and charm. The widening space – proudly if a little
lengthily named Plokata 19 aprila 1921 (the date commemorates
the decision of the Treaty of Rapallo that Korčula should finally
be Slav and not Italian) – is indeterminate, half street, half
public square; the buildings unremarkable, three- and four-
storeys high, narrow, all but devoid of any kind of architectural
accent or enrichment. On our left, fissured gaps leak into a
labyrinth of cranked lanes and stepped alleys hidden in which
are the town's shops – butcher and baker, bars and boutiques,
mini-market, photographer and cobbler – and, unjustly
disregarded in its quiet square, the small octagonal church of St
Justine (Sveta Justina) breaking the skyline with a halo-ed figure
of the resurrected Christ. Ahead, opening to the sea beyond, is
Trg pomirenja, the town's memorial to the dead of World War

Two, a small circular arena partially ringed with three concentric tiers of marble benching enclosed by low curving walls on the outer faces of which are *bas relief* carved panels depicting the trades and crafts of the town – stonemasonry, viniculture, boatbuilding and fishing – and a single plainer tablet recording with incised Trajan precision, the names of the fallen. Square in name, if only in translation (Trg pomirenja translates as Square of Reconciliation), this open, almost amphitheatrical, urban space, designed in 1987 by local architect Bernardo Bernardi, appears to take its circular shape from that of the nearby Prince's Great Tower whose battered circumferential bulk forms the western bastion of the Old Town only twenty metres away. Passers-by pause on the warm, stone benches to rest and perhaps remember, while children shout and play, oblivious to the silenced lives that linger in this ring of memory. To the right, a broad gap opens north, funneling towards Punat, the grand staircase-bridge that rises in an elegant arc like some oversized perron to enter the walled town through the Tower of the Land Gate (Veliki Revelin). And because this in-between space we are in is the space that binds the old to the new, it is above all a meeting place, a focus for much of the town's commercial and social life. The old inner town is still the centre of civic and ecclesiastical administration as it has always been. The offices of the municipality lie up the steps and just within the gate. On the hilltop are the cathedral and *župski ured*, the parochial office – religious power as unequivocal in its location as its ubiquity (over the years I have counted nine churches within the walls and still I cannot help feeling I may have missed some small chapel buried in the stony shadows). Up in the Old Town the sights, sounds and smells of family life still spill out of the old multi-level houses and palaces packed back-to-back along narrow, parallel lanes. But down here outside the walls is where business is done, here on Plokata is where one keeps a rendezvous. Looking left and right, I make a simpler tally: two banks, two newsagents, two travel bureaus, two cafés. It's no surprise to see the cafes doing good business.

Ten minutes later we are sitting in one of those cafés. We have parked the car as always on the long pier that flanks the west side of the old town and have walked back along the waterfront. A few expensive-looking yachts ranked stern-on to the quay nudge one another gently, their rigging whispering in the light breeze. Rounding the massive base of the Prince's Great Tower we are back at the centre of things.

The *Caffé Arula* sits on a corner, its terrace tented under a blue-and-white, twin-masted canopy decoratively scalloped at the edges. It's busy but we find a table by the terrace wall. Nada sees us, a glint of recognition enough to tell us she'll take our order in a moment. There are usually two, sometimes three, waitresses on duty but Nada is our favourite. She's small and slim, she smiles a lot and, in her white blouse, Saxe blue *gilet* and short dark skirt – a uniform her colleagues appear to wear with ill-fitting reluctance – she's smart and attractive. It's difficult to guess her age. Good legs. Late thirties perhaps? Her dark auburn hair has been carefully back-combed but the colour is false, dyed, like that of most Croatian women. Over forty? As she wipes our table the skin on the backs of her hands wrinkles like crushed tissue paper. Maybe fifty. Maybe more.

'*Dobar dan. Dobar dan.*' She greets each of us in turn as she always does, somehow managing to combine politeness with urgency. I smile our acknowledgment and order the coffees. My added request for a doughnut provokes mock reproof; a *faux* frown then a grin. When it comes it's fat, powdered with icing sugar and oozing with jam. More raised eyebrows. Nada turns away feigning a despairing shrug.

So we sit drinking our coffee. If, as it seems from the town's crowded cafés and bistros, half of Korčula is doing the same, then the other half is at large on the streets. A kind of musical chairs is in play. While those who are seated sip the last of their wine or spoon *cappuccino* froth from their empty cups, deciding at length to continue their stroll, complete their shopping or go home to lunch, others watching wait to pounce. Each feels the other's gaze. We too. I pick up the tab Nada has slipped under the ashtray and, catching her eye again, pay the bill.

It's a short walk to Tino's. We cross the square and join the crush of people filing through the narrow street opposite *Caffé Arula*. The corner is papered and overpapered with torn notices of local events, most of them out of date. A freshly applied black-bordered rectangle announces a death – *u dubokoj boli javljamo*, in deep pain we announce... *vrijeme prolazi, sjecanje ostaje*, time passes, memories remain... The street walls themselves, stone or stained stucco, crack and peel in a palimpsest of memories. Above a shop, a fading fascia, the painted, barely legible name of a forgotten proprietor long since out of business and out of life. We pass *Cukarin*, an Aladdin's cave of delectable confectionery. As always we pause, tempted by the array of 'calorie bombs' on display. From her doorway Smiljana, the ebullient proprietrix, gives us an inviting smile; but we resist. I notice the name of the street, carefully cut in classic Roman letters into a stone block set high on a corner. Ulica Hrvatske bratske zajednica. The words carry a faint echo of Tito's once ubiquitous and socially importunate appeal for *Bratstvo i Jedinstvo*, Brotherhood and Unity. But in the shop windows no nostalgia now for the Communist utopia. Instead, evident, if not always affordable, proof of the new material well-being; full shelves and, preserved for the tourist, the crushed spirit of socialism reduced to the red rag of a Che Guevara tee-shirt.

We buy our wine and oil. Turning left out of the shadows we step down into Prolaz tri sulara, a narrow lane running back to the east bay. At the far end of the street light glitters on the clutter of masts in the marina, glistens on the sea beyond. A banner slung above us advertises the *Caffé Bar Galerija*. It seems hardly necessary. The pound of pop music is loud enough and the *Galerija*'s patrons are crowded around the tables and chairs that have spilled onto the lane in front of us. It's difficult to pass – a more persuasive ruse, perhaps, than the banner overhead.

The chrome-framed void of the café front has cut away what must once have been the ground floor of the three-storey dwelling above. But an old stone doorway has survived. It has moulded architraves, a good cornice, and a scrolled armorial tablet carved with two *putti* cavorting around what seems to be a globe. Not the grandest entrance in Korčula by any means but one that does at least preserve some past pretension to familial pride. The door to Tino's, on the other hand, is plain, squat in proportion and easily missed. The lintel is low and again we

119

step down, this time out of the sun into a dark interior. It's a small space, the ceiling not much above two metres, but, like the café, it's busy. A counter top runs along one wall; there are five computers, six chairs. All are occupied. Tino pops his head round a corner in the shadows at the back of the room. He signs to us to wait; it won't be long till a machine is free. So we wait, wondering whether it will be the German yachtsman in the far corner or one of the young backpacking Australians busy trying to book rooms in Dubrovnik or Hvar or Split who will be first to give up their seat. We don't have to wait long. It's the Ozzies. A tall tanned girl gets up and, stretching herself unselfconsciously, offers us a place. I smile our thanks, sit down and log on.

We have mail.

As Jasna guessed, both Andrew and Ian have written. I open Andrew's letter first. As usual it's crisp and business-like, the preliminaries brief, the bad news abrupt.

'...you were right about the régime. I have had the first of four chemotherapy treatments and hope to be well enough to do it again later this week. Three nights in the hospital for one twelve-hour and two eight-hour sessions. The first went well in that I had almost immediate relief of symptoms and have been eating without difficulty ever since. Last week my blood count was low all round and I was poorly for a couple of days but building again towards being fit for the next dose. The hair will be all gone soon but not a problem.

Beyond the four chemo sessions planned at three weekly intervals, I have had my mask made and the computer programmed to deliver thirty radio therapy doses so it will be some time yet before holidays might seem attractive. But that also feels OK.

Margaret is becoming more and more formidable, especially with visitors, and anyone with the least cough doesn't get beyond the garden gate. You two will be an exception to her rules as long as you bring photographs and stories. We're looking forward...'

It all seems so straightforward, almost clinical. As always Andrew is in control. The whole horrific business is almost objectively documented: the length and intensity of the treatments recorded, the loss of hair reported with an almost bland acceptance, the surely gruesome preparation of the protective mask noted without a trace of morbidity. And nothing is said that might reveal what he and Margaret must be thinking as they hug each other to sleep each night. Nothing. It's as if to betray emotion, still less any hint of negative speculation about the future, even to us who are among the oldest and dearest of their friends, might be a flaw of character, a weakness to be seized on by the disease. Crisis? What crisis? Things take their course; nothing to get upset about. I can picture Andrew sitting alone at his computer typing this latest report to us, choosing his words with care, intent on a kind of honesty that tells us the truth but never the whole truth. If only he would share the pain. If only he were not so Scottish. The more I read the words – the more I read the words between the lines – the more my throat tightens. Jasna, standing behind me, has her hands on my shoulders. I can feel the pressure of her fingers as she reads. I close my eyes, trying to escape, but it's useless. A helpless sadness makes us cling to the words on the screen.

It's Jasna who breaks their melancholy spell; leaning over she presses 'Back'. The Inbox reappears. Another click and Ian's long letter comes up. More pain?

'Dear Frank and Jasna

The waiting is over. Susan finally saw the consultant yesterday. It was like going to her execution, she said. For me it was like hearing the result of an examination I knew I had failed.

The cancer was not an aggressive one, whatever that means. It was "hormone sensitive" which is apparently a good thing. But it had spread to the lymph glands – three, I think. But these have been removed and now all -all! – that needs to be done is a course of chemotherapy to mop us any rogue cells. We meet the oncologist next Thursday when Susan will learn the full extent and nature of the chemotherapy to be given.

All this sounds quite matter of fact! But for Susan yesterday it was pretty traumatic. Mention of the word chemotherapy *was enough to press all the panic buttons simultaneously. She fell apart! The C word – not the cancer so much as the chemo – was the death knell. Today, however, with help from the children, even from me, she seems a little more put together. So, as you said in your last letter, all will be well. Indeed, is well. Having said that, Susan is dreading the next weeks and months. Already your support has meant much and I know that will continue. Thank you seems inadequate but I mean it.*

I am truly sorry your yesterday was a melancholy, even dismal, day for you. It is the lot of Calvinists, of course. My own dismal days, however, are not, I've concluded, theological, but genetic. On my father's side. Deo volente, he would offer, as we said our farewells. Carpe diem, he could never quite seize. I suffer from that, too, somewhat. But less so now. So my fight is not with God but with my genes – for which, I suppose, I can fairly blame God. No escape.

Now to that phrase I used last time, "The meaning is in the waiting". You wanted to know where it came from. It's from a poem by R.S. Thomas. Thomas was a minister in the Church of Wales and most, indeed all, of his poetry is austere and gloomy. The poem is entitled Kneeling.

> *Moments of great calm,*
> *Kneeling before an altar*
> *Of wood in a stone church*
> *In summer, waiting for God*
> *To speak; the air a staircase*
> *For silence; the sun's light*
> *Ringing me, as though I acted*
> *A great role. And the audiences*
> *Still; all that close throng*
> *Of spirits waiting, as I,*
> *For the message.*
>
> > *Prompt me, God;*
> *But not yet. When I speak,*
> *Though it be you who speak*
> *Through me, something is lost.*
> *The meaning is in the waiting.*

So, the meaning is in the waiting. I have taken it out of context; the meaning, for Thomas, is in the silence of prayer. To verbalise thought in prayer is for him to lose the meaning.... the presence. But doesn't the same truth apply in the lives we all have to live. With Susan, for example, I have tried all the platitudes: don't worry... you'll be all right... everything will be fine. Perhaps I should have offered her silence, a presence, a waiting-with-her. Would not meaning have somehow been transmitted? And in my own waiting for Susan's results I have hurried on towards the end, the consummation. Whereas the waiting in the now *is the strengthening now, and to know that strength is so profoundly meaningful. Hope, as you yourself said, is the corollary of waiting. More than ever these waiting days I am glad for my/our faith.*

This comes with affection and love

Ian'

It's a wonderful letter. It *is* what we have to do – *wait*. Andrew, Margaret, Ian, Susan – us too. But it's not waiting *for*. No anticipation. No brooding on the next chemo session. No picture in the mind's eye of Susan without her thick dark hair. No lived-in future, joyful or, still less, tragic. Ian has it right, it's waiting in *the now*. It's waiting *with*. It's waiting *on*. A verse comes back to me out of my Presbyterian youth: 'they that wait upon the Lord shall renew their strength...' Easy to say; glib, pompous even. And why bring God into it? But that, I can't help. And Ian knows it, for deep down – indeed, maybe not so deep – we both share the same bible-schooled baggage of duty and guilt that goes with a parlous, doubt-tempered Protestant faith. God may be our familial obligation, a moral onus, a get-out clause, a habit, all these and more. But we have waited in the pews all our lives and He still seems to be there. It is duty – a duty born of long friendship, not the compulsion of childhood Sundays, but all the more a duty – that makes us write to Andrew and Ian now. We need to look into their wounds. We have to touch them, at least with words. There's guilt too. Not some simplistic piety that finds false penance in pain, but a

123

subtler puzzled shame that we, waiting here in the sun, are free to read or write the words – and go. Sometimes the lotus has a bitter taste.

Back in the lane outside Tino's it takes a moment or two to grow accustomed to the noon sunlight. It will be a longer wait before we come to terms with the grim news from home and longer still till we find the words we need to respond to our friends. I have printed both letters knowing we will want to read them again and again as if perhaps, by doing so, the truth might turn out to be different or, if not, we might at least draw closer to Ian and Susan. And knowing what we might rather not have known, I find it difficult to step back into the Korčula streets without a disturbing sense that for this, our inexplicable, inequitable, good fortune to be here, some atonement must be made.

> *'...the sun's light*
> *Ringing me, as though I acted*
> *A great role...'*

But this is the greatest conceit. To think that there might be some *quid pro quo* in the dilemma of suffering, to imagine that were it possible through some self-sacrificial performance of ours we might cancel the pain and despair of others, is to play God – or rather, it is to assume that God plays to our text. There is no 'great role'. No 'far far better thing'. We can only watch and wait in the wings, unsure of the *dénouement* to come but hopeful that our being there might somehow matter to those we love. I put my arm around Jasna and she leans her head against my shoulder. It's a closeness we need and, as we each sense in the physical comfort of the moment, a metaphor, too, for the embrace we long to share with our friends.

Prolaz tri sulara ends as it began – with a café. At the corner, where the houses step back as if in spatial respect to two tall old olive trees, the *Caffé Olea* sits a little incongruously in the recess. It's not much more than a glass box, a greenhouse oddly capped with hip-ended tiled roof. Outside, under the shade of the olives, the tables and chairs are busy. Across the road is the marina and, beyond the long harbour mole, the sea. Out across the water, not much more than a kilometre distant, green on blue, the low convex outline of Badija island. We turn left towards the eastern quay, crossing the harbourside road, the same road along which we drove into town an hour or so ago. It's well named, Obala Korčulanskih brodograditelja, in honour of the island's long tradition of shipbuilding – though the local shipyard (still in business, just) is kept well out of sight two bays away to the east beyond Punta Križa. There is no pavement but a long line of dumpy hemispherical bollards, like half-buried concrete footballs, marks a walkway by the water's edge.

At the pier expectation is growing. Three lines of vehicles wait for the ferries. Most will be headed north: cars with a variety of registration plates – German, Croatian, Slovenian, Czech, Hungarian, Italian, rarely British – two are trailing gargantuan motor launches (German), there are three immense camper vans (French), a lorry from Split ostentatiously advertising *Karlovačko* beer, and, making its regular return trip back to base beyond Rijeka, the familiar white van of *Vera Buzet*, an Istrian furniture company with branches all along the coast. A single bus is in the queue. The closely packed rows are crowded with people. Nervous drivers lean against the bonnets of their cars or hang on open doors. Some already have their flimsily counterfoiled Jadrolinija tickets in their hands; others kick their tyres, not in anger but nodding knowingly, as if the consequences of this primitive gesture were of some vital technical significance; a few open car boot or hatchback, rearranging, probably not for the first time this morning, the cases, bags and bottles they have stowed there. Temporarily decanted from air-conditioned comfort, perspiring bus passengers (none of whom, it seems, is under fifty) cluster together, ill at ease in the noonday heat. They stay close to their bus, taking advantage of its shade. Unburdened backpackers, tanned, tired and untidy, drink from plastic bottles of mineral water with practised economy. Some local tradesmen and shopkeepers are arguing amongst themselves as to whether the goods they have ordered from catalogue or prospectus will arrive on the ferry this time. We recognize a number of familiar figures, *Korčulani* and others like us, unfailing spectators whenever the boat comes in. There, sitting astride their moped, the middle-aged German couple who never miss the show. There – beard, waxed moustache and fraying Panama – the trio of white-haired old gentlemen whose everyday tryst on the same quayside bench to smoke and reminisce with one another about other ships on other seas gives them a front seat advantage. And there the town's ever-optimistic landladies, black-clad and grandmotherly, but for a single bottled blonde with a high-heeled hint of more than rooms for sale, take up their positions ready for the dash for disembarking customers. Only the smartly dressed local travellers, deck passengers on business or family trips to Split or Dubrovnik, appear relaxed, isolated from the invisible miasma of *Reisefeber* that is swirling across the quay. They alone appear indifferent to the palpable sense of imminent theatre. But all are waiting. I think of the poem in Iain's letter – 'all that close throng' waiting. And to the east, emerging from behind the curtain of islands that screens the open sea, the *Liburnija* is already in sight.

Finding a way through the crush we reach the shade of some palm trees growing at the back of the pier. It's a place to pause but hardly the best vantage point. To find that we turn away from the crowd, walk back uphill under more tall palms almost as far as the Land Gate and then, turning again towards the sea, continue up Rampada. The wide gently inclined carriageway, built against Korčula's ancient landward defences in the late nineteenth century to provide vehicular access to the tree-lined promenade on the eastern walls, breaks a little inelegantly through the circumferential parapet of All Saints Tower (Kula Svih Svetih). Now, however, there are neither carts nor cars; bollards block any traffic and the slow ramp has become a favourite place to begin or end a leisurely stroll around the Old Town. The tower is also the best location from which to watch the comings and goings on the pier below. Perched on its broad parapet between two of the three carriage-mounted cannon placed here in 1994, we watch the *Liburnija*'s cautious approach.

She edges nearer and nearer, slowly, in a turmoil of foam. Starboard side nudging the quay, the white ship shudders as hawsers fore and aft slacken and tighten. Along the deck, passengers crane over the rail watching the narrowing gap. Finally, close to the stern, the steel door to the car deck yawns open, its motor whining to control the slow descent that is transforming it into a vehicular ramp. A dark inner cave is revealed. A single car, a German Mercedes (I imagine its driver fearful of the hair-raising demands made by the mainland route from Dubrovnik) emerges into the light, negotiates the lip of the ramp with exaggerated care and begins its contorted stop-start escape through the waiting ranks. Immediately, loading begins: first, the vehicles for Stari Grad on Hvar, then those for Split, and finally those going all the way overnight to Rijeka; a sequence which, it quickly becomes apparent from the chaotic manoeuvring entailed, seems to have been unknown or more likely totally disregarded by the pier control. Familiar with the drill – or lack of it – lorry and van rumble aboard confidently. The bus, however, makes heavy weather of it. Half on, half off the ramp, it stalls, re-starts, then, warned by the shouts and gestures of the crew who are swarming around it on all sides, comes to a second abrupt halt. At the rear the bodywork has all but grounded on the pier. From somewhere, hefty battered planks of wood and oil sodden coconut mats are brought out to be wedged under the rear wheels. The engine growls into life again and the bus inches forward elevating itself just enough to clear the surface of the quay. Gasping its relief in a cloud of exhaust it disappears into the dark depths. A few last cars follow.

Meanwhile foot passengers are clattering down the staircase gangway slung amidships. They spill onto the pier in a swelling flood of confusion that only gradually begins to coagulate into a number of smaller pools. Each group presses close to its leader, twenty or thirty hot tourists held together by the reassurance of a clip-board held aloft, a waving flag or a rolled umbrella flourished by their guide. These are the day-trippers, here for lunch and a few hours touring the town then back by bus making the short ferry crossing to Orebić and the two-hour mainland route by Pelješac, Ston and Slano in time for dinner in their Dubrovnik hotels. Others, locals burdened with luggage or packages, disappear into waiting cars or temporary shade.

How familiar all this is! How many times have I waited to watch the ferries come and go! Yet there is always something irresistibly elemental about it. The sense of arrival and departure. Expectation, excitement and bathos. Life and death on the pier. For the watcher, of course, there is no direct engagement, no change of scene – only an isolated detached waiting as events take their course and time passes, the meaning – if there is a meaning in this waiting – hanging in the still air somewhere between ship and shore. And now, transfixed in the torpid afterglow of it all, my gaze sightless in the middle distance between us and the *Liburnija* steaming out of sight around the blunted promontory of the old town, I find myself thinking again of Susan and Andrew.

Is this sudden return of sympathy genuine, or is it no more than self-righteously imposed by these musings? I'm not sure. In either event, does it matter much? The remembrance of friends' pain is surely what counts. Perhaps it is love that has found a way back to them through the metaphor, a better way for sure than any mapped out by moral projection. Perhaps. For a moment or two, I juggle with this dilemma. The pier has lapsed into stillness again, waiting for the *Marko Polo*. Life then death, then life again after death. Watching and waiting too, I begin to ponder what, if any, might be the parallels implicit in these quayside scenes.

Abruptly, the second ship appears. Her approach, like the onward voyage of the *Liburnija*, hidden from view by the town behind us, is both sudden and slow. Stately, high in the water and multi-decked, the *Marko Polo*, named for Korčula's most famous son, is a much bigger ship, so much so she (can Marko be a she?) cannot lie alongside the quay but must approach stern-on. The manoeuvre is soon completed. Foam churns below us eddying into the rocky skirts of the pier. White-shirted officers in black shades kiss instructions into their mobile phones. The ship sashays hesitantly, then advances. On the pier, mirroring these adjustments, men are moving to the left, then right, then left again, waiting for the ropes to be cast. A last white-water eruption and it is done. Heavy hawsers are looped over the pier's cast iron bollards, the rear of the ship tilts out away from the hull in a slow descent to the quay, pausing at the last to allow the deckhands time to push forward each of the ten individual tapered steel teeth of the car ramp. They crash noisily on the hard stone. The drama can begin again.

This time the sequence is reversed. Cars roll off, not on. Then motor-bikes. Buses, too, three of them. All goes smoothly. Only two cars drive aboard. Then come the passengers, necessarily disembarking from the car deck but held back by the crew until the vehicular exchange is completed. They swarm out of the darkness on a broad front, most, though not quite all, tourists of one kind or another, anxious to be ashore: clustering bus passengers; mothers and children, obliged to walk off rather than overload the car on the ramp, screwing up their eyes to see where Dad has parked to wait for them; regular visitors waving to friends or relatives on the quay; locals quickly off through the crowd and into town; backpackers momentarily perplexed over which way to head until the eager landladies pounce. Running against the tide of arrival, the handful of local men who have spent the last hour or so estimating their respective chances of finding the goods they have ordered aboard, disappear into the darker recesses of the ship to emerge carrying, pushing or pulling their various prizes. A bedstead emerges, somehow manhandled to a waiting pick-up. Pipework, electrical cabling, kitchen fitments, a bath and lavatory basin, endless boxes of varying shapes and sizes get loaded into and onto cars that look as if they have been here before. A large potted palm is trundled off the ramp. A small, decidedly distressed-looking lorry backs on to be loaded with a dozen or so sacks of who knows what.

And then, as suddenly as it all began when the ramp clanged onto the pier, it is over. The cars and buses have gone. The people too. A young ship's officer strolls casually across the deserted pier, a cigarette cupped in his palm. Deckhands lounge against the car ramp rail. There is a sense of redundant time as the minutes tick to one o'clock and the *Marko Polo*'s scheduled departure. Now there is nothing to see, nothing but the silent pier and ship. We, too, find ourselves alone – the last watchers on the tower.

'It's a boy's thing.'

'What?' I ask, somehow offended, without knowing why, by this Parthian shot of Jasna's. She has already gathered up her bag with its supply of wine and olive oil and has turned away from the parapet.

'This obsession to watch until the very last minute. As if you had to possess it all. As if you might miss something, some unexpected incident, some collector's item. Like trainspotting –' and then, whether to soften or sharpen the insult, 'without the anorak'

'Hardly.'

'At least you didn't draw it yet again.'

That's true. Over the years I've made dozens of sketches of ships at the pier. And there beside me on the parapet is the sketch book I've been carrying all morning – unopened. I pick it up, not quite sure why I haven't thought to make another drawing.

'It was different today... waiting... I...' But Jasna is out of ear-shot halfway down Rampada. I swing myself off the stone wall and follow her, quickening my pace to catch up.

It's hot. But more than that, it's quiet. After all the noise and activity of the quay Korčula seems to have fallen asleep. There are few people about. Someone is hosing down the ring of concrete tables at the open market. The souvenir stalls below the old walls are deserted. The cafes are empty. The tourist groups up from Dubrovnik for the day are nowhere to be seen, whisked off by bus to a hotel meal of veal and *blitva* before their island tour, or up in the old town wondering why they have had to endure a pre-prandial history lesson from their over-enthusiastic guide. Everyone else is at home at lunch. The heat is burning up the town

> *'...the air a staircase*
> *For silence...'*

Slowly we walk back to the car, an implacable pall of melancholy hanging in the sun's stillness.

I look back and catch a last glimpse of the *Marko Polo* sailing south, already far in the distance. It *was* different today. Two ships. One gone, the other still in sight. Two friends.

* * *

Six weeks later, home in Scotland, we learn from Margaret that Andrew is in a hospice. He has beaten the oesophageal cancer but secondaries have spread to his liver. Two weeks more pass and he is dead.

Susan has finished her long course of chemo- and radio-therapy. Her hair is growing back – auburn-coloured. Ian has organised a wig-burning barbecue for a few special friends. At last he's able to talk about a holiday for them both. Korčula, he thinks.

THE RETURN OF MARKO POLO

'...from the number of imaginable cities we must exclude those whose elements are assembled without a connecting thread, an inner rule, a perspective, a discourse. With cities, it is as with dreams: everything imaginable can be dreamed...'

Italo Calvino
1974

If, as Italo Calvino surmises in *Invisible Cities*, Marko Polo held in his head 'a model city from which all possible cities can be deduced', I like to fancy he had in mind his Dalmatian childhood in the island town of Korčula. But, of course, it is Venice that gets Calvino's vote: 'Every time I describe a city I am saying something about Venice', he has his hero tell Kublai Khan. No doubt as he penetrated deeper and deeper into the dry heart of Asia, Marko must many times have recalled *riva* and loggia and all the arcaded panoply of the canals coiling to the lagoon. *La Serenissima*, her marbled body contoured with lubricious light or shadowed with allure; no doubt the pulse of fantasy pounds faster beside her. Lost in labyrinthine imaginings, the Great Khan must have listened to his alien guest tell of eye-splitting piazza and dark disorientating *calli*. Did he listen and dream in Marko's memories?

Venice is intoxication, a metaphor for miasma. Yet misty dreams make poor models for city-building, and if, as Calvino would have Marko say to the still importunate Khan, 'To distinguish the other cities' qualities, I must speak of a first city that remains implicit', might he not have known that first city in the lithic body of Korčula? For, small as it is, Korčula is rigorously urban. Its geometries are explicit, clean-cut in plan and filigreed in façade from the hot hard local stone. As much as Venice's ravelled mysteries do at length reveal themselves to her meandering lovers, so much more does Korčula seduce with an immediate unequivocal embrace of stone and shadow ordered in space. Instead of the maze, the matrix. Besides mystery and memory, reason.

Korčula is a city set on a hill. Its logic is visible, it cannot be hidden. Walled and towered, it erupts from the sea fashioned in a girdle of fortified stone. The plan is both organic – fishbone, feather or leaf – *and* geometric, an axial north-south spine cross-draped with narrow streets cut in parallel alleyways. These deep fissures threaded through the stone are tuned to wind and sun: steep lanes dropping sunset-straight to the north-west, open to the cooling summer breath of the *maestral*; tight vennels falling west to east in a slow curve that is just enough to check the winter gusts of the *jugo*. Densely packed, double-banked rows of tall houses, humble dwellings and palaces from a patrician past, rise side by side in blocky cubic prisms through ogee arch and dark half-shuttered voids. Up above cornice and corbel there are flower-filled terraces, kitchens smoking to the sky and a spreading parasol of orange-tiled roofs. In the darkened lanes, lines of washing are hanging bunting-bright like limp ensigns of familial possession. On balcony and lintel, scarred escutcheons betray the lineage of another time.

Marko's childhood home is here too – or so the *Korčulani* say. Up the hill from the Land Gate, past the Cathedral, there is a tiny tilted square that fronts the little Church of St Peter (Sveti Petar). To one side of the church the square is flanked by the gaunt north wall of the Cathedral as it runs down into the stepping defile of Ulica Don Pavla, one of the ten fish-bone alleys that fall to the eastern walls. On the other, palm and lemon trees tumble over a high wall, bare but for the long stone bench at its base. Hidden behind sleeps an ancient garden while above, just visible in the skyline angle between the cascade of fronds and branches and the open gable bellcote of St Peter's, is a small, pyramid-roofed pavilion. This, the *Korčulani* claim, is the House of Marko Polo, the family home of the great explorer.

Today the visitor approaches the walled garden from Ulica Depolo, the next narrow street to the north, climbs some steps, then passes under a pergola into the cool green darkness. It costs a few kunas to enter the house. But there is little to see; in effect no more than a tight timber staircase returning in short flights as it climbs in its tower above the lane. Opposite the garden is the derelict void of a substantial three- or four-storey dwelling, once presumably accessible from the bridging stair. The masonry shell is more or less intact – cusped bifurcated Gothic windows, round arches too, cornices with crisp billet moulding – but inside only rubble. A door opens from the stairwell out onto the final flight, cantilevered stone treads rising under the sun to the shaded loggia on the roof. Light-headed and a little out of breath, I reach the top and look down on the town.

Beside me I can picture the young Marko clinging tiptoe-tense to the parapet, ardent eyes staring out across the sea. Aloft and alone, is he dreaming here of distant worlds? Do invisible cities find fantastic form in his young imagination, spurring the far-flung adventures of later years? And if so, was every dream – and later every memory – a transformation of his own town, the stone-cut city below his childhood gaze?

But the dream is mine. These walls cannot be seven centuries or more old. This House of Marko Polo is a fabrication, the fanciful construct of local legend turned to tourist use. Or is it? Is it quite so simple?

Myth it may be, in whole or part, but like every traveller's tale distilled in the telling through time and space, like the very memories of home that Marko shared in Xanadu or those fantastic journeys remembered with his amanuensis Rustichello in a Genoa jail, something of the intoxicating spirit of truth remains. The house may be a sham but not the place and not the people. Decidedly Dalmatian in origin, the Polo or Depolo family (the name has a number of correlated versions both Italianate and Slavic, *e.g.* Pavao, Paulovich, Pavlović, De Paulis, Di Polo, Depolo) are known in Korčula from before Marko's birth in the middle of the thirteenth century. Through the years local records identify them as sailors, sculptors, merchants, priests, lawyers and, in particular, shipbuilders. In this last capacity many *Korčulani*, including some bearing the name Polo, found work in Venice. Were Marko's father and uncle among those who came and stayed? It is impossible to say, but the combination of circumstantial evidence including the fact that Marko himself lies buried in the Church of St Lawrence in the Castello district of Venice, a part of the city intensively settled by Croats, suggests that the family might indeed have had links with Korčula. That one sixteenth-century editor-biographer of the great explorer's *Description of the World*, a certain Giambattista Ramusio, should record that Marko's commital to a Genovese jail – the very event which was to precipitate the writing of his amazing story – followed upon his capture at the naval battle fought between Venice and Genoa off the island of Korčula in 1298 adds a further coincidental symmetry to these speculations. Whatever the truth of the matter, the myth is compelling. I am not alone up here on this small canopied platform above the trees and tiles. Screwing up his eyes against the sun, a dark-haired boy is searching the horizon for his future.

We dream different dreams, Marko and I. He of a future that is for me a past. I of a past that is still his future. We live in different worlds. But below us we see one city. The moving picture of the crowd breaching the circling wall at the Land Gate, filing up through crevasse-deep lanes into the hot light of the town's hilltop square, drifting down again to the clattering shimmer of the quayside. We hear the city's sounds: children, church bells, the bright morning chatter of caged finches hanging in window reveals, a snatch of evening mass out of the dark open cave of the cathedral, a sigh behind a shutter. We smell the sea, flowers, dust, and grilling fish. We sense the wind or sun around one corner, shelter or shade round another. We touch the ubiquitous stone.

Born in 1254, the very year when the Zorzi family, re-establishing themselves as *kneževi*, Venice's hereditary proxy rulers on the island, began the programme of urban reconstruction that would lay the foundations of modern Korčula, Marko must have lived with the city, watching it take shape as completely and irrevocably as he himself grew into manhood. As often as he gazed out from his attic eyrie on the open seas that stretched to Venice in the north and Greece, the Levant and Asia in the south, so often he would look down on the feverish construction activity around and below him. A fortified wall thrown around the town. Ten high square towers set at intervals in the *enceinte*. A regularized pattern of streets. A visible city.

It has changed, of course. The walls and towers have been repeatedly strengthened, their thickness and profile altered. By the nineteenth century only eight towers were standing. By the twentieth, a stretch of the western perimeter defences had gone while only one square tower and four others, now massively machicolated and drumlike, remained. The buildings that I see are those of the fifteenth, sixteenth and seventeenth centuries – Cathedral, churches, palaces, the town's tall houses – not those of Marko's time. But the urban space, combed in parallel clefts through the stone or opening up behind the Land Gate and again before the Cathedral on the crest of the hill, must be Marko's too. His to remember, his to share with the Great Khan.

Ours too.

From Plokata and the disordered bustle of the modern town, the approach to the old city of Korčula is already calculated and auspicious. A balustraded staircase spills forward from the Land Gate tower, a widening cascade of twenty-nine stone steps inviting ascent. To the right, the city walls are screened by a stand of six tall palm trees, to the left by mulberry and bougainvillea. The steps are new – or at least, in the time-scale of the city, recent; the arching structure of the stair, built to replace a timber drawbridge that crossed the ditch separating the island town from the mainland, was completed in 1863. At the same time a new round-arched opening was cut through the base of the old square tower. The portal is plain and unadorned, with simple imposts and keystone, its inner promise hidden in the depth of shadow. Above the archway are two superimposed stone tablets. One bears an inscription marking the 1925 millennial commemoration of the coronation of the Croat king Tomislav; the other, a fragment from the centuries of Venetian rule, carved with the winged lion of St Mark confined between armorial shields (it is one of only a few remaining Venetian lions on Korčula, the others defaced or removed by islanders embittered by the Italian occupation of World War II). Higher still, the rubble surface of the tower merges imperceptibly into a parapet of four square-cut merlons, disarmingly austere above the baroque rhetoric of the stairway below.

We cross the dark threshold and, passing below the mid seventeenth century Mannerist archway raised against the interior face of the tower in honour of the Venetian military leader Leonardo Foscolo, enter the city. We are in Radić Square. The sense of enclosure is sudden, abruptly claustrophobic after the expansive flattery of the twenty-nine steps. But then comes reassurance, the strange primeval realization that we are safe within the walls. It is intimate, too, this small square we have so often entered, Jasna and I – and this intimacy is the intimation of something fundamentally urban, of stones and space. It is as if one stood just for a moment at the limbic stem of that first city locked in Marko's memory. Rectilineal in form though imperfect in its symmetries, the square first encloses then proposes, its elongation to the north, where a two-step rise creates a kind of inadvertent public dais, implicitly directional. Ahead is the main avenue of communication through the town, the spine of the plan, an absurdly narrow passageway, but straight and rising, conduit to the Cathedral on the hill. The street is proudly named, Ulica korčulanskog statuta 1214, recalling the *Statuta et leges civitatis et insulae Curzolae* which, as only the second such document in the Slavic world, gave to Korčula the code that, even before Marko's birth, defined civic conduct and administration and enshrined the island's commune autonomy within the Venetian imperium. Leading right and left from the square, precisely opposed at each of its four corners, are the first of the fish-bone lanes traced across the hill. Subtly, the plan begins to reveal itself in a logic that perambulation will confirm.

The lane immediately to the right, running downhill behind

the land wall past the truncated Mali Revelin tower and the old arsenal to the Church of All Saints, is Ulica dobrotvornosti, Charity Street. Of the ten lanes that fall east it is the only one which is not stepped, a distinction which has led some local guides to suggest that this was a favourite place for the town's thinkers to take the air since here, heads in the clouds or buried in books, they might stroll free from any fear of a fall. Facing the square at the corner is a three-storey-and-attic dwelling dating from 1530, originally that of the town physician and now a jeweller's shop perfectly located to trap the tourist. Beside it, a little recessed, the Church of St Michael (Sveti Mihovil), its ashlar front gabled and belfried yet no higher than the doctor's house. The façade, completed in 1651, though the church itself is first mentioned in 1412, is characteristically Dalmatian: three-arch bellcote, a small eight-spoke wheel window set centrally in a heavily moulded bowl frame, and, flanked by darkly staring *oeil de boeuf* windows, a doorway with tapering pilasters and a broken pediment. From the north side of the church a short balustraded bridge arches over Kaporova ulica to connect at first floor level with the treasury of the Brotherhood of St Michael.

To the left, tucked against the Land Gate tower is a small chapel unexpectedly dedicated to Our Lady of the Snow, Kapela Gospe Snježne. Its single-bay vaulted porch linking it to the Town Hall (Gradska vijećnica) marks the beginning of Knežev Prolaz. This narrow alley, directly opposite Kaporova, was originally reserved for the ruling *knez*, the route by which he, the high representative of Venetian power on the island, might reach his palace and descend by a final flight of steps to his private jetty on the western quay. Filling the block between this still shady and secretive lane and the next of the west-falling streets, Žitnica, is the Town Hall, centre of Korčula's administrative affairs since its construction in 1520-25 on the site of its ruined predecessor. Three round arches spring from short columns set on a low wall, the central bay opening to a cool porch or loggia. Above this arcade two flags are flying: the ubiquitous Croatian tricolour with its red chessboard and the flag of Korčula, royal blue with a castellated tower set in the yellow outline of a shield. A continuous stone bench provides seating around the porch and along the entire western side of the square. Close to the entrance to Žitnica, placed on a low plinth straddling the two-step change in the level of the square pavement, a single free-standing fluted column honours the memory of *knez* Battista Michieli, Venetian governor of Korčula, 1569-1571.

I remember this square when we first came to Korčula nearly thirty years ago, not so much for its urban clarity or for the architecture of its buildings pressing in on a space not much larger than some of the private courtyards opening off the lanes above, as for the people thronging through the July evening heat in search of food and drink. Crowds, squeezed through the Land Gate, lingered to take their bearings, the night air thick with cigarette smoke, a confusion of perfumes and the sweet scent of sun-creamed sweat. Progress was difficult, for the tables of the Gradski Podrum, the Town Cellar restaurant located at the upper right-hand corner of the square, had taken up most of the space. There were tables immediately outside the kitchen making it almost impossible to pass down the already tight defile of Kaporova ulica; others had been placed two steps down in the main body of the square below the baroque façade of St Michael's; still others on the opposite side were laid out alongside the short arcaded loggia of the Town Hall. Every table was occupied. White-shirted waiters darted and dived through the swell. Outside the restaurant a queue had formed, an added obstacle to the crush of people passing between the tables and on up into the old town. We too were waiting, but across the square from Kaporova on the western side where a small private restaurant struggled nightly to keep pace with an incessant demand, its handful of tables lined one after the other down Žitnica.

We knew the proprietor as Rade, a tall thin Serb with dark sleeked-back hair receding dramatically at the temples. He and his Croatian wife toiled in a kitchen no more than three metres square. The food was simple without pretension but it was food well worth the wait – fish and meat from the grill, fresh salads, and those staple accompaniments of every Dalmatian meal, good bread and wine. What's more, because it was Yugoslavia then, we could eat such dishes as *Srpski pasulj*, a thick filling soup of beans, pork and onions laced with plenty of paprika pepper, *Bosanski lonac*, a stew of mixed meats and vegetables

140

equally spiced up with paprika, and the best kebabs and meat balls, *ražnjići* and *čevapčići*, in Korčula. These last can still be found today, but not, alas, the others which, like Rade's restaurant, have vanished from the scene. It is a sad reflection of ethnic enmity and, indeed, insecurity that Croatian cuisine now abjures anything with the slightest flavour of Orthodox Serbia or Moslem Bosnia. Confronted by such absurdity, it's as tempting to be smug and dismiss this rejection – a rejection that was most absurdly evident in the careful 'whiting out' of the words *Srpski* and *Bosanski* from all hotel and restaurant menus in the early 1990s – as it is to think that the atrocities of the Balkan war could never happen in civilized Britain, until, that is, one remembers not only how, following the First World War, German biscuits were re-cooked as 'Empire' biscuits and the teaching of the German language disappeared for decades from secondary school curricula, but also, in more sombre and more immediate reflection, how socially inflammable is the potential of those Northern Irish hatreds that not only burn in Belfast and Derry but continue to smoulder in Glasgow and Liverpool. 'Balkan' is an epithet to use with circumspection.

I remember, too, a more recent April evening when it seemed that the whole town had assembled in the square to watch or take part in the celebrations held on the evening of Good Friday, *Veliki Petak*. Men dominated the crowd; in particular, the men of the Brotherhood of St Michael and the Virgin of Consolation, the so-called *mihovilci*, one of the three historic lay confraternities in the town. Dressed in their white gowns, gathered at the waist by a leather strap and covered at the shoulders by a blue cape, they spilled out from the church onto the square. Men of all ages: white-haired and stooped, tall and short, bearded and clean-shaven, young boys with their first close-cropped haircut of the season, even a child or two in his father's arms, and all in the same medieval robes. Many were carrying candles, called *torci*, some no bigger than the votary lights that could be seen burning in the shadowy interior of the church, but most larger, thicker and longer, sheathed with a circular tray to catch the dripping wax and held aloft like flagstaffs. A single four-shaft monster towered over the scene, for the moment steadied on the paving slabs by two muscular bearers; over four metres high and eighty-eight kilos in weight, so we learned later, it had been manufactured in honour of the Brotherhood's quatercentenary jubilee. Its huge silver-ringed wax-catching tray rose above the crowd like an inverted blue parasol. It remained understandably static, while the other candles moved in fluctuating constellations of light as the men of the Brotherhood circulated casually, chatting and smoking in the gathering twilight, waiting for the order to form ranks.

When it came, it came mysteriously and silently. No military imprecation, no evident explanation why the moment had come, but a line formed. No more than two deep, for more would have made it impossible to negotiate the narrow processional route up through the city to the Cathedral, the column took shape. Crosses, stars, ceremonial lamps and candles were raised. Above all was the great jubilee candle, the *veli vosak*, hugged erect by one of its two guardians, the other alongside ready to take the place of his partner should he tire or stumble. And then, as it had done for centuries, the procession began.

Side by side the brothers filed through the square. Some heads bowed solemnly but most smiled or looked around acknowledging family or friends in the watching crowd. Thirty or forty passed. We recognized faces we had seen behind counters, in cafes, on the *riva*. Fifty, sixty. A waiter from Hotel Korčula. A deck-hand from the Orebić ferry. Perhaps eighty. Tino, from the computer shop where we check our e-mails, looking a little ill at ease in quasi monastic garb rather than jeans and tee-shirt. He saw us and grinned wryly. By now we had lost count of both men and candles. But the procession continued until, just as it seemed that the square might empty, around the corner from Ulica dobrotvornosti there appeared a second body of men bearing aloft more religious treasures. Robed in cream-coloured Capuchin gowns with cowls on which a red cross had been embroidered, the Brotherhood of All Saints were fewer in number yet seemed to carry themselves with an assurance and a candle-lit dignity that may have had something to do with their being the oldest of Korčula's lay fraternities. From their Church of All Saints, first built close to the walls in the southern corner of the old town at the end of the thirteenth century shortly before the foundation of the Brotherhood itself in 1301, they too were walking to the Cathedral. There, as the Good Friday mass drew to a close, they would receive a blessing. And later they too would complete a circuit of the town maintaining this ancient Korčulan tradition.

That night we went with the flow, borne along in the surging crowd that followed the procession up to the Cathedral. People crushed together in the dark narrow street. Here and there, pools of light from a café or a shop window filled with filigree jewellery shone on the worn paving stones. And then, climbing a last few steps, we were in the upper square awash in a sea of jostling spectators.

Despite its grandly evocative name, Trg Svetog Marka, St Mark's Square, there is nothing beyond the allusion of a few architectural details to remind one of Venice. On all sides confined by stone, the space is elongated but tight in width; perhaps fifty metres in length, continuing the north-south spine of the town plan, but with little more than ten metres between the Cathedral portal and the Arneri Palace opposite. With some effort, suppressing any lingering deferential politeness, we worked our way through the crowd to a position between the Arneri and the City Museum. Here we could see that, though the last of the All Saints brothers were already disappearing into the Cathedral, a third group of celebrants, robed in cream-coloured capes with a red ribbon at the neck, had entered the square from the north. These were the *rokovci*, the Brotherhood of St Roch, founded in 1575 in gratitude for the saint's protection from the plague. Like the others they were carrying crosses, lanterns and a forest of tall candles which, combining reverence with necessity, they too dipped carefully below the low lintel of the Cathedral doorway. Two by two they passed into the dark church.

Now the crowd waited. From inside the Cathedral the sound of the choir's singing alternated with the undulating intonation of the priest. Wafted outside, incense hung on the evening air mingling with the smoke of cigarettes that glowed like candles hidden in the dusk. People talked together, voices muted, whispering greetings and gossip. Some found room to stroll and gradually a slow arm-in-arm sequence was set in motion, back and forward through the square, like the interval parade in theatre or concert-hall.

Suddenly, up in the campanile towering between the gabled façade of the church and the lower, plainer front of the Chapel of St Roch that forms the fourth aisle of the cathedral, the bells began to chime. From the interior came a stunning detonation of sound as the organ released a final salvo of joy. The mass was over. Blessed by Holy Church, congregation and Brotherhoods began to emerge onto the square. The waiting crowd were pressed back. Slowly and deliberately, crosses and candles were raised. Where wicks had been extinguished they were relit. Perspiration was wiped from foreheads, arms were stretched, robes re-adjusted. The procession re-formed: St Michael, All Saints, St Roch. Now the annual circumambulation of Korčula would begin.

For some time we watched the men of Korčula leave the church in the candle-lit darkness and slowly make their way back downhill towards the Land Gate. But we did not follow. A little tired, we turned away from the square into the quiet emptiness of one of the vennel-like streets that slope and step down to the western quay. I can't recall which street it was – probably Miroševica, or perhaps Arnerija – the parallel rigour of the plan makes it difficult to distinguish one from the other. Tall curtains of darkness pressed in from each side, high houses shuttered, silent and secret. But ahead, below, clustered above the *riva*, the glimmering lights of café tables drew us on, down to the Sea Gate.

The truncated Tower of the Sea Gate (Kula Morska Vrata), first constructed in 1265 when Marko Polo was ten years old, but largely rebuilt in 1448, still survives – just – its interior adapted as a small art gallery. So, too, brushed by palm fronds, do two tall square piers commemorating *knez* Alviseo Polani, 1598, and *knez* Pellegrin Pasqualigo, 1680. The gate itself and much of the western wall have, however, gone, victims of the peace dividend that followed a declaration made by the Viennese War Ministry in 1863 that the town's fortifications were no longer deemed necessary defences and would be handed over to the care of the local administration. To this decision Korčula's Town Council reacted by demolishing several of the old towers and, along the western quay, a considerable length of the town wall stretching from the large drinking-water cistern known as Trepoca, 1437, in the south, to the Bokar Tower in the north. Linking what had been the wallhead walk with the quayside below, an elegant neo-baroque staircase was built in 1907. Its two curved upper flights, clasped symmetrically around a semicircular terrace shared by the two thriving bistros whose table lights had led us down from the Cathedral, come together in a central landing. From this falls a single broad staircase, widening with each step between the convex arms of stone balustrades carved with acanthus whorls. So, staring out over a black sea, we reached the *riva*, as always a little exalted by the final grandeur of the descent.

As if to sanctify this mood, out of the night there came the low soft sound of voices chanting. The Brotherhoods' procession had already rounded the Prince's Great Tower at the south-west corner of the town. We could see the first lights of their lanterns and candles. Soon we could see faces, some illumined by the yellow light of the candles in their hands, others, whose candles burned on the ceremonial staffs held high above them, still shadowed and mysterious. As the robed figures passed in the darkness, the rhythmic throb of their prayers and hymns seemed to cast a spell cancelling time and space, an impromptu Easter miracle drawing us back into a medieval world. For a few moments the past was resurrected and it seemed that we were once more in that older simpler city which Marko Polo must have known as a child. Lost in this dream, I thought again of the boy looking out over the rooftops and then of the man who left his island world to cross a continent. Surely he remembered. Perhaps, travelling at times in despair or delusion, blinded by the sun of Takla Makan or the riches of Xanadu, he may have conjured a consoling memory of Korčula's ancient streets much as we did that Easter night.

Now we are once more at the Sea Gate staircase. It is late May, late in the day but still light, that last low golden light before dusk. Tonight the town is crowded, no less than it was over Easter. We have to pick our way carefully down to the quay for a team of teenagers, tee-shirted and bare-footed, have claimed the final flight as tiered seating. Children are playing on the steps daring one another to make longer and longer leaps to the pavement below. Nearby, their parents and grandparents have gathered under the palm trees or sit watching from the long stone bench that runs below the Town Loggia. The tables on the terrace of Hotel Korčula are full. Along the *riva* locals and visitors are enjoying the evening *korzo* or *passeggiatta*, making what the *Korčulani*, with their Dalmatian delight in slavicising Italian, call the *đir*.

It's a familiar enough sight this slow drift of families and friends, old and young, taking a turn around the old town, but this evening there is something different about it. The customary slow stroll is slower as arm-in-arm groups adjust pace and direction to avoid bumping into one another, their relaxed progress stuttering now and then as if executing the advancing figures of some complex folk-dance. There are many more people than usual about tonight – a sure sign that something is about to happen. We share in the expectation, for we know this to be a special day in the Korčula calendar – *Povratak Marka Polo;* this evening Marko Polo returns from far-away China to his native city. And already, as a shout goes up and the crowd turns to the west, we can see a two-masted galley approaching the quay, darkly silhouetted against the setting sun. A single cloaked figure stands tall at the prow.

Thanks to the imaginative enterprise of the town's tourist association, the annual pageant is underway and, in the name of Marko Polo, Korčula's summer season is about to begin.

We can hear drum-beats across the water, muted at first but growing louder as the vessel nears the land. Then there is silence, oars are shipped and the boat glides against the quay. A bearded Marko raises an arm to greet the crowd waiting on the shore. Cheers erupt. He doffs his plumed cap. Cameras flash. Men, women and children, teenagers too, wave back. Now we see that on the quayside a large group of *Korčulani*, dressed in a variegated wardrobe of cassocks, tabards, doublets, breeches, pantaloons and other medieval attire, have been waiting. Greens and browns predominate, though there are four pikemen ostentatiously clad in scarlet. As Marko steps ashore, one of the waiting group offers him a chalice. More flashing cameras. The great explorer acknowledges the welcome and, as he toasts the crowd, raises the glass high towards the Cathedral on the hill – or is it perhaps (for from this landfall the direction is the same) towards the Polo family home?

An informal procession begins to take shape. At its head, Marko and those who have sailed with him, accompanied by the welcoming delegation. The costumed citizens follow, waving to the crowd lined along the *riva*. Then the crowd itself joins in. Spread out in a dense train behind the protagonists, they too are now part of the drama. Some among them know what is to come: they have seen it all last year and the year before and the year before that; they have a son or a daughter, brother or sister, taking part; they may even have played a role themselves in the past. They are here out of civic pride, filial loyalty or simply to make comparisons with previous shows. But for others, like us, this is the first time. Enchanted by the way the city of Marko's birth has become the very *mise-en-scène* of these events and thrilled to find ourselves involuntary extras in what we take to be an urban masque, we follow on, intrigued. From up ahead comes the dull beat of Marko's drums marking time.

Past the arcaded offices of the port authority stretched along the line of the old fortifications, the procession reaches the Prince's Great Tower, largest of Korčula's surviving towers. Where once its strongly battered mass of ashlar blocks rose directly out of the sea, a roadway now rings its base drawing the *riva* into the heart of the modern town. There are crowds here too: some are struggling to keep a foothold at the quayside; others pack the pavement outside the row of small shops that face the western bay; a few, younger and more daring, in search of a better view, have climbed onto the parapet wall of the war memorial at Trg Pomirenja. Plokata, too, is thronged with people. For the moment at least, no cars are able to pass through. But for Marko and his patrician hosts with their entourage of drummers, pikemen and medieval revellers, official and unofficial, the crowds part willingly. At the foot of the staircase rising to the Land Gate, the procession halts.

Ranged against the balustrading of the twenty-nine step flight are two lines of sentinel-still young men, one to every second or third step. They are dressed in the colourful costumes worn for the *Moreška*, the traditional dance performed in Korčula from the sixteenth century. Part of this strange and not altogether understood dance entails the ritualised conflict between opposing armies represented by two bodies of twelve men who confront each other through a series of subtle steps and movements, clashing swords with near lethal ferocity. Each side is identified by its exotic dress, similar in design – skirted tunic with leggings, wide cap sleeves and a strange headdress that might be described, though inadequately, as a cross between crown and turban – but differing in colour, one red and gold, the other black and silver. It is these two 'armies' who, short swords in hand, now present themselves as a guard of honour for the returning Marko Polo. Slowly, inclining his head now and then in a dignified aside as if to acknowledge the respect being shown him, the explorer ascends the staircase alone. Two trumpeters, silhouetted above the battlements of the Land Gate tower, announce his arrival. Below, the town's dignitaries wait to receive him; members of the local council appropriately costumed and the mayor of Korčula, robed in the role of *knez*, personification of the Venetian power that once ruled the island. He is the first to speak.

> *'Oj ti sine, korčulanski vrli*
> *Pozdravljam te poslanice prvi*
> *Perjanico rodo od starina*
> *Lozo drevna, korkyrskog kolina'*

> 'Worthy scion, all hail to thee,
> Greet we Korčula's first emissary,
> Honoured of birth from ancient time,
> Noble in lineage as Korkyra's vine.'

Declaimed with some bravura and an exaggerated emphasis on the rhyme, which seems to imply how clever the speaker of this brief salutation has been, the mayor's speech meets with the crowd's approval. The full meaning, however, eludes me, though from the words I do recognize and the demeanour of the two figures face to face centre stage below the tower, it is easy to grasp that Marko, scion of Korčula's noblest

148

lineage, is being hailed as the town's greatest ambassador. Whatever the historical truth, the *knez*, Korčula's mayor, has got it right; in the promotion of the island's tourism the role played by this latter-day, born-again Marko is considerable.

Somehow neither the pretension of the language nor the incongruity of the boom microphone slung above the speaker, nor even the intrusion of press and television cameramen fighting for the best angles on the staircase, diminishes the crowd's attentiveness nor their willingness to be a part of the illusion. No-one takes the solemnity of the encounter too seriously, but everyone is prepared to play along so that when out of the throng there emerge not only Marko's own group of followers but a colourful succession of 'delegations' who have come to acknowledge the achievement of Korčula's local hero – emissaries from Zagreb, a troupe of musicians and dancers from Dubrovnik, acrobats and jugglers from Split, crossbowmen from the island of Rab – each receives a cheer as it climbs the staircase to pay its respects. For each there are warm embraces from Marko and from the *knez* an appropriate couplet or quatrain whose rhymes meet with amused applause from locals in the crowd below. Finally Marko steps forward. He, too, it seems, speaks in rhyme, though rather less pompously.

> *'Svima hvala! Od srca vam velim.*
> *Grad moj rodni, razgledati želim.'*

> 'To all. My thanks! Heart-felt for thee,
> Now let me once more my home-town see.'

This we can understand. He thanks everyone for the welcome and then, turning to look into the dark archway of the Land Gate, expresses a wish to see again his native city. With an expansive sweep of his arm the *knez* then indicates to his guest that the procession may continue and, taking the lead together, the two enter Marko's Korčula. One by one the groups who have assembled at the head of the staircase pass through the vaulted portal below the tower. Finally, relinquishing their minatory positions, the guard of honour follows. At this, the attendant onlookers, no more intimidated nor any longer bound

149

by a *faux*-plebeian deference unconsciously assumed in the make-believe of the moment, surge onto the steps and up into the old town.

But this is no more than an intermission. The break in the spell is short-lived. Once inside the town, Korčula as always works its medieval magic. Perhaps it is the sudden change from the openness of the space outside the walls to the closed intimacy within, perhaps the physical constriction of the Land Gate entry acting like a time-lock between the present and the past, or it may simply be the ebbing evening light playing tricks with the imagination; whatever the reason, crushed into the little square that lies behind the tower, we are once more in thrall.

The soft sound of unaccompanied male voices – tenor, baritone and bass; each note pure, each vowel and consonant clear – floats over the murmuring crowd like an evening blessing. We might be listening to compline and, indeed, through the open door of the Church of St Michael we can see the Baroque altar afire with candle-light. But the church is empty. The sound comes from across the square where, in the shadows of the Town Hall porch, a *klapa* is singing; six men in affectionate harmony. There is a gentleness and a precision in their music that makes it seem almost sacred and yet, while the origins of what has for centuries been a distinctive feature of Dalmatian life may well be ecclesiastical (though the word *klapa* might be thought a corruption of the Italian *a cappella*, it seems more likely that it draws its provenance, not inappropriately, from Trieste slang for a group of friends) such unaccompanied singing is now very much a part of popular culture, the focus of friendly competitive endeavour among the towns and villages of the coast and an indispensable element in any local celebration. It comes as no surprise to find Marko welcomed in this intimate traditional way.

Marko, of course, has already passed on up into the city. We, on the other hand, are still adrift on the tidal swell of the crowd, crushed in a vortex of confusion as more and more people pack into the little square behind the Land Gate. In temporary disarray, we are soon squeezed into the narrow defile that leads to the top of the town where by now the procession must be reforming itself in front of the Cathedral. At length, helpless in the surge uphill and drowned in the sweats and scents of the crowd, we too reach the Cathedral square.

It takes some time to orientate ourselves to events already underway. At the far end of the square a dais has been raised, perhaps a metre and a half above the stone paving. Microphones have been rigged and though we can hear that something is happening it is impossible to disentangle the words and just as difficult to see the action for our view is inhibited by distance and the shifting parapet of heads between us and the stage. In an attempt to get nearer we push our way along the side of the square until, unable to force a path further forward, we find ourselves wedged against the west door of the Cathedral. The church façade is flat with none of the deep rippling reveals of Gothic nor the undulating recesses of the Baroque; the portal itself (the work of Bonino of Milan in 1412) is shallow, flanked by twinned barley-sugar columns that rise in a pointed-arch frame above the sculptured figure of a seated saint set in the traceried tympanum. On each side of the doorway, however, a slim cluster-shaft stands free from the wall surface. Each supports a ponderous corbel-stone, these in turn carrying lions couchant, guardian symbols of St Mark. Below these, carved in full relief on the face of the corbels, are the figures of Adam and Eve, each straining forward from the stone, hunched, hands on knees, in what can only be described as a defecatory position. We are standing, a little uneasily, immediately below Eve.

All eyes are drawn to two figures positioned at the edge of the stage. A tall young woman, dressed in a crimson tabard that reveals a less than medieval display of elegant legs clad in black tights, is addressing Marko who is seated beside her. Her speech is brief and, as she invites a small group of singers on to the stage, it becomes clear that her role in the proceedings is to introduce the sequence of entertainment which the city has arranged in honour of its returning son.

And so the evening's events unfold. The singers sing: another *klapa*, female this time, eight tall dark-haired women gathered in a semi-circle of close harmony, their identical full-length gowns merging into a continuous curtain of silk and voile. The musicians play: a single violin; a colourful folkloric group with *tamburice*, violins, guitar and bass; a Renaissance

151

band of recorders, viols, violins and lute, cornet and sackbut. To this last the dancers from Dubrovnik dance; three couples in a slow and stately pavane, and then, in quick succession, two sprightly but still elegant galliards. The archers from Rab present their crossbows in a dignified charade, miming their skills to show how they might arm and fire their weapons were they ever to be called upon to do so. The drummers drum a relentless beating, slow and hypnotic, but then, in a sudden burst of sound, switch to a more sensual rhythm as the jugglers take to the stage and begin to swing their flame-laden spheres in daringly choreographed displays that light up the square and the sky above in flashing arcs of fire. This is the culmination of the show. Finally, as daylight begins to fail, the stage is empty save for Marko. For a second or two he treads the boards in silence, apparently deep in thought. And then, opening his arms in a wide gesture that in the magic of the moment seems as honest as it is histrionic, he opens his heart to the crowd. He reminds his rapt audience of the loneliness and privation of his Asiatic journeys, how often he had been hungry and thirsty not just for bread and wine but for the sacramental stones and sea of his native island, how though he saw countless wonders on his travels he found nothing to supplant his dreams of Korčula. He thanks the city, his 'first city', for its memory. He rejoices at his return. He invites everyone to share in his joy.

Slowly, almost reluctantly it seems, the crowd begins to disperse seeping into the shadowy lanes that fall to the sea from each side of the Cathedral square. High up, darting in the attic gloaming, bats wheel and dive like black shooting stars. Lamps glimmer in windows. Torches have been lit. Burning in bronze sconces, the flames flicker on the ancient stone lighting the darkening town. In the bars and restaurants, now thronged with people eager to toast Marko Polo's return, glasses sparkle on candle-lit tables.

We idle aimlessly in the square, easing our cramped limbs back to normal. We have had enough of crowds and when Jasna suggests a quiet drink back in Lumbarda at *Feral* the thought of that pleasant terrace overlooking the still pool of Tatinja bay seems like the perfect end to the evening. But, though the show is over, the spell of Marko Polo's little city is not easily broken. Turn a corner and the magic begins again.

A few steps and we are in the small square that opens before the Church of St Peter. The paving stones are older here and the little church façade no more than a gabled wall of ancient stained stucco, the rough uneven texture now accentuated in the wan torchlight. Pink snapdragons are growing in the belfry. A single ocular light pierces the wall in a black Cyclopean stare. Below is the entrance doorway, domestic in scale and detail; on the lintel, a small stone tablet carved with the figure of the key-carrying saint is all that betrays the sanctuary within. Architecturally, this is the least prepossessing of Korčula's churches, yet its very simplicity and antiquity exert a special charm. A first archival mention dates it to the early fourteenth century but, as with the Cathedral itself, a place of worship must have existed on the site long before. The small unblinking window, deeply sunk in the old wall, fixes us with its gaze. We stop but cannot enter for the locked door refuses revelation. We know, of course, what lies within: bare stone walls, a simple timber roof carried on corbelstones, worn stone-flagged floor, a plain block altar set in the arched recess of the sanctuary. The restoration is recent, 1957-58, but fittingly modest and severe, without pretension. But now, in the afterglow of Marko's return, I imagine something else. An older interior. A distant mystery. The rough walls are whitewashed, here and there bright with the rush-wick flame of open oil lamps; there is no music, no congregation, only the priest and a kneeling dark-haired boy. He takes the host on his tongue.

'Look! Up there!'

'What?' Enchantment vanishes, my mind tumbling out of its reverie. And then I see what Jasna is pointing to.

Up beyond the church's façade in the angle between its open bellcote and the thick foliage of palm fronds spilling along the north side of the square, the rooftop loggia of the House of Marko Polo is brilliantly illuminated. Suddenly floodlit, it seems to float on the night air. Familiar figures move in the wide-screen gap between parapet and eaves. They wear medieval costume. One, bearded, taller than the others, stands a little apart. At arm's length he holds a goblet that glints in the beam of light coming from below. For a moment his arm is still, extended above the city. Then he takes the cup to his lips.

BORIS'S PARTY

*'In this new experience you may find temptations both in wine
and women. You must entirely resist both temptations, and,
while treating all women with perfect courtesy, you should
avoid any intimacy.'*

Horatio Herbert Kitchener
1914

'Here!'

Mirjana's shriek gets a quick response. Nebojša swings the
Seat abruptly to the right. A rutted junction, shadowed in the
early evening light and all but hidden in a break between garden
walls. An unexpected ramp. We jolt off the ferry road onto a
poorly asphalted track, narrow between hedge-height bushes but
straight. Mirjana's back-seat navigation confounds proverbial
scepticism. Feminine insight – or simply good eyesight? It
scarcely matters – though who knows on what marital score-
sheet she may later cite this minor success. For the moment at
least, we are still on the right road.

We are headed for a party organized for some of Korčula's
English speakers by one of the island's lovable fixers. The
invitation is for seven o'clock and we are already late. Boris's
card had said five, but an apologetic call earlier in the day has
deferred events. Some problem with the wine or the food. Or so
we were told. Perhaps Boris simply overestimated his own
capacity or desire to sustain the role of host. An hour or two less
of obligatory bilingual chatter might well have seemed
attractive.

'Where now?'

'Left.'

Asphalt still, but no better. The road even narrower. Fewer
houses. We are in Soline heading east from Korčula town not

155

far from the northern shore of the island. The thick *makija*, still green in April before the summer sun, presses on creamy verges of rough limestone chips. On our right, a dense tangled mass of low vegetation sweeps up to a low ridge then dips into the wide saucer-rimmed plain of Donje Blato, a flat fertile expanse gridded with green lines of vines. To the left, there is no cultivation, only the impenetrable *makija*. Tiny cyclamen glimmer in the shade. Cistus, buckthorn and bushy holm oak pack together in rolling thickets that can tear the legs and make progress through the matted undergrowth all but impossible. Ubiquitous and luxuriant, the shrubland preserves its viridian secrets all the way to the sea. In the distance, an incongruous gantry – the island's shipyard at Dominče, ancient in origin but for decades now a mass of cheapskate concrete sheds, the tawdry legacy of underfunded socialist enthusiasm. We catch glimpses of the channel and the fir-quilted island of Badija. A single belfry steeple rises among orange roof-tiles on the old Franciscan monastery. Beyond, in hard grey-green detachment, the mountainous mainland peninsula of Pelješac.

For some minutes it seems we may have taken a wrong turning. The road continues, curving now, but revealing nothing. There are no houses. The persistence of the broken asphalt track barely reassures us. We come closer to the shore, though the water's edge remains out of sight. Then the villas begin.

'Which one?'

'No idea. You're the one who knows Boris.' Mirjana, a little indignant, or perhaps just annoyed that she cannot repeat her earlier coup. 'You've been here before, haven't you?'

'Yes…' Nebojša's response is an unwilling admission, but reflective too. He is trying to remember. 'It must be on the left. The garden falls to the sea.' But this is less than helpful since most of the houses built along this bumpy road have naturally taken advantage of the coastal plots. There are no numbers, no names. We are crawling now. Then, rounding a slow bend, we come upon a row of cars haphazardly abandoned along the verge.

'There! The flag!'

It is Jasna who sees it first. An intense splash of red, white and blue behind the low trees. Mirjana exchanges an ironic look with her husband. They share an amused shame that they as locals

156

should have failed to identify the house. Then her smile widens. She sees the flag – or rather, the flags – for, draped from Boris's window sill, is a large Union Jack and beside it a smaller Croatian flag. The reason for Jasna's sudden perception is clear. Sensing a second victory for her sex, Mirjana grins with good-natured smugness. Smiling, she leans over to flick Nebojša's hair in mock reproof as the car draws to a halt. I look away, opening the car door as if to excuse myself from this playful intimacy.

Croatians love flags. They love Croatian flags in particular. They love them to the point of iconic indulgence. In the early years of the nineties' war the flag was everywhere, flaunted with a superstitious abandon like the miracle-working amulet of some primitive cult. Both secular and religious authority embraced the same naïve ostentation. Above every village, every church, sometimes it seemed almost every building of any social consequence, the national tricolour with the distinctive red and white heraldic chequer board of the *šahovnica* crackled in the breeze. Ten years and more on and things are a little different. The flags still fly, but less aggressively now and in fewer places. It is as if, for all the economic uncertainties of the present, there is a greater maturity, a belief that the battles have been won, that there is at last physical and psychological security. The *šahovnica* none the less remains a pregnant symbol. At once potent and equivocal, it recalls for some the heraldic banners of the medieval Croatian kingdom, for others the first independent Croatian state of modern times, the virulently fascist régime of the Second World War years. For most, and the younger generation in particular, it is no more than a reminder of new passports, football colours, airline livery, and much else that is comfortably trivial in today's democratic Croatia. But besides its implicit evocative power, earnest yet never entirely free from historic equivocation, the red and white gridded heart of the flag has a direct graphic charge that few other national banners can match. One that does is the Union Jack, its three crossed crosses uniquely recognizable even if their constituent symbolism is for most Brits at best irrelevant, at worst meaningless. We see both now. We read them as signs, not symbols. They draw us into the garden. Ducking below the orange blossom past a lank wisteria

157

whose clouds of tiny mauve flowers are fighting through the trailing vestiges of last year's growth, we hear Boris's greeting.

'I'm sorry. I couldn't get a Scottish flag for you.' Then, as we round a corner of the house and find our host waiting for us, 'But since your Scottish saint, Andrew, has his cross in the British flag, you can forgive, I think.' This love of flags is clearly well informed.

'*Naravno*. Of course,'

We shake hands. Our first face-to-face meeting with Boris, so no kisses on the cheek. Nebojša and Mirjana, acquaintances already, are more affectionate. There is a momentary crush and confusion as politeness and friendship collide on the threshold.

He is dressed in unexpectedly formal style. Until now, for Jasna and me, Boris has been no more than a voice on the telephone, once or twice a year perhaps, confirming our ferry or flight tickets, more often than not it seems, reassuring us that the tickets will be in the post tomorrow, that the Croatia Airlines timetable has not been altered (and even if it has, *nema problema* – no problem, no problem) and that there will be someone at the airport (a cousin he says – it is always a cousin with Dalmatians) who will have the car for which we have prepaid a small fortune ready and waiting for us, even though our scheduled arrival time is a quarter after midnight and may well turn out to be much later. Fitting face and figure to voice is always tempting, particularly if one is entranced or exasperated. Speculation almost always gets it wrong, yet it seems that the mind's eye cannot resist; we inevitably build an image however indistinct or blurred. Boris's appearance is indeed unexpected, and it is a surprise that charms. He is edging into middle age, yet animated and boyish. Late forties perhaps, probably more. Light brown hair, still generous but not thick, bounces off his forehead as he speaks. The eyes are brown, a little watery but alert. He has a smile that spurns exaggeration. But it is his assertion of urbane smartness that is for me, and I suspect for all four of us dressed in casual wear on a warm April evening, completely unexpected.

Boris is wearing a grey suit imperceptibly pin-striped, a crisp white shirt and collar, and a scarlet bow-tie. Perhaps this nonchalant Englishness has been assumed out of respect for his choice of guests. At any rate, the affectation, if such it is, is innocent enough, there is no guile, no pomposity. I find it odd, a little gauche, but endearing too. Indeed, there are winning deficiencies in Boris's attempt at cultural disguise. The bow-tie is too clearly 'clip-on', too stiff, too precise; it lacks insouciance. Shoes, too, betray; respectably black, they are neither highly polished nor expensively casual. Do I patronise our host with this silent doorstep critique? Is my amused affection only a mask for latent conceit? Am I, as a Scot, smugly delighted to find the *soigné* poise of the English gentleman off balance? Perhaps. And what am I to make of Boris's hands? Below crisp white cuffs the backs of his hands, dark already with hair, are streaked with what seems to be a darker stain, the fingers almost black at the tips and under the nails. I exchange a puzzled look with Jasna. But there is no time to ponder the mystery. Boris has launched into an enthusiastic one-sided conversation. When did we arrive? Did we fly to Dubrovnik this time? We came by car! Really? How many kilometres? There is a momentary lull as our arithmetic skills struggle with the eight-over-five conversion. But Boris races on, the good host interested in his guests. Where is our house? How many rooms? How many square metres? Another pause for calculation. Have we travelled much on the island? Do we sail? Boris's mastery of English is impressive. He is fast and fluent. But it is the kind of fluency that quickly becomes the Achilles heel of linguistic exchange. Stimulated not just by his articulate command of the language but every bit as much by his awareness that, though he may make the occasional grammatical error, his frequent and ready recourse to some suitable English idiom to cover the gaffe will, as he might say, remove the cat from among the pigeons, he rushes on from observation to opinion, from enquiry to epigram. There is no time for answers, let alone contrary views. Discussion is not on the agenda. He looks at us only briefly as he speaks; his eyes dart from one to the other and then beyond. He does not engage. It is as if he is directing the conversation in another sphere, following a script only he can read, an auto-cue positioned somewhere above and behind us. I try to catch his eyes. But they cannot be caught. They look beyond, around, above. I am tempted to think that this too is a very uppercrust English trait – a politeness scrupulous but distant, asking everything while revealing nothing, that cold mannerliness that has made the English such good diplomats. But I am imagining things. He has simply been watching for his next guests. For suddenly, with more smiles and an encouraging push, Boris is gone and we are all four swept from the little entrance hallway into the main room of the house.

The room is crammed with people, so much so it is all but impossible to sense either its dimensions or décor. White walls. White ceiling. A picture or two: mostly misty shore scenes but, above the couches symmetrically opposed at each end of the room, some violent, almost abstract, landscapes by the Lumbarda painter Stipe Nobilo, brash variegated patchworks of Mediterranean colour. A parquet floor that squeaks under our feet. A long windowed wall giving onto a terrace. Glimpses of the sea. But we are engulfed by the throng. Glasses are thrust into our hands and filled to the brim with Pošip, the crispest and clearest of Korčula's white wines. Nebojša and Mirijana are quickly in conversation with friends. We are introduced to Nikola, whose wine it is. He has vineyards at Čara, a forty-minute drive away and one of the main centres of wine production on the island. Boris, pressing past us with some new arrivals, points to the cases stacked by the door explaining that they have only just been delivered, that an hour in the fridge is scarcely enough, that we should temper our judgment. Nikola, tall and dark-browed, not much more than thirty-five, smiles diffidently and shrugs his shoulders. Emptying the last drops from the tall slender bottle he holds in one hand into the glass in the other, he asks our opinion. The question is directed towards Jasna rather than me, though whether this is out of gentlemanly politeness, or a mildly flirtatious gallantry, or simply because her glass is (I am tempted to say, as usual) almost empty, it is difficult to say.

'Wonderful', sighs Jasna, as if Nikola's wine were the long-anticipated reason for our presence at the party. And, indeed, after the hot late afternoon drive, the wine is fresh and invigorating. 'Last year's?'

'Yes, it's very young. But good for this kind of drinking,'

says Nikola, casting an open palm at the crowded room.

'Too easy to drink', agrees Jasna and drains her glass. She licks her lips with a certain lingering ambiguity.

This suddenly annoys me, not so much for its hint of sensuality, which I take to be no more than playful, but because this very playfulness is so open and undisguised. But the ruse works for her. Boris returns from the kitchen with a new bottle for Nikola. Jasna's glass is replenished – the wine poured a little too slowly, or so it seems to me. Glasses are held up to the light, the wine a warm, pale golden colour like the low evening sun. Cheeks are pulled in to savour the acidity. More licking of the lips. More critical pleasantries. I begin to feel *de trop* and start to mingle.

I know only a handful of Boris's guests. Several of his local friends are here, of course. Some I recognize, like the tall, balding owner of one of the local restaurants. He, too, it turns out, is from Čara. He, too, like Boris, has opted for Anglophile garb – knife-sharp fawn flannels and a light sports jacket with a dark brown herring-bone check. He, too, speaks English, but it is a fast and garbled English spoken with a confidence that seems simultaneously to impress his diminutive, twin-set trim wife and embarrass his daughter. In conversation I realise that while his wife has only Croatian and admires in ignorance, his daughter, home for the summer from university in Zagreb, knows better. Like many of her generation, she has acquired a mastery of English, so accomplished indeed that it is perhaps more correct, if less colloquial, than that of many of her student contemporaries in London, New York or Sydney. Raised eyebrows betray her disgust at her father's sometimes incoherent fluency. Well capable of navigating her parents through the linguistic shallows of perfunctory conversation, she seems an unwilling pilot. She says little. In response to my enquiries about her studies, she is languidly polite, all the time evidently intent on escaping elsewhere as soon as possible. But it is I who flee. With an empty glass as an excuse, I move on. Mother and daughter seem relieved. The father, at first unaware of my departure, talks on, but then, momentarily bereft and in search of an explanation, casts a puzzled gaze around the room as if to find a vacant table in his restaurant for some new and valued visitor.

161

My gaze finds Zora. Another English speaker. A teacher in the local school, she must be well into her fifties; she looks younger and is far from prim. Small and dark, still conscious of her physical attraction, her comfortable figure a little uncomfortably imprisoned in a plum-coloured suit, she smiles in recognition without interrupting her conversation. She and Mirjana, not so long ago her pupil, are talking houses.

Mirjana and Nebojša, I know, have just given up their attic flat in the old town and have moved into a new, or almost new, home, one of several villas built on the hillside at Medvinjak, a deep inlet immediately to the west of Korčula town not far beyond St Nicholas monastery. Begun by a Serb in the late 1980s, this three-storeyed house lay empty through the war years of the nineties, roofed and glazed but neither decorated nor furnished. Like almost all Serbian-owned properties on the island, it remained untouched throughout the conflict. None the less, though the destruction or illegal acquisition of Serbian property on Korčula was as negligible as the physical impact of the war, the psychological scars of ethnic bitterness were such that there was little prospect of any original owner daring to return. With hostilities over, the best recourse was to find a buyer. But this was far from easy. Not that there were not those with the money to buy. The problem was how to complete the transaction. While the legalities of any deal done between two countries barely on speaking terms were difficult enough, the secure transfer of money was all but impossible. The only reliable option was a face-to-face encounter but, since it was as inadvisable if not downright dangerous for a Croat to travel to Serbia as it was for a Serb to venture into Croatia, the likelihood of any meeting on 'home territory' was zero. In the event, now some years ago, both Nebojša and the Belgrade-based seller had travelled to meet in northern Bosnia where an envelope stuffed with German marks had exchanged hands.

I supposed that Mirjana might be telling Zora what progress they had made in making the new home habitable. In fact, it is Zora who is doing all the talking. It seems that she and her sea-captain husband are also moving out of the old town. Unlike Mirjana and Nebojša, however, they are building from scratch. The site is nearby – we must have passed it on our way

162

down the tight track to Boris's house – a narrow plot tumbling to the sea.

'It belonged to my grandfather. Part of the family land lost to the state in the fifties. Most of it got built on, of course, except our plot. Too small and awkward, I suppose. We got it back a couple of years ago, just at the time Ante decided to retire. Then last year, after months of wrangling, the *općina* finally agreed we could build on it. Ante's there just now,' Zora adds, explaining her husband's absence from the party. 'They're pouring the first floor this evening.'

'Who?' I ask. I have a picture in my mind of Ante, his brothers and a few friends wheeling barrows of slurping concrete over timber ramps back and forward between the shuttered deck and the family cement mixer. That's the way of things here; do it yourself or, rather, do it with the help of family and friends.

'I'm not sure who'll be there tonight.' Zora considers for a moment, looking into her glass and then at the ceiling. 'Probably Marko and Stipe, Ante's brothers. Stipe's brother-in-law, who usually comes down from Žrnovo. And Nikša Batistić from Lumbarda – he brings the cement and sand in his lorry.'

'When do you expect to be finished?'

'By nine or so. But Ante won't come here. He'll be too exhausted.'

'No, I mean when will the house be finished. This year?'

'Ah. Good question…'

It's a question to which I know there is no good answer. All down the Dalmatian coast there are impatient local authority inspectors, disgruntled builders, dismayed spouses and children, irritated neighbours and puzzled tourists asking the same question. The unfinished house seems almost to have become the talisman of Adriatic life. Certainly it is much to the credit of the former Yugoslavia that Croatia has avoided much of the commercialisation and high-rise excesses which have cheapened so many tourist developments along the coasts of Spain, Italy and Greece. Strict controls on materials, prompted at first perhaps by the stringencies of a socialist economy but later maintained to protect the visual environment, have limited builders to local stone, render and terra cotta tiling. The results, from Istria in the north to Dubrovnik in the south, are coherent townscapes that have escaped abuse and survive free from any infringing feature – except, that is, the unfinished house. This constructional procrastination is everywhere. There are elegant villas, their ground floor smartly shuttered, windows drenched in floods of red geraniums, walls palatially clad in polished travertine, yet with reinforcement-spiked stub columns waiting for the upper floors and roof to be added. There are three-storey houses, beautifully roofed in bright orange tiles but with unrendered external walls of crudely pointed insulating blockwork. There are balconies without balustrading, windows without glass, gutters without downpipes. At times it seems as if, at the entrance to every village, a concrete skeleton stands guard. And why?

'...It depends', continues Zora. 'Maybe the bank won't come up with the money. Maybe we'll have difficulties with materials. But we won't be in this year.'

There's a certain Mediterranean resignation about all this, though it's not so much Latin indolence as a world-weary Slavic forbearance. *Mañana* does at least carry a sense of delayed optimism; here, on the other hand, the future could easily be worse. Yet people do build. Against all the political and economic odds – admittedly shorter now than ten years ago – they take the risk. If things deteriorate, they pause and wait. Hence the unfinished business on the streets.

'But why is it everyone here seems to want to build a completely new house?' It's a question I've wanted to ask for a long time. 'Didn't you think about converting some old property? Seems to me there are plenty lying empty, especially up in the hill villages. And it would cost less. You could move in sooner.' Then, thinking to appeal to that undiluted nationalism that lies only just below the skin of every Croat, 'You'd be helping to save your local heritage'.

Mirjana is quick to become involved. 'But who wants to live away from the sea?' With two teenage children and a husband whose family are renowned across the island and beyond as superb swimmers and water polo players, she has a case.

'And anyway it's not so simple', says Zora. 'The building

might be sound enough but you might find you had only cistern water, no electricity, no drainage. And why live away from the town, from Korčula itself? The only people who convert these old cottages are foreigners.' It is not said offensively but, conscious that it must have sounded unnecessarily dismissive, she swivels round searching the room for someone who might prove her point. 'Like Richard', she exclaims, raising her voice to attract the attention of a tall, fair-haired man of about thirty-five, locked into an animated group at the end of the room.

This is my cue to make another move. Catching Richard's acknowledgement of Zora's cry, I push across to introduce myself. Now I know no-one. I discover that Richard is an American working for the State Department in post-Dayton Bosnia. Delicate and deferential in his demeanour, utterly conventional in dress in a white shirt and grey stone-washed jeans, he is polite but diffident. He has nothing to say about his job. Gradually, however, I learn that this is his third visit to the island on 'R and R', that he regularly meets up here with his friend Wayne and that together they have indeed bought a crumbling ruin which they are in the process of converting into a holiday home. The house is located on the edge of Žrnovo, a straggling inland village up on the hills above Korčula. But before there is time to discover how near the mark Zora's assessment of such property might or might not prove to be, the rest of the group begin to introduce themselves.

Wayne is as short and plump as Richard is long and lean, all the more so as he is wearing a white tee-shirt, shorts and hefty trainers. They make an... interesting... couple. Odd would be the wrong word. Gay, possibly. Then again, perhaps the inference is unwarranted. But since Wayne, too, is on government business, attached to the US Embassy in London (in what capacity also remains mysteriously unclear), I feel an irresistible urge to set their relationship within that duplicitous domain of the imagination which, Philby or Bond, seems created as much by the facts as by the fictions of diplomatic activity, sexual and otherwise. This fancy is compounded when I am introduced to Višnja. A woman of sixty or so, self-possessed and possessing, hardly a Mata Hari figure but with a physicality at once immediate and hypnotic. She has the heavy eyes and full lips of Jeanne Moreau and the same tired, up-front sexuality. She, too, has an interest in the house at Žrnovo. Quite why she forms part of this *ménage à trois* is unclear but intriguing. It appears that she and Richard met in Sarajevo. She, a Croat, was already widowed by the war, her Serbian husband killed by Karadžić's snipers. Did she find comfort in the younger man? Did he provide a way out, an escape from Bosnia's horror? These are not questions to be asked. She is, she says, a poet and there is something about her loose-fitting clothes and the slender-fingered hand she has a habit of passing across her forehead into lank grey hair that seems wholly in keeping with this unlikely activity. Žrnovo is a haven for her. She writes there. Far from the memories of a life broken in Bosnia, she can sit on the ruinous terrace of the house they have bought, looking out across a low meadow of wild flowers to rolling fir woods spiked with the tall cypress trees that are so characteristic of that part of the island. There is poetry in her description, something almost Petrarchan about this eulogising of the rural retreat. Her young companions, silent under her spell, listen as she speaks. I know the Žrnovo area well and picture its landscape, a stony Tuscany, clearly.

'You must come and visit us.'

'I will.'

I have the strange feeling of having taken an oath. Not to make such a visit – something easy enough to do, almost expected indeed, were the invitation to have come from a fellow Brit – would be unthinkable. There is a compulsion about this strange woman which I cannot refuse. Looking into her green eyes, I imagine myself on that terrace, her hand stretched across the stone table to rest on mine, a sensed intimation, the climb to the bedroom.

'And bring your wife, of course,' adds Richard, unwittingly shattering my fancy.

It is only now that I realise Jasna is already part of this large group. She smiles, amused by a momentary discomfiture on my part that perhaps only she has noticed. Women of a certain age... I can see she has been watching my encounter with Višnja. She knows exactly what is going on in my mind, that the respectful disinterest I hope I have assumed is really no more than the disingenuous mask of the romantic. She herself is no poet but she can play the game too. I see Nikola still beside her, still with a bottle in his hand.

More introductions.

Mina, a pale Finnish girl, reticent, timid even. Months in Bosnia working with some international aid mission have left their mark. It is clear that she, too, has a story to tell. But she reveals nothing, speaking reluctantly even of Korčula and how she too is restoring an island house. Hers is an old, two-roomed cottage at Kneža on the north coast. Hesitant and devoid of self-assurance, she keeps close to Višnja, clinging almost, content to remain in the shadow of her commanding personality. Is there a relationship here too?

Rupert and Olivia, brother and sister, decidedly English, decidedly aristocratic. Both have been on some kind of voluntary work in Sarajevo. Somewhat incongruously it seems to me at first sight but, on the other hand, in tune with the spirit of Boris's party, he is in county uniform: blazer and flannels, a scarlet kerchief tied tightly at the neck, a tiny cancer relief daffodil in his lapel. She in a long, billowy dress, cream linen cut low at the neck. Learning that Jasna and I are from Scotland, they mention Fitzroy Maclean and the Marquess of Bute, not so much because these are names well known on the island but because they are family friends. I consider the possibility that I am being taken in by upper class bluff? Of course, neither brother nor sister has been in Scotland. Is Bute very far north? Is it an island? I answer their questions with barely veiled impatience.

Debbie, another American, clearly knows exactly where the island of Bute is situated but does not get involved. She, too, like Wayne, is with the Embassy in London. No, she has nothing to do with Bosnia or Kosovo; her patch is Northern Ireland. Yes, she is well aware of the cultural ties between Northern Ireand and south-west Scotland. She makes intermittent visits to Glasgow to check on the politico-religious vibes. Not surprising, I suppose, but a bit disturbing none the less to discover the Yanks are watching in that theatre too. No wonder she knows where Bute is.

And Niamh, as Irish as they come, down from Mostar where she works with the War Crimes Commission. Her hair cut

167

very short, she is dressed in a multi-pocketted jerkin and jeans, more like a *Lonely Planet* backpacker than someone who has seen the final gruesome face of the Balkan conflict. But what, I ask myself, is the look of someone who has looked on such things? Seconded from the Dublin police to serve in Bosnia for a spell of nine months some four years ago, she stayed on to join the Commission overwhelmed with compassion for the many families who had lost their men yet needed to know the time and the place, needed some token of identification however slight, to exorcise the trauma. She speaks quietly about the interviews she has had to carry out, the catharsis people experience and how, when the support she and her colleagues can offer is removed, the trauma simply returns. Her view of the future for Bosnia is grim. Yet she loves her job and has no idea when she will want to go home to Connemara.

As we talk, someone switches the lights on, low table lamps by the couches. It is already dark. On the balcony, where the smokers have assembled, cigarettes glow, pin pricks of light bleeding in the gloom. Out on the sea, scattered in the deeper darkness beyond the terrace, there are more lights, local fishermen hoping for a good night's catch. There is a moon. Stars appear, and the white cloudy sweep of the Milky Way. I push the glazed sliding door aside and escape for a moment into the night.

About a dozen of Boris's guests are on the balcony. Of these the majority are locals; it is no surprise to see that they are the ones who are smoking. I pick up snatches of conversation. Another scandal in Split, this time something to do with the management of the daily paper, *Slobodna Dalmacija*. Complaints about the delay in bringing the summer timetable for the local ferry services into operation. A whispered intimation that Vesna is pregnant – a second time. I have no idea who Vesna may be nor whether this piece of gossip is congratulatory or shaming. But it pleases me, as I keep to myself looking across the water to where Badija is hidden in the blackness, to think my limited Croatian is good enough to admit me to such secrets. A young couple next to me, distracted from their own physical intimacy by overhearing this same snippet of local news, share a conspiratorial smile with me. For a moment, the smoke from their cigarettes invades me with nostalgia. I suddenly remember a small tennis-club hall, crowded with teenagers intoxicated with Saturday-night cider and traditional jazz. The push and slide of the Players pack. The careful removal of silver paper. The tap, tap, tap to hold the open threads of tobacco in place. The first inhalation of adolescent *savoir faire*. But only for a moment, for no-one is more addicted to righteous smugness than the reformed smoker. I turn away into the light evening breeze, taking a few deep breaths to clear lungs and memory. I catch the scent of pines in the air and a hint of the sea. Then, rising from the garden below, the soft clean fragrance of roses, for me always the perfume of innocence rather than seduction. Memory springs back to life: my grandmother's garden, the wood-log summer-house and the neatly laid out beds with their diagonal paths criss-crossing between the tea roses. Me, only six or seven, my nose buried in the head-height blooms, drunk with delight at the changing smells.

'A penny for them.'

'Jasna!' Surprised, I look round. '*Ništa*. Nothing. *Baš sam mislio da...* I was just thinking... the roses,' stumbling from dreams to reality, from Croatian into English, looking for the right words. 'Where's Nikola?'

'Oh, he's captivated by Olivia.'

'Not you?'

'No, not me.' A self-deprecatory laugh. She gives me a knowing intimate look, amused by my friendly sarcasm. 'Must be her Nordic looks.'

'Or the cleavage.'

'Mm...' Then, changing tack, 'I brought you some food. Boris is dishing out in the kitchen. See what it is?'

It's risotto, black risotto.

'So?'

'Boris?'

Then it dawns on me. Boris's stained hands. Mystery solved. He must have prepared the risotto himself only an hour or so before the party began – evidently not long enough in advance to enable him to get rid of the cuttlefish ink from his fingers. So both the wine and the food had been late. No wonder he had phoned to postpone things by an hour or two.

We move back inside, settling down on the floor to eat. The risotto tastes good. Fresh and fishy with just the right trace of nutmeg. Nebojša arrives with another bottle of Pošip straight from the fridge. With the food the wine is even better than before. I have lost track of the number of glasses I have drunk and am beginning to feel a kind of benign indifference to events around me. The buzz of a dozen different conversations continues, barely diminished by the arrival of food, but I have stopped eavesdropping. From the terrace comes the sound of gentle singing: four or five unaccompanied male voices in harmony, an impromptu *klapa*. There is nothing more Dalmatian than this. Each year, all along the coast amateur groups of tenors, baritones and basses, compete to bring honour to their village. You may hear them – fathers and sons, brothers, cousins and friends – practising in the evenings in a local hall or restaurant or better still come upon a group on the *riva*, pleasantly drunk, their arms locked at shoulder height in a closed wheel of intimacy, each supporting the other, at times as much physically as musically. Locked in this ring, they listen for the lead singer's first note then begin. Inebriated or not, they sing with precision, following the beat set by the leader, shaping their words with care. The songs themselves, simple folk melodies, have a mellow intensity, rich in harmonies. Some seem almost Neapolitan, others Greek, some more melancholy have a Hebridean cast, a few a stranger, more eastern quality. They are the songs of fishermen, about the sea, about gulls and doves, about the mountainous Dalmatian coastline with its fir woods, olive groves and vines, about lost or parted love. Strains of familiar airs reach me from Boris's balcony. I lie back beside Jasna, resting my head on a pile of embroidered cushions. Soon only the music matters. A warm tide of dreamy cadences washes me back into imagination's spell. I am adrift in a small boat eddying in the smoky haze of an afternoon sun, my fingers trailing in a cool rosewater sea. My thoughts ebb. My eyelids close.

When I wake it is already past eleven. I must have slept for over an hour. The singers on the terrace have gone and the room is much less crowded. The Americans appear to have left, presumably with Višnja and Mina. Zora has gone too. Nikola has Olivia trapped in a corner. Robert is asleep on the floor. Boris, however, is still full of life, cosseting the last of his guests with untiring politeness and a full bottle. Following his progress from one bout of animated conversation to the next, I see faces I had not noticed before. I recognize a few. Mr Winthrop, a retired surgeon from the north of England who for some years has lived alone in Korčula in one of the tall, narrow 'palaces' close to the Cathedral. The writer, Celia Irving, also in her seventies and another resident Brit. And seated in rather stately detachment on the couch at the far end of the room, the Bennets, a distinguished couple of indeterminate means and advanced years who, no doubt dependent on Boris's services, make their annual pilgrimage from London to stay an unfailing six weeks at Hotel Korčula. They sit erect, as they do every morning when they take coffee on the terrace of their hotel: he with clasped hands resting on the crook of his cane walking stick; she, a little taller, with a stiff-necked, anachronistic dignity, self-assured and intimidating. I have never spoken to them – it has always seemed too daring a thing to do, as if approaching royalty merely to pass the time of day – but I think about it now. What is their story? Was he, as I imagine from his demeanour of assumed *gravitas* and muted wealth, 'something in the city', or perhaps a senior civil servant or diplomat? Is she, with her high chin and thoroughbred looks, the daughter of some impoverished Italian count? But just as I get up from the floor, Jasna intervenes on my intention.

'Let's go home', she says, catching my elbow. A flirtatious glint flickers in her smile – but her words are matter-of-fact. 'I spoke to Mirjana while you were sleeping. They were thinking of leaving half an hour ago. I told her it was OK, I'd wait till you woke. She didn't want to go without us, of course. But I said we would walk.'

'Walk?'

'Well why not? It'll do us good after all the wine.'

That was true enough, I conceded, without saying anything. I knew, of course, we could probably get a lift from someone in the

171

room, though looking round again I could see no-one from Lumbarda. Even so, wherever anyone was headed, since there was only one route back to the ferry road, we were bound to be taken at least part of the way. In any case, we could always call a taxi. But then, emboldened by vanity and wine, I thought how attractively absurd the whole idea was. A needless night-time hike. And we knew the road well. How often, driving between Lumbarda and Korčula, had we told each other we could walk the eight kilometres or so blindfolded if we had to. Why not now – in the dark? There was no danger. Why should we not walk home?

Ten minutes later, having said our goodbyes to Boris, we are alone on the moonlit road. The night is scarcely warm but cloudless and still. We breathe in the scent-laden air and set off, hand in hand.

In half an hour we have reached the ferry road, Dubrovačka cesta. Turning away from Dominče, we pass a long row of darkened houses on our left. Here and there a dim midnight light shows at a window. Bats dart through the trees, their flashing flight illuminated by an occasional streetlamp. Beyond the canopied car parks and tennis courts of the Bon Repos Hotel, we come to the junction for Lumbarda. Now the road home stretches out straight before us, its asphalt track silvered in the moonlight. On the right is a deserted camping site. Tall stone gate piers mark the entrance with what seems an unnecessary grandeur. Before the trauma of the nineties civil war this was the site of a Yugoslav army barracks. Always a place to pass without pause, now in the darkness it regains its sinister aura and we quicken our step. To our left, a few last houses straggle along the roadside. A tall prickly pear cactus explodes out of the gloom. We catch the kitchen-garden smell of rosemary hedges. Back from the road, silhouetted against the grey sky, two parallel stands of tall cypresses climb to the little hilltop Church of Sveti Antun. Between the trees, hidden by the night, is the one-hundred-and-one-step staircase that the pilgrim must ascend to reach the tiny paved forecourt on the summit. A double reward awaits him there: first, the spectacular view across the Korčula archipelago to Pelješac and then, through the dark doorway of the twin-eyed, Venetian facade, the cool restorative cave of the church itself. But not us. However rash our midnight adventure, we are in no mood to make the climb and press on along the road out into the country.

As time passes and the way begins to wind east in a series of slow bends rising and falling through the *makija*, we seem to fall into a trance. Clouds pass across the moonlight and for a time there are no more landmarks to be seen. Soon nothing is discernible in the rolling shadows around us. Only sounds. A bird's screech. A dog barking somewhere in the hills. The regular tread of our footsteps. Our breathing, coming and going against the silence.

I turn my gaze inwards, reflecting on our midnight foolishness. With more than an hour gone I can feel the ache begin at my hips. How could I have been so easily persuaded to set out for home on foot? But soon I am wondering not just why we are here walking on this lonely island road but, as is the way of reverie, why we are here at all. Why here on the other side of Europe? What is it about this place that brings us back? More than twenty years now, time after time on Korčula. Is it the landscape, the scenery we cannot see as we make our way through the night? Stark hillsides striped with ragged ranks of rough stone walling, like multi-tiered auditoria falling to the sea. Spidery groves of gnarled, grey-green olive trees, low tethered vines and splashes of burnt sienna earth. A warm, ice-clear sea shining with ochre shingle in the shallows. Blind in the darkness, I can still see all this clearly, just as I can imprisoned in the depression of a west-coast winter in Scotland. The lure of the south – centuries old. Not the Grand Tour, of course; no Goethe-conscious *Italienische Reise,* no list of monuments, museums and galleries to be visited. Not now, at any rate, after more than two decades. To be sure, there is culture here, Venetian and Slavic, for those who seek it. All through the summer, the tour parties come and go, spilling out of bus or cruise ship behind the local part-time, parasol-pointing *ciceroni.* I listen to what they have to say, these tellers of tailored tales, testing my French or German. I am no linguist, but there are English-speaking guides, too, and sometimes I learn something new. Occasionally I try to sketch some important building or architectural detail, making a record more of the moment than the subject. I am no Ruskin, but sometimes, just sometimes, I judge the result worth looking at again. But it is not the churches, not the cloistered monasteries, not the modest patrician palaces with their fascinating mongrel fusion of Gothic and Renaissance, that hold the secret. What holds us in thrall is the life lived here. The simple life: sun and sea, food and drink, the people we count as friends. Not the kind of people we have left at Boris's party. At least, not the émigré English-speaking community, transient and permanent, who all too often seem able to sustain native prejudices abroad. Not the Americans, with their innocent New World confidence undefiled by foreign travel, their judgments of others trivially measured in categories of cuteness. Nor those young, rucksack-loaded Australians, second- or third-generation Croats on a whistle-stop tour of the 'rellies', who, equipped with their *Lonely Planet* guide and high on vitamin C, manage to find their way around without ever attempting to speak one word of the language. Certainly not the Brits, most of whom are no better on the language front and often hopelessly ill-informed (notoriously unclear, for example, about the distinction to be drawn between Croatia and Yugoslavia – not to speak of Slovenia and Slovakia), while others, fluent enough to get by informally if not intellectually, and well enough versed in Rebecca West and Misha Glenny, seem to cultivate an aura of detached superiority in all their dealings with local society. It is, I realise, exactly this gentlemanly *hubris* that Boris must covet.

Then I remember that I am myself a Brit. Jasna, too, despite her measure of Slav blood. Am I – are we – seen by others in this same stereotypical light? I suppose we are, in some eyes. But not, I have to hope, in the eyes of those *Korčulani* friends we have made over the years. And isn't there, in any case, an affinity, unexpected and paradoxical perhaps, between west-coast Scotland and Dalmatia? Forget the climatic differences, take away the sun (a factor I find easy enough to ignore as I walk on into the blackness with the soft chill of the night on my cheek) and the two regions are not so dissimilar. A mountainous coastline. Unnumbered islands. A simple life dependent on the sea and a rarely fertile land. The export of people. Respect for learning, the honouring of religion and tradition, a love of family. Is it all this that holds the friendships we have made together? But before I have time to convince myself, there is a cry from Jasna.

'Look, Sveti Spiridion!'

On a low hilltop to our right the thin spire of the church stands out against pale clouds. A rustic saint for a rural setting; no grand apostle but a fourth century sheep farmer. It means we are on the edge of the village.

'Not long now'. She takes my hand again.

I look at my watch. We have been walking for more than two hours. Over a rise we come to Račišće bay, the sea barely visible in the weak moonlight. We veer right, away from the water's edge on to a single-track road that climbs slowly between silent houses buried in black. We pass piles of rough-sawn planks, the crusty bark still on them, stacked outside the joiner's workshop. Across the road the skeleton of the half-built fishing boat lies in the shadows. Laid along the verge are huge quarry-cut slabs of travertine and, ranged in the mason's yard, stands of polished facing stone white enough to reflect some of the moon's feeble light. At *Zure*'s, the small family-run restaurant where we go when we want to eat good fish, the gates to the courtyard are long since closed. We tread more softly now, afraid to disturb the neighbours. At length we reach home.

The pomegranate tree marks the corner of our lane. These warm late April days it begins to blaze with scarlet blossom; but now, in the night, it is colourless. We duck below its branches, watching our step on the old ramped path that leads down by the belfried gable of Sveti Bartul. Once through the white-painted courtyard doors, we exchange a wry exhausted smile. The key enters the lock and turns slowly. I put my hand on Jasna's forearm. We climb to the bedroom.

THE OLD GENTLEMAN OF
PRIGRADICA

'...many Mediterraneans go in for horoscopes...'

Predrag Matvejević
1987

Arriving in Blato around two or three o'clock on a late summer afternoon is not something to be recommended. The sun is at its height and the town is very, very hot. Here in the interior of the island, away from sea and sea breezes, over forty kilometres west of Korčula town and only two or three short of Vela Luka, a dense, jigsaw cluster of low, orange-roofed houses sprawls across a riverless valley up onto the hillsides to the north and south. Blato soaks up the afternoon heat with a remorseless thirst. The streets are still. Everyone is indoors, already asleep after an enormous lunch or drowsily sipping a last glass of wine before siesta. Behind the shutters, the town is dreaming of evening.

But Blato is hardly a town. Though ancient in origin, founded perhaps by the mysterious Illyrians and later colonized by Greeks, Romans, Avars, Croats and Venetians, it is better described as Korčula's largest village. Now by far the most populous inland settlement on the island, it seems to have grown in a haphazard agglutinative fusion. In a sea of undistinguished domestic building saved from banality by the ubiquitous mantle of the town's tiled roofs, its patrician houses are the exception, their decorative stucco façades crumbling around a Baroque portal or buried behind orange trees. Its narrow streets, winding and climbing in disorientating confusion, are not named but numbered, a distinction the inhabitants are quick to tell you it shares with downtown New York. No doubt this has the

176

considerable merit of eliminating any need for that re-naming of streets and squares which appears to be necessary in much of post-communist Europe, where the honoured heroes of the old regime – many of them once rebels who, as Cees Nooteboom puts it, poured their 'blood into addresses' – have been so discredited as to become the non-persons of the new. This rewriting of history on every street corner may reassure those old enough to recall the *status quo ante*, but it irritates almost everyone else, not least the stranger who finds last year's guide-book plans already out-of-date. Numbering the streets may avoid that confusion, but it is hardly a basis for any convincing claim to urban sophistication. None the less, Blato is not without its dignity.

I sense it immediately. We have been here before, of course, many times, but now, driving off the road that leads on to Vela Luka, I am again somehow surprised by the change from rural to urban, the nature of the transition abrupt and unexpected. With no more than the briefest threshold of perception, we plunge into Zlinje, the dark avenue of pollarded limes that stretches in a long green axis through Blato from east to west. This intimate *allée* is the town's main street, but it scarcely seems so. The trees, spaced closely in parallel arcades, are thick with luxuriant summer foliage leaning in a leafy vault over the narrow carriageway. It is not quite single-track but there is barely room for two cars to pass comfortably. An oncoming lorry or bus necessitates immediate evasion between the trees. Despite the formal straightness of the route this is no grand boulevard; the scale remains rural rather than urban. We are in a village street. Through the trees we catch glimpses of quiet stone and stucco houses, a deserted café terrace, an empty school-yard, a football pitch forlorn in its weekday silence. A cat streaks across the road – the only sign of life. Five hours from now it will be a different story when the *passeggiata* begins.

Halfway down this shadowed tunnel, the trees to our left merge with those of a small wooded park; pine, lime and chestnut. Beds of red salvia and redder, taller Canna lilies sprout among battered benches. Crude concrete edgings delineate a network of paths. What grass there is is lank and sparse, for the neat, close-cropped lawn is as unknown here as wayside figs might be in the Trossachs. Hidden beyond and a little above the park is a large paved square, elongated and irregular in plan and dominated by the parish Church of All Saints (Svi Sveti). This is Blato's only architectural set-piece, the spiritual heart of the community. Here the *Kumpanija* is danced and the town's religious and secular festivals celebrated. Wide but brief flights of steps negotiate a succession of level changes from the street to the square, from the square to the church and on to the streets and houses on the hillside above. The church, though begun in the early medieval period and several times altered and enlarged since, is largely the result of building carried out in the seventeenth century. Nave-and-aisles in form and Venetian in style, it is constructed with typically provincial, solid-walled severity, minimally lit from a few narrow, round-arched windows and *oeil-de-boeuf* openings punctuating the clearstorey and flanking the doorway on the gabled west façade. Steps rise from the square to a second doorway at the centre of the north aisle; above it, a small wheel window and raised transept gable. A detached belfry tower, erected in the eighteenth century, stands a few metres to the south-west. Further west across the square is the town loggia, an open rectangular structure, the low enclosing wall of which carries a series of regularly spaced stone pillars supporting the heavy larch timbers of a hipped tiled roof. Dating from the beginning of the fourteenth century, the structure was completely rebuilt in 1700, repaired in the middle of the nineteenth century and again in 1920 when the present roof was constructed. No longer court or council chamber, though still the outdoor focus of Blato's civic life, it serves as a shaded place for children to play or old men, and occasionally old women, to linger.

We have no time to linger – or is it that Jasna and I are a little unwilling to risk that epithet 'old'? At any rate, we do not stop. We are on our way to Prigradica, a small village gathered around a cove on the north side of the island. To get there we must pass through Blato to find the narrow road north over the hill to the sea. An unprepossessing, hardly legible sign directs us through the trees on our right and we begin to negotiate the slow climb up through the town. The gradients are not steep but the tight streets bend abruptly. Corner succeeds corner. We have to pause at each junction, changing down into a low gear, not so much to cope with the incline as to take our bearings. There is little to choose between one street and the next and no indication of which might be the right route. Labyrinthine confusion sets in and our directional hunches become less and less reliable. But at length, working on the problematical assumption that those asphalted surfaces marginally less degraded than others are likely to be those used by whatever, presumably modest, amount of through traffic may exist (though the opposite might just as easily be the case) we find ourselves on the open road above the textured carpet of tiled roofs. Below us is the wide depression of *Blatsko polje*; 'muddy field' is the free translation, though in the summer heat the valley is parched and much of the vegetation burnt to a dull fawn fur drawn out between the green vines. On the hillsides to the south there are dark slopes of scorched *makija*, the moon landscape legacy of last year's fires.

We have decided to pay a visit to Jakša Kalogjera. This name, Kalogjera, is well known in Croatia, as it is in Greece and Sicily and no doubt also in the diaspora societies of Australia, South Africa and the United States. But it is particularly renowned on Korčula and especially in Blato. The family has a long and honourable history that still commands respect locally and, indeed, beyond – academic, cultural and professional life in Zagreb, would be much the poorer without Kalogjeras. It was there, in the capital, many years ago now, that we had our first encounter with a branch of this distinguished clan when, on an early visit to what was then Yugoslavia, we were guests in the home of Dr Marko Kalogjera. I remember the house on Medvesčak, a flat-roofed thirties villa, tired and distressed in the sixties but still refreshingly modern, and Dr Marko, as we always addressed him, extremely tall, a little remote not only in height but manner too, always well dressed in a sober, business-like way as befitted an international lawyer of some European renown. Utterly cosmopolitan, he was equally at ease in Paris, Vienna, Milan or Bucharest, whether working for the Communist government or employed by some multi-national oil or shipping company to ease their contractual negotiations with Belgrade. Yet each year he would return to Korčula and the family home in Blato, or, to be more accurate, to Prižba a few kilometres away on the south coast where he, his wife, Erna, and three gifted daughters spent much of the summer. Besides Croatian (or Serbo-Croatian, as we knew it then) he spoke French, German, Italian and Russian, all fluently. His English was pedantically perfect and spoken with a precise but slow enunciation. This could be intimidating, for it gave his every measured word a judicial gravity. He was, however, very much the good uncle, extending to us the friendship he had, as a younger man, shared with Jasna's father.

Through Marko we later met a Kalogjera cousin – there are always cousins in Dalmatia. This was Ante Kalogjera, with whom we spent several summer holidays in the mid-sixties in his home on the coast at Crikvenica. A lawyer, too, Ante was otherwise entirely unlike Marko; casually dressed, convivial and far from sober (often in all senses of the word) he was always full of mischievous fun. Motor-boat trips laden with a dozen or so plastic jerry cans filled with the local red and white wine (a mere month's supply) drawn from the casks of peasant family clients at Vrbnik on the island of Krk, invariably ended in song and an erratic crossing back to the mainland. When we drank and laughed together, attempting to translate jokes from one language into the other, it was hard to believe he had spent years in a concentration camp. His story amazed us, his spirit more so, for he had somehow contrived to transcend tragedy. Missing, presumed dead, he returned to Croatia at the end of the war, unexpected and unannounced, only to find his wife had remarried. Perhaps his escape from prisoner-of-war camp gave him the resolve, in those first days of the rest of his life, to seize and enjoy the moment with neither a backward nor a forward glance; perhaps he was even amused at the trick fate had played on him. At any rate, he refused to rock the matrimonial boat, wished his wife well and got on with living his own life. In Crikvenica he settled happily with two friends, Ljubica and Milan, in a contented *ménage à trois*. Whether innate or assumed, there was, I think, a paradoxical nobility about his light-heartedness and it endeared him to us.

There was nobility, too, though of a different kind, in Katica Mirošević, another cousin whom we first met, again at the instigation of Dr Marko, a decade or so later. Looking for a place to stay on our first visit to Korčula, some twenty-five years ago, we had come to the home of the Batistić family in Lumbarda. We had two young children then. Nikola Batistić and his wife Katica had three. Nikola's mother, Katica too, already long since widowed, lived with the family. She was then well into her sixties, strongly built from years of labour in the vineyards and olive groves yet with a straight back and a still proud carriage. She continued to work in the family fields and in the garden. Unbowed physically and emotionally, she had never fully submitted herself to the black de-sexing trappings of Mediterranean widowhood, though she always dressed in dark colours and on Sundays would revert to black for mass. She had long, silver-grey hair gathered in a roll at the back and a strong, high-cheekboned face, barely lined and of great womanly beauty. Born and raised in Blato, she never left the island until in later years illness obliged her to spend a few days in hospital at Dubrovnik. Yet there was nothing parochial nor small-minded about her; on the contrary, with long life she seemed to have acquired a matriarchal wisdom to which all deferred. Her nobility was simple, reserved and gentle.

Dr Marko, Ante and *baba* Katica, all long-lived, are dead now. But Jakša, Marko's younger brother whom we have never met, is still alive and vigorous. Now in his nineties, he lives most of the year alone in Zagreb but regularly leaves the summer heat of his city flat to spend some months on Korčula. It seems that, like Dr Marko, he, too, has a house not far from Blato, though the location at Prigradica on the island's north shore is considerably less fashionable than the villa-ribboned south coast at Prižba. He is there now. No-one in the Batistić household has ever paid him a visit, nor, with *baba* gone, does anyone seem to know much about him. We hope to solve the mystery.

Gradually the road begins to level out, holding a straighter track as it does so. A dense pine wood presses to the verge on our right, blocking the view down to the valley below but filling the air with a fresh, resinous scent. The hill we have still to cross continues to rise on our left and, perhaps a kilometre off, we can see the road as it re-appears climbing through the afternoon haze. Dead ahead, some two hundred metres distant, framing the diminishing perspective of the carriageway, we see an open gateway flanked by tall, masonry piers. It comes nearer, its symmetry hypnotic, quickening our puzzled anticipation as we approach, leading us on, inviting our entrance until, when we are almost upon it, the road makes an abrupt ninety-degree turn to the left. I make the turn but only just in time, raising the dust as we slew to a stop beneath a stand of cypress trees. Breathless and relieved to have avoided colliding with a high stone wall less than a metre to our right, I realise with a wry irony that we have all but gate-crashed the local cemetery.

'Thank God', gasps Jasna. She is shaking. I put my hand on her knee, pressing gently in reassurance, but say nothing. I have my own racing pulse to master.

Some silent minutes pass. A swallowtail butterfly settles briefly on the wing mirror. It flickers into flight, yellow and black against the chrome, and is gone, vanishing in waves of feathery fennel growing below the trees. I throw open the car door, take a few deep breaths and make a decision.

'Let's take a break. Maybe it's fortuitous. We haven't seen this one anyway, have we?'

Visiting cemeteries is not exactly a habit of ours but on Korčula it has become a kind of casual temptation, something we often find ourselves doing on a long country walk or drive. There is nothing morbid about this. Nor is the experience a melancholy one. We are a long way from those gloomy northern churchyards where rain-soaked yews weep over the tombs and every meandering step is made with superstitious care as if to tread on the mossy inscription of some half-hidden memorial were to waken the dead. Here in the sun everything is different. Pine and cypress give a welcome shade. Paths are neat and straight. There is no grass. The grave slabs, blonde travertine and gunmetal granite, shine in the heat. On every tomb there is a vase of flowers.

Through the gateway, the straight line of the road runs on, skirting the edge of the cemetery for a bit before petering out on the hillside. The way up from Blato must once have ended here at the town's burial place with no more than a stone-crushed track continuing over the hill to Prigradica. There is an arched opening in the wall to our left, the keystone carved with skull and crossed bones, the ironwork of the graveyard gate wrought with the date 1905. Suddenly we are in cloistered shade, walking between tall regularly spaced conifers towards a small chapel. The line of this main avenue is reflected west and east in parallel paths running between the burial plots. Narrower cross links create a regular grid-iron plan. God's paths are made straight. As elsewhere on the island, the cemetery is a rigid, rational construct. Nothing dilutes its simple classicism. Burial is, as one might say, a grave matter. No grass, no romantically contoured paths, no indulgence in the picturesque. If the apotheosis of this rigour is to be found in the cemeteries of the great cities – notably in the avenues of Pere Lachaise in Paris 'laid out like a modern grid-form metropolis', but ultimately nowhere more so than in the New World necropolis of Recoleta in Buenos Aires with its dense, deeply depressing matrix of posthumous display – its beginnings lie in the old Old World, on quiet Mediterranean slopes like these where death was first deceived by geometry. And here at Blato the lines of this last battle are clearly drawn. To the left, the older plots lie on flat ground, a gridded field of horizontal and vertical stone, flashed with flowers. Ahead of us to the north and east, the graves are tiered up the slope of the hillside in a series of long terraces crossed at regular intervals by short flights of stone steps. Walking round, I see that some of these graves have sensibly taken advantage of the slow slope to the valley below, the roof over their repetitive vaults forming a raised level platform, patterned by the cemetery paths. A high wall, lowered in height towards the south to reveal the valley view, surrounds the graveyard on all sides. In the brilliant afternoon light, the warm ochre of its polygonal masonry glows and intensifies against the banks of pines, firs and cypresses rising behind. Conscious of its enveloping protection, I experience a sense of peaceful enclosure no less intense. The realization that, but for the dead beneath our feet, we are alone in this enclave of funerary order evokes a strange, almost claustrophobic calm. We seem to have found a second Blato, not gathered in careless intimacy like the village below but ordered and shriven; a world transfigured by the disciplines of death, a world in waiting.

We stroll aimlessly from path to path, listening to the ceaseless cicadas and the crunch of our steps on the gravel. The flat rectangular slabs of the graves are identical in material, dimension and profile, differentiated only by their inscriptions, the varying pretension of the headstones which rise from them and the freshness of the flowers they bear. Here and there, especially on the upper terraces, some new tombs have been constructed, cut into the stony ground. Looking down into these empty vaults we can see they are no more than shelved concrete boxes, room for three coffins, one above the other, on each side of the chamber, as if the dead had booked *couchettes* to heaven. We stop from time to time to read the dedications on some of the older graves, noting the recurring family names and translating the familiar expressions of grief. Among the headstones there are the usual cross-topped steles, obelisks, broken urns and angels. But some memorials are more idiosyncratic.

One grave in particular catches our eye – a composite monument raised in commemoration of Ivan Sardelić and his family. The headstone itself, a plain slab of grey granite cut to a segmental arc at the top, is unremarkable, except perhaps that it is more restrained than most. In a small elliptical frame, it bears the customary sepia photograph of the deceased below which a sober inscription symmetrically inset in black lettering records names and dates. On one side stands an urn; on the other, a shaft of granite incised with the most ascetic of linear crosses. On this shaft, however, added with graceless and disturbing daring, sits a curved pedestal of granite carrying the realistically modelled representation in stone of a 1960s jet fighter, one wing broken symbolically. In the shadow of the broken wing is a second photograph, that of Ante Sardelić, Major-General in the Yugoslav airforce. Out of respect, I try to convince myself that this is an imaginatively modern departure from the traditional imagery of death. But the toy plane teases me from its perch and I cannot escape the cloying odour of *kitsch*.

Nearby is another distinctive if less unconventional grave, a tall pedimented monument hollowed out in a round-arched niche within which is the life-size, half-body statue of a well-dressed young man. A wide-brimmed hat sits back halo-like on his forehead. A little stiffly erect in his collar and tie, waistcoat and lapelled jacket, he meets our gaze with composure, hands clasped before him in an attitude that could be patient resignation but might equally well be that of an attentive teacher, doctor or municipal functionary. It is all but impossible not to imagine the lower half of his figure embedded somewhere in the tall stepped plinth, for the sculpture is placed almost eye-to-eye with the observer. Immediately below the clasped hands a small round-arched recess houses a tiny red candle. On each side, the inscription, dated 1914, records that this is a memorial raised by a grieving mother for her only son. He is Petr Farčić-Priša, known to his mother and friends, it seems, as 'Franko'. It is always touching this island custom of giving lithic permanence to everyday or pet names. But to see my own name... I read the letters carefully – six to my own five – with an odd sense of reverent recognition. St Augustine's plea for divine postponement comes into my mind. I want to light the little candle, but have no matches.

Chastened by this reminder of my own mortality, I decide I have had enough of tombs and begin to walk back to the car. To break the spell of the place I kick the stony grit of the path, quicken my step and, looking up through the trees to the hill we have to cross, begin to wonder again what we will find at Prigradica. But there is no escape just yet. This time I *hear* my name. It is Jasna calling me.

'Frank! Come and look at this.'

She is standing in front of one of the graveyard's largest pieces of memorial sculpture, not far from the main entrance.

'How could we have missed this? Look!' she points, directing my attention to an inscription high on the monument. 'Read what it says!'

'Kalogjera!'

How *did* we miss it? It is impressive. The plot is expansive, raised as a moulded stone platform and surrounded on all four sides by small, square columns from which at some time protective chains must have hung. Set back within this field of low standing stones, the monument itself rises erect like some tall dolmen. The base alone stands almost two metres, reducing in stepped splays to support a broad plinth bearing a framed inscription. A heavy cornice forms the elevated table on which sits the third and final element of the composition, a round-topped headstone. Above this rises the cross, nearly six metres from the ground. Represented on the headstone, carved in bold relief within the horseshoe embrace of a laurel leaf wreath, is the shawl-wrapped head of a woman. Below the ribbon-knotted boss at the base of the wreath are the words I have read. This is the grave of the widow, Marija Kalogjera.

The main inscription is a terse panegyric. *Uzor. Žena. Majka. Krščanka.* Paragon of virtue. Wife. Mother. Christian woman. These expressions of affection and admiration come, the monument records, from her seven loving sons who 'with flowers and tears' promise to honour her saintly memory.

'It must be Dr Marko's mother.'

'No, I don't think so,' counters Jasna. 'Look at the dates. Born 1850, died 1925. Dr Marko could only have been about fifteen or sixteen in 1925. I doubt if she could have given birth at sixty. And he wasn't the youngest – there's Jakša.'

'His grand-mother then?'

'Must be.'

The discovery pleases us; I have the feeling we are both glad to be here looking up at the nun-like face above us, the lines carved on her brow thin but precise in the sharp shadow of the afternoon sun. I watch a faint smile pass across Jasna's gaze and fancy her drawn to this old woman through the threads of family and friendship that link her to Dr Marko, and him to Jasna's own dead father. She stoops to re-arrange some dried flowers gathered in a vase at the base of the memorial. Then, rising up and leaning forward, she extends her right hand to touch the black inlaid letters of the inscription with the briefest brush of her finger tips. It is an unexpected gesture, made quickly but tentatively. It is not furtively done, there is no guilt in it, no sense that to presume such intimacy might invoke retribution, divine or otherwise; on the contrary, though it passes in an instant, the movement is one of almost fearful respect, as if the stone itself held a charge of affection too strong to bear. The moment gone, she turns and walks towards the gates. I follow, musing that my wife, the least superstitious of women, should act in this strange way.

Back in the car, I think about reproaching her on this score. But I guess I am on shaky ground. For it is I who am the superstitious one, inheriting a whole range of taboos and propitiations from my mother, an intelligent woman who, the youngest of an eleven-child family and the only one to complete a full five years of secondary education, would none the less fly for refuge under the dining-room table or into the windowless hall of our council-house home whenever a thunderstorm struck. I can remember crouching in the darkness with her waiting for the last clap of thunder and the last frightening flash of lightning. Did she imagine some kind of retribution in these dark skies? From her, and from her mother too, I learnt never to put shoes on the table, open an umbrella indoors or say 'thank you' to someone picking up a dropped glove. I still turn the money in my pocket whenever I see a crescent moon through glass. So I say nothing and turn the key in the ignition.

The road is narrower now but the surface good. Now and then we have to slow down to allow a car to pass in the opposite direction. But there is little or no traffic; few people come and go to Prigradica. We skirt the walled grounds of a large villa, a relic of Austro-Hungarian wealth long since conscripted to serve as a retirement home. Low stone bollards, like fossilized sand castles, march along the roadway edge, the only barrier to some disastrous drop into the *makija* below. They come intermittently, first to the left, then the right, reinforcing their visual warning in a repetitive slipstream echo – thump, thump, thump, thump – an aural reminder that punctuates the drive with metronomic regularity. As we climb, bending back and forward across the contours of the hillside, we can look down on the valley vineyards stretching back eastwards in the direction we have come. Far to the west it is just possible to see the sea and the long widening gulf of Vela Luka. But in a matter of minutes we have left these long inland perspectives behind. We are over the hill and the road is falling fast. Below is the north coast of the island, suddenly near. The vast expanse of the Adriatic floods out before us, ink rich in Prussian blue. Out in the distance Hvar hangs on the horizon. Cautiously we edge downhill into the village.

It's a small place, orange roofs scattered among the olive

trees. Tiny fields cultivated with rows of vines or tall-stalked *blitva* interrupt its tumbling randomness. Most of the houses we pass are new but modest in size and detail; two-storeyed villas, some gabled, some hipped, many with the gap-toothed dentilling of the eaves still so favoured all along the Dalmatian coast. They are arranged with no logic other than that dictated by the fall of the land and the lure of the sea. View succeeds view, spilling over the roofs below us and out over the turquoise waters of the inlet. Trailing back from dark, pine-carpeted headlands, a yellow-grey selvage of stone borders the water's edge deep into the heart of the village, ragged at first over the rocky shore then smooth along the ashlar masonry of the *riva*. A stone slipway runs down into a tiny inner harbour. But this is no more than a claw-shaped pool, big enough to protect perhaps a dozen small boats from the swell. We reach it in low gear after a slow descent.

Skirting the quayside slowly with a caution heightened by the hazards of the journey over the hill and the memory of the cemetery skid, I am gradually aware we have driven onto a stage. There are few people about in the afternoon heat but, for those who are, we are the event of the day. Not much out of the ordinary may happen in road-end places like this but when it does, it seems that observers take unabashed note. A young fisherman, tinkering with the inboard engine of his boat, looks up, brushes the sweat from his forehead with the back of an oily hand and stares relentlessly. Further on, a trio of older men turn their heads as one as we pass. Behind a balcony profusion of red and pink geraniums a full-figured, middle-aged woman puts down her watering can to tighten her dressing gown at our intrusion. Some children stop playing, stock-still with curiosity. All this is familiar enough but, as always, discomfiting, and all the more so for us northerners schooled in a self-deprecating Scottish society where the natural inclination to stare or point must be curbed. However much we might like to fade into the background, we have inadvertently made a spectacle of ourselves. We have become a fleeting scene in Prigradica's everyday drama. In a moment or two the village will blink and we will be released. For now, however, we must play our parts, prepared to hold the stage until some new arrival steals the show or, more likely, our audience returns to its quotidian torpor.

I nose the car forward. But not for long. A stone wall, extending inland from the seaward side of the short stubby pier that terminates the long *riva*, blocks our way. Steps recessed into the stonework lead up to what appears to be a shore path across the rocks, but we can go no further in the car. So we park on the quayside finding what shade we can under some wispy tamarisks. Conscious of our sparse but still attentive audience (now joined by a group of seagulls preening themselves on the pier wall) I look around wondering whether Jakša's house is here at the heart of the village or up on the hill. Behind the trees is an irregular, gable-to-gable row of two- and three-storey buildings. Perhaps here near the water's edge. These are older houses, their plain façades scarcely more imaginatively organised than a child's drawing but as honestly constructed. They possess the kind of tarnished vernacular dignity adored by the city dweller keen to conceal the creature comforts of conversion behind specious neglect. I imagine the attraction such properties might hold for someone from Zagreb – the location, the view, the price. Several, however, are in desperately poor condition. A few have even been abandoned, no more than hollow shells. Two, still occupied at first floor, have forestairs, their cantilevered treads arched precariously. The stucco is spalling on some, revealing the crudely bonded brick below. On others it is still intact but scarred and bleached. Faint memories of the past survive: a painted shop sign, the family name long ago obliterated by socialist zeal; war-time grafitti, faint, too, but still legible – ŽIVIO DRUG TITO. But there are other houses, perhaps a hundred years or more old, but solidly built and well cared for, their windows and doors characteristically framed in finely dressed stone blocks. Some have simple cornices over the first floor windows. Wedged into this parade, not far from the harbour pool, is a small hotel. Constructed with the utilitarian enthusiasm of the nineteen fifties, it looks as if it may once have served as an *odmaralište* for some industrial enterprise elsewhere on the island – perhaps workers from the marine equipment factory at Blato spent seaside weekends here at the Yugoslav state's expense. The bedroom shutters are drawn and no one is drinking at the half dozen or so tables crushed together on a small terrace crowded with potted palms and oleanders. But perhaps this is a good place to start our enquiries.

Plate-glass doors with a broken push-bar. Terrazzo floors. A boarded pine ceiling. A frayed poster of Dubrovnik; the familiar aerial view of the old walled city. The nauseous cocktail of stale cigarette smoke and disinfectant. On the reception desk, a television set with the sound turned down; mid-afternoon folklore censored. There is no-one about. I look over the counter. A copy of *Slobodna*, an overflowing ashtray, a large leather-covered book that is presumably the register, or possibly the obligatory but always nugatory complaints book. No bell. I wait. Silence. I think about trying to find the office or kitchens but decide against it.

Back outside, momentarily blinded by the sun sparkling across the shimmering cove onto the quay in front of me, I stop to rub my eyes. Where is Jasna? Then I see her talking to the old men whose concerted gaze we bore earlier.

'Any luck?' I call, trying not to sound too loud.

She raises a hand in acknowledgment and answers 'Yes', interrupting her conversation only momentarily and not bothering to turn her head as I approach. I reach the bench and nod deferentially to all three. The response is perfunctory: a serious look, raised eyebrows, a barely perceptible tilt of the head, my arrival evidently a distraction. The talk is of travel. Not our travel but theirs. Surprised but delighted that a stranger – a woman – is attempting to speak to them in their own language, they are first keen to find out our background, where we have come from, how we got here, what we think of Korčula, then keener still to tell their own stories. Yes, two have been in Scotland: one, as a merchant seaman, on several occasions when his ship called at Leith, Aberdeen or Greenock, the other on a single hard-drinking visit as part of a trade union delegation during Tito's time. The third has never made it but seems particularly well informed about our football teams and whisky. He longs to see the island distilleries. Are the Hebridean ferries like those on the Adriatic? Does it rain all the time? Jasna's Croatian is soon overwhelmed by this volubility. Not that this worries her elderly companions, who, animated by recollection, begin to engage in a competitive exchange of increasingly imaginative memories and anecdotes. She nudges me and we edge away.

'Well?' I ask as soon as we are out of earshot.

'Yes. They knew him. He's here,'

'Where?'

But Jasna is already heading back towards some low houses opposite the harbour slipway. There are three crushed together under a common eaves line, sandwiched between the hotel and a range of two-storeyed dwellings peppered with dilapidated and dangerous-looking balconies. All three are identical, little more than a room wide. But while the two outer dwellings retain their original window and door, in the central property these, and the short stretch of wall between, have been dismantled to form a single broader opening under a flat arch of tightly jointed voussoirs. Flanked by the dressed stone pilasters of the doorway, one in its original position, the other resited at the window jamb, this carefully contrived opening is perhaps three metres wide by two high. A boathouse? In front, the quayside has been invaded by planting – geraniums, French marigolds and cineraria maritima housed in a variety of cans, pots and rough stone troughs on one side; on the other, big enough to provide noonday shade as well as privacy, a large shiny pittasporum rooted below the paving. This, it seems, is Jakša's bolt-hole.

The folding door facing us is divided into three vertical panels, the glazed upper halves of which are screened by hinged louvred shutters. One panel lies slightly ajar at the pilaster jamb; the door has swung in, the louvred shutter out. We peer into the gloom, inquisitive but careful not to cross the threshold. It's difficult to discern things with eyes used to the glare of the quayside but, after some moments' impertinent scrutiny, we can make out enough to see something of the chaos within. There is a boat, of course. An old clinker-built vessel takes up most of the floor space. But there is much more. Several small wine barrels, some car tyres, ladders, oars, coils of rope, stacked chairs, a bicycle, a good deal of timber in varied sizes of planks and boards, a broken bird-cage, numerous bottles, cans of paint, a fishing net hanging on the side wall. Jakša, however, is nowhere to be seen. Perhaps he is upstairs in the attic. I knock heavily on the door.

There is some movement overhead and the sound of footsteps. Evidently there is a staircase somewhere in the shadows at the back of the boathouse. A figure emerges out of the darkness. He looks a little sleepy, more puzzled than annoyed to be wakened by our intrusion.

'*Gospodin Kalogjera*?'

'*Jesam*', he replies, the affirmative immediate and polite, his voice rising with curiosity on the second syllable.

Jasna launches into an explanation of who we are and why we are here in Prigradica – her childhood in Zagreb, her father, Dr Marko, me, our visits to Korčula. I listen, smile occasionally by way of silent support and wonder what this elderly man whom we have called on unannounced will make of our presumption. Not that there is anything intimidating about his manner or appearance. He is dressed carelessly and comfortably: a crumpled pale-blue shirt, zip-fronted and buttoned at the cuffs, pockets and epaulettes, hangs over scuffed blue jeans; thrown around his neck, what looks like a white pullover or cardigan; on his feet, black trainers. He might be ready for a lazy hour or two's fishing. And perhaps he is – or, rather, was. For, watching his expression soften from bemused surprise to one of surprised delight, I have the growing feeling that, charmed as he evidently is to find an attractive woman on his doorstep, he is even more captivated by the unfolding of the Kalogjera connection. I fancy I can see the family look. Like Dr Marko, Jakša has a high domical forehead from which thin silver hair has receded, though it still covers the crown. But he is not tall like Marko. Not small in stature either, yet his thick-set upper body and large head make him seem less than average height, an impression oddly intensified by a smile which creases the skin on his nose in a mischievous grin that must have been irresistibly puckish in his youth. Now, in old age, the smile is less conspiratorial as if the pleasure shared were not so much wicked as just a little naughty. This, too, is quite unlike Dr Marko, though it does make me think of Ante in Crikvenica. Jakša, of course, is much older than Ante was then, more gnome than elf. One of the Seven Dwarfs perhaps. Impudent and disrespectful as it is, it's an analogy I cannot resist.

It's clear we are welcome. Having established our credentials in Croatian, we have switched to English – or, rather, Jakša has, aware that his fluency makes for livelier conversation than our respectful stumbling. Seats are carried out from the boathouse: a rather spindly straight-backed kitchen chair, an antique deck-chair with torn striped canvas, and a large paint can on which our host, making it clear this is not for us to sit on, places a piece of carpeted blockboard. Next comes the drink, brought from the attic with three small glasses, all different. It is *travarica*, the grappa-like, urine-coloured brandy privately distilled all over Dalmatia. In the bottle, the necessary mix of herbs and grasses, the selection of which varies from family to family. Jakša fills our glasses and, looking us in the eye as a good host should, toasts us with the customary '*Živjeli*'. I can see he is watching us with that almost ritual attention islanders give to their guests, largely from a natural concern to be hospitable but also out of a barely veiled curiosity to see how the stranger copes with the fierce spirit in his glass. Every toast is a test. Not drinking with bravado but not sipping either, I fancy we pass the test. The initial impact of the *travarica* is one of freshness, the nose clean and predominantly lemony. There are hints of the various herbs immersed in the liquid – rosemary, fennel, thyme. Then comes the first strong rough cut of taste, almost unsupportable until it passes over the palate and upper throat. And suddenly it releases its deeper secrets, glowing under the breast bone with a warmth that makes the initial shock more than worthwhile. The herbs linger in the mouth like a *digestif* while a pleasant composure settles on mind and body. Perhaps another? And, indeed, Jakša has already refilled our glasses.

Sitting on the quayside beside the flowers, warmed outside by the sun and inside by the spirit we have drunk, I am tempted to fall asleep. But I am also hungry, the more so since the *travarica* has sharpened the appetite. Guessing that Jasna must be feeling the same, I suggest we might all three try to find something to eat at the hotel. Of this, however, there is no possibility for it seems, if Jakša is to be believed (and, from my own experience of half an hour or so ago it appears entirely credible, if inexplicable) that the hotel does not serve meals or even drinks until the evening. But our host has the answer. If we are willing to put up with a lack of meat, fish and sophistication, then he can prepare a simple meal for us. And without waiting for any response to this offer he gathers up the glasses, a finger in each, grasps the bottle and invites us to follow him into the depths of the boathouse. Embarrassed to have further presumed on Kalogjera hospitality and goodwill, but well aware that unless I eat something soon the rest of the afternoon will slip away slowly but surely into a miasma of alternately raised glasses and the journey home become impossible, I usher Jasna ahead of me. Climbing the worn treads of the staircase, I wonder what lies above.

The attic is hot. The single skylight has been pushed open, presumably to encourage some through draught to the staircase void, but there is no perceptible movement of the stifling air. The light seems barely adequate at first but our eyes quickly adjust to the gloom. We are in a low-ceilinged, tent-like space. The roof timbers and lateral walls have been crudely covered with plywood sheeting, as have the flimsy partitions that enclose a small compartment next to the stair well. Apart from this makeshift cubicle, which has evidently been added at some time to provide basic sanitation, Jakša's summer home is an intimate one-room world. On one side is a couch, cushions plumped together, a crumpled sheet thrown aside in haste. On the floor an open suitcase serves as a wardrobe. This is the bedroom. In the middle of the room a small trestle table positioned to catch the best light from the dormer. The waxed table-cover is torn and frayed. There are two chairs. This is the dining room. Running along the wall beyond the head of the staircase, a hefty shelf with cupboards below and more shelves above. A small sink has been cut into the worktop and there is a gas ring. This is the kitchen. It is a condensed world into which the necessities of everyday life have been compressed with cavalier expediency and none of the calculated economising care a practised caravaner or camper might bring to such confined living. There is nothing spartan or minimalist about this room; on the contrary, cluttered with what seems to be the accumulated detritus of an indiscriminately acquisitive life, Jakša's attic is drowning in disorder. Bulging shoe-boxes are stacked beside the sofa-bed. Spilling piles of journals and newspapers restrict the free floor space to an island around the table. Below the table, an ancient typewriter. Books are everywhere; on the floor, on the table, on both chairs, beside the sink. Pinned on the walls, some tourist posters, a clutch of newspaper clippings and photographs, and what looks like a large astrological chart. Jakša has thrown off his pullover scarf and is standing by the sink, arms outstretched, palms uppermost.

'This is all there is, I'm afraid'

His shoulders rise as he smiles at us in a mocking, self-deprecatory way. On the bench in front of him are the few bits and pieces that are to form our lunch. Two eggs, a small salami already half consumed, a fat, burgundy-purple aubergine, a large onion, and a handful of parsley, the coriander-like kind that has so much more flavour than the crinkly variety familiar at home in Scotland. It isn't much; but before we can respond with a polite, if mendacious, reassurance that it is looks appetising and will be more than adequate, Jakša has pressed us into service. Jasna is switching up the eggs. I am slicing the onion. Jakša tackles the aubergine. Within minutes the meal has taken shape. An omelette, into which the salami has been diced, cooked quickly in olive oil and topped with parsley. A salad of purple-streaked crescents of onion and chopped green parsley drenched in a dressing of olive oil, wine vinegar, salt and a large amount of black pepper. Cut into long thin strips that have been dipped in olive oil, drawn through a bowl of sesame seeds, then fried, the aubergine is presented as a hot side dish. It is scarcely a loaves-and-fishes transformation and the portions are small. But there is, as there always is in Croatia, plenty of bread and wine. The chunks cut roughly from a gnarled loaf are fresh and filling. The local white wine, golden in colour, is viscous and potent. Since there is only one wine-glass available we drink from used yoghurt cartons. The plates are chipped, the cutlery varied, the shiny table-cover ringed with the memories of previous meals. Ours is delicious.

As we eat and drink together, we learn more about the Kalogjeras and about Jakša in particular. The house in Blato where he and his brothers were born and raised, still there but no longer wholly in the family's ownership; school in Korčula and university in Zagreb; work as a civil engineer all over

Yugoslavia; marriage, the children's early emigration, his divorce; the brothers' return to Prižba and Prigradica. We do not ask about the war, but that, too, is part of the story: the help Jakša gave to two Jewish families enabling them to escape from Zagreb to the more benign Italian occupation in Dalmatia, his betrayal and subsequent months of incarceration in the notorious Jasenovac concentration camp, the efforts – ultimately successful – made by Marko to gain his release. It is a Central European life with its personal joys and sadnesses and more than its fair share of drama and tragedy. Yet there is something strange about the way the story unfolds. Jakša remembers without evident emotion – no nostalgia, no regrets, no affirmation, no recrimination – it is as if what had occurred, however unique to his experience, were outwith his control, as inexorable as the impersonal measure of the days, months and years that have passed. Gradually, it becomes clear in conversation that what lies behind this calm retrospective acceptance is not the religious resignation of old age, still less the unredeemed party member's stubborn belief in philosophical determinism. The explanation is (or so it seems to me) more naïvely fatalistic, sadder than late-onset piety and odder than any pig-headed addiction to discredited politics. It is there in the Zodiac signs, symbols and planetary tables on the wall and, as I see now, in the books and almanacs piled on the floor. Jakša is consumed with a passion for astrology.

At first I am intrigued by this unexpected faith. How strange the symbolism on the walls around us is, abstract and pictographic, colourful and complex. How arcane, almost hieratic, Jakša's language becomes as his confessional continues. How confidently he moves from chart to chart tracking the fated course of his life with quasi-religious intensity. I cannot take it seriously, this irrational star-struck trust in cosmic destiny, but I am disarmed by his assurance and ask no questions. Debate would be more than discourtesy. And so, concealing as best I can my smug amusement at what I take to be the absurdity of it all, I listen in polite silence.

But if my detachment is first passive and perhaps also patronising, it soon becomes speculative and critical. How was it possible that an educated man, the kind of man continental

Europeans call 'an intellectual', could so completely espouse this astrological mumbo-jumbo? A hobby, perhaps. Prigradica is a quiet place given to drowsy indifference and one might just as well infer fortunes from the movements of the heavens as idle away the days in the unfulfilling oblivion of erotic novels, wine or sleep. But Jakša's is a deep-rooted obsession, addictive, life-possessing. What had fostered it? Did it begin over seventy years ago when the boy from Blato lay dreaming in the family vineyard gazing up into black summer nights star-pricked with the glimmer of hidden worlds? Or was this the zeal of provincial Croat catholicism running to superstitious excess as readily as it so often did to chauvinism? Had the long lonely years that followed the loss of wife and children brought this charming old man to senescent foolishness? Tempting to guess but impossible to tell. On he went, the impish smile all the time more engaging and persuasive than the litany of his convictions. No journey without a favourable augury. No friendship without some zodiacal affinity. A life circumscribed by portent and presentiment. It was hard to believe his boast that, as an independent consultant, he had only ever hired those engineers whose star-signs matched the omens of the moment. It was as if in building a new professional team, as much on the foundation of each individual employee's horoscope as his or her *curriculum vitae,* he were repeating that combination of divination and common sense invoked by the Romans in the inauguration of a new camp or settlement – though it had to be admitted that Jakša's method of taking the auspices did at least avoid the messiness of haruspicy.

I could see what was coming, sense the swing in the conversation away from the particulars of Jakša's life to the generalities of the faith then back again to the personal: how would *we* score? Would some astrological bond validate and deepen the Kalogjera family friendship upon which we had presumed? I began to feel uneasy at the increasing likelihood of a psychic examination – star sign, tarot cards, the whole circus tent business. Jasna, on the other hand, was entranced.

Making my excuses that I needed some fresh air – and it was insufferably hot in the attic – I left them to it. Neither seemed put out at this somewhat abrupt leave-taking and we agreed to meet on the *riva* in half-an-hour's time. From the half-landing I looked back. A pool of sunlight spilled onto the two figures seated opposite each other at the little makeshift table below the roof. For a moment, a Vermeer-like stillness of light and shadow transfigured the attic. And then I was swallowed up in the gloom of the boathouse below. Out on the sparkling quayside I stood for a long time looking down into the dark water, now watching the shoals of tiny fish sweeping over the sea-bed below, now twinned in reflection, the mirror melting on the surface. It occurred to me that, had Jakša asked, I should have to have owned that I was a Gemini.

Two hours later we were on our way home. We had scarcely spoken since thanking Jakša for his hospitality and for the bottle of his *travarica* rolling behind us on the back seat of the car. But now, halfway between Čara and Pupnat, we had reached one of the island's few straight stretches of road. I made myself more comfortable in my seat, regripped the steering wheel and put my foot down.

'Well, what did he say?'

'What do you mean, what did he say?'

'I mean what did you talk about after I left?'

'Mmm…'

'Did he read you fortune?'

'It wasn't like that. It was different. It was…'

I let her think. Below us to our right, far out across the grey glaze of the sea, lay the silhouettes of Lastovo and Mljet, veiled in the late afternoon heat, their island landscapes as distant, mysterious and ill-formed as Jasna's thoughts. Minutes passed. The road began to climb and bend again. Down to the south I caught a glimpse of a tiny blue bay remote and beautiful under the wooded hills – Pupnatska Luka. Jasna saw it too. Stirring from her reverie, she looked young. I fancied that, like me, she was remembering how years ago we had clambered down through the forest to swim in that golden pebbled water. But when she spoke her tone was troubled.

'The strangest thing,' she said, pausing as if unsure whether to go on. 'Jakša told me his grand-mother was Cancer too. Born on the same day as me.'

'Coincidence,' I said dismissively. And then I remembered the finger-tip caress in the graveyard.

THE OLD LADIES OF
DUBROVNIK

'A pretty girl in Dubrovnik is called skladna; *this not only means she's physically attractive, but also that she has her own harmony with her surroundings, with both the City and the landscape.'*

*Božidar Violić
1993*

What is it about old ladies? Am I somehow subject to some aberrant delusion? Gerontophilia? Is that the right word? If it is, then its multi-syllabled ugliness sounds condemnatory enough. Yet this is not an obsession; I simply like old ladies. I find some of them alarmingly attractive. Not all, of course. No, only those who seem to possess – what shall I call it – a certain presence, a kind of physical self-awareness. Surely this is not some deviant phase of my own ageing. Think thirty, I often tell myself, dismissing as best I can the depressing limitations of the years, and the amazing thing is that I can still convince myself. But perhaps there is a penalty to be paid for this persuasion. Or is it some harmless compensatory thrill that time affords its long-term addicts? The thrill is still physical; something to do with the eyes, the voice, the skin, above all the posture. I think of a Scottish friend in her nineties who, walking with a stick, never forgets to stiffen her body with feminine poise and pride. I remember one of Lumbarda's loveliest women, *baba* Katica, Niko's mother, who kept that same erect carriage to the end. And Jasna, my wife – almost an old lady?

Then, too, there is Mrs Kralj. Gospoda Kralj – *teta* Marija, we would like to call her, for we see her as a favourite aunt, but fear that were we to do so we should break the bounds of respect. She is over eighty but her skin is unlined, milky white and unblemished, touching cool and fresh on the cheek when we meet and kiss – with due restraint. She is not tall, not stooped, and though she walks with a straight-backed elegance she walks slowly for her knees are now arthritic; this the ambivalent legacy of a life in folk dancing. Like almost every Croatian woman of every age, her hair is dyed; it's a dark, earthy brown with a faint sheen of auburn, almost outrageously daring for her years but at the same time defiant and unequivocally feminine. Nor does she dress in black though she has long been a widow. She is our landlady in Dubrovnik.

When we visit the city, as we do every time we are on Korčula, we rent one of her spotless rooms. The house, which is not large – three storeys high, three small rooms on each level – is tightly wedged into the irregular street wall of Od Tabakarija, a narrow alley in the dense network of lanes that lies below the Pile gate just outside the western walls of the Old Town. The area is known as Brsalje. It's an intimate, almost secret neighbourhood which even in the late 1800s still housed centuries-old weavers' workshops, dyers' yards, a tannery and a soap factory. Now it's a quieter, lazier place frequented by colonies of foraging cats, little old ladies climbing the steps to and from the city, and the occasional tourist lost or curious. Below the busy road that leads over the hill to Lapad and the city's modern port at Gruž, the old houses tumble down to the sea around two picturesque coves dramatically divided one from the other by the towering, rock-curtained crag of Fort Lovrijenac. A green cushion of pine trees softens the skyline along the rising ridge that links the town's orange-tiled roofscape to the gaunt, grey-golden walls of the fortress above, walls that in places are as much as twelve metres thick. To the west, under the precipitous back of the Danče promontory, a deep-water creek pulls the sea's slow surge onto a small shingle beach; a handful of swimmers – and there are not many who know of this hidden inlet – take the afternoon sun before it disappears behind the cliffs. On the fortress's eastern side is a tiny harbour protected from the Adriatic swell by a barrier of random rocks that rise out of the sea between Lovrijenac and the immense cylindrical bulk of Fort Bokar on the western perimeter of the Old Town walls. A number of small boats used by the local fishermen bob at the jetty, though more – or so, it sometimes seems – upturned and half painted, litter the quayside. Raised a metre or two above the water's edge, the tables on the open terrace of the *Orhan* Restaurant, lined up in regular rows and neatly laid with cutlery and glassware ready for the evening, reproach this attractive disorder. A ramp runs up from the quay into Od Tabakarija. Less than fifty metres away Mrs Kralj's house juts into the narrow street.

We have left our car under the sun up on Danče. It is all but impossible to find a parking place in Dubrovnik unless one can beat both rush hour and tourists by being on the prowl at the crack of dawn and this hilltop spot, rutted, dusty, sun-scorched and untended, has little to commend it beyond its proximity to our room (Mrs Kralj's house is no more than a ten-minute walk away, downhill) and the fact that most tourists don't know of its existence – it is both difficult to find the entrance to the lane that leads to it and even more difficult to negotiate the lane's narrow cranked course. This invisibility and inaccessibility means there is always a chance that there will be a space and it is this that makes the dust, the risk and the final struggle back up the hill worthwhile.

Mrs Kralj has made us coffee; Turkish coffee, of course. With what seems an almost ritualistic care she spoons a little of the froth from the enamelled coffee pot into each of our cups then pours the dark treacly liquid. It tastes good and strong, like gritty espresso, bitter but sweet from just the right amount of sugar she has added during the boiling process. There's cake, too; wedges of a light sponge-cake made with ground walnuts. Mrs Kralj takes neither coffee nor cake and I have the embarrassing impression that this is because she thinks it would be impolite for her to eat or drink with her guests and, though she sits with us, keen to hear news of friends on Korčula, she is careful, too, to keep her chair marginally but deferentially distant from the edge of the table.

These forgotten courtesies have an odd effect on us. At first ill-at-ease and more than a little disturbed to be treated so graciously by someone whose age and manner should command *our* respect rather than the other way round, we nevertheless soon feel ourselves honoured by such simple acts of kindness and esteem. A consciousness of the privilege it is to be a guest in this home overcomes our embarrassment and it occurs to me that this civility, too, is part of the beguiling charm of not a few old ladies.

A shuttered window to the street slices the fierce afternoon light in zebra diagonals falling across the walls. The little lace-covered table at which we are seated takes up most of the room. This is Mrs Kralj's living-room and the main apartment on the ground floor of the house but it's still a small space. It serves as bedroom, too, and on the low upholstered couch that lies along one wall cushions and rug have been hastily tidied; like everyone else in town – except, of course, the tourists – she has been sleeping through the early afternoon heat. Above the couch are two pictures banded with sunlight and shadow. Not pictures, in fact, but framed reminders of Mrs Kralj's past, part of the traditional costume she must have worn in her folk-dancing days: embroidered ribbons from the Konavle region south of Dubrovnik. On another wall a pencil portrait recaptures her youthful beauty. But the signs and solaces of old age are more in evidence: a missal lying open on the sideboard, photographs of grandchildren, a shelf of books (some, in German and English, evidently left by her guests), a picture of the pope taken when he was in Dubrovnik on his last visit to Croatia, a large television set filling a corner of the room. A display cabinet, its glass, dark-stained ash and chrome fittings combined with the outmoded confidence of nineteen-sixties' design, holds family treasures. A dinner service. Gold-rimmed Bohemian glassware. Some Meissen plates. A few faded wedding favours. All frozen in memory's aspic.

But Mrs Kralj is interested in the present too. Is Korčula busy? How are all the members of the Batistić family? Our own children – are they well? And their children? How many now? Will they come to Croatia soon? How long will we stay this time? Two months – three? Why don't we stay longer in Dubrovnik? Two nights are not enough. A pity to miss the chamber music concert in Sveti Spas (the Church of the Holy Saviour) later in the week. But at least we'll be able to visit the exhibition of architectural drawings in the Sponza Palace. More coffee?

We answer as best we can, speaking with deliberation and what we hope is precision, not from any patronising concern for the deafness or slowness of old age but (for Mrs Kralj hears well and is altogether quick-witted) out of respect and the corresponding desire we feel to make the effort to be as correct with our Croatian as we possibly can be. We take care to use the polite second person plural 'you'. We try hard to get the cases right – adjectives and nouns, singulars and plurals. And we remember, too, to enquire after health and family, to ask if the season has been a good one and if the town's economy continues to recover. We express our thanks. And yes, we'll make a point of seeing the Sponza show. But, no, no more coffee.

Later, up in our bedroom on the top floor, I marvel once more at this old woman who has so many times welcomed us with coffee and cake. Can she really be in her eighties? She seems not old but... ageless. In all the years we have been coming here she has been the same, a gracious lady able to assimilate and annul the distresses of time in a deeper inner dignity – much like the city I can see through the open window. It is now ten years since, armed with the indispensable recommendation of a mutual friend, we first pressed the doorbell on Od Tabakarija. Mrs Kralj is unchanged. It is more than forty years since, at the end of a gruelling two-day bus journey that began in Skopje and took us over the mountains of Montenegro, we first arrived above Dubrovnik, astonished by sea and stone. And Dubrovnik, too, is the same. Despite the trauma of bombardment, the Old Town has not lost its loveliness. Here and there a raddled rooftop complexion of bright new terra-cotta tiles lays a brash cosmetic over past pain but, in the streets beneath, the stone face of the city looks as it always looked, calm, serene, beautiful. Tomorrow we will see it all again. For the moment, looking out from the bedroom window down the worn stepped paving of Od Tabakarija and across the little harbour, I gaze at the city's ancient carapace: stretches of the western fortifications, much of it the work of the fifteenth century Florentine architect Michelozzo Michelozzi, drawn in a stone curtain from the great drum of Fort Bokar up over the cliffs; these walls, too, as beautiful, as ageless.

Next morning we are closer to the walls. A short walk down past the scattered harbourside boats and up the stepped lane by the little Church of St George (Sveti Juraj) has brought us to the urban bustle at Pile. Crowds are streaming to and from the Old Town. Orange-liveried buses bearing the municipal motto *Libertas* release their stifled passengers into the throng before wheeling around the square to head back to the western suburbs. Multi-coloured tourist coaches manoeuvre for space to disgorge their groups. Taxis wait; short of business at this time of day, their drivers sleep or smoke. On the pavement, at the approach to the Pile Gate, the rows of parked scooters and motor cycles grow steadily longer, steel and chrome foreworks to the fortified city across the moat.

We are having breakfast – coffee, *croissants* and honey – under the trees on the streetside terrace of the *Kavana Dubravka*. There is, it always seems to me, something thoroughly Gallic about this place. It is not merely that watching life go by here at Pile gives one the pleasant sated sense of the world-weary *boulevardier* but that there is a distinctly Parisian feel about this shaded spot with its leafy pollarded trees, gravel parade and the stone drinking-fountain over which a naked *odalisque* is poised voluptuously (not to speak of the notice in the café window that *croissants*, *brioches* and *pains au chocolat* arrive every morning by air fresh from the French capital).

Pondering these links, notional and actual, I wonder if perhaps Napoleon's General Marmont, honoured with the manufactured title *Duc de Raguse* in 1808 after French forces had forestalled the Russians in bringing to an end the city republic's centuries of independence, might have contrived some affinity with home. Certainly, for whatever reason, Marmont fell in love with the city. He admired and respected its beauty, considered its citizens of 'sweet disposition… industrious and intelligent' and did much to foster local culture, becoming patron of the newly created *lycée* for boys, founding elementary schools, establishing a theatre and playing a part in the publication of a Croatian grammar and a Croatian-Latin-Italian dictionary. Nor were certain decisions, driven by military expediency, without a long-term benefit to the city: it was Marmont who, intent on improving communications in the new Illyrian Provinces, began the construction of a coastal road, the forerunner of the modern *magistrala,* now such a vital artery in the economy of Dubrovnik, Dalmatia and Croatia as a whole. Could it be that the very place where we are breakfasting is part of his legacy, too? True, it does not have the full *à la française* formality of, say, the Tuileries Gardens, yet sitting here under the trees drinking the first coffee of the day it is impossible not to feel that relaxed and undeniably smug sense of civilized urban living so characteristic of French café culture. No matter that this may be no more than fancy, Marmont's brief administration left its positive mark on the city. And if the view which he later expressed in his *Memoirs*, declaring Dubrovnik to be 'an oasis of civilization amid barbarism', rang true in the pre-Congress, Balkan confusion of the Napoleonic Wars, it tolls with a more terrible truth almost two hundred years later.

But there are only a few remaining signs of the nineties' war here. A hundred metres or so up the hill from Pile the rehabilitation of the oldest hotel in Dubrovnik, the Grand Hotel Imperial, whose roof and upper storeys were badly shelled in November 1991, is still not complete. Just across the street from our table, a fine seventeenth-century patrician palace which, before the war, served as the offices of the city's tourist agency, lies empty, its symmetrical three-storey façade blinded by boarded windows. Crossing the bridge over what was once the moat but is now a pleasant tree-shaded park, we spot some patches of new stone – repairs to the moulded quatrefoils of the balustrade. The great city walls, however, inviolate still, rise above all this, magnificent.

The Pile Gate, built in 1537, commands the axis of the bridge, symmetrical and massively convex, bulging forward like some shore-defence bunker left over from World War II. Set centrally above the gate's arched entrance-way, the carved figure of Sveti Vlaho (St. Blaise) stands in a cockle-shell-canopied niche flanked by fluted pilasters. Here, as at the Ploče Gate in the east, the saint watches over all who enter and leave the Old Town. The city has long honoured him as its patron, revering too, in its very Catholic way, those anatomical relics of the Armenian martyr that first came into its possession in the late tenth century. This is the oldest surviving effigy of the saint. In his left hand he carries a model of Ragusa/Dubrovnik, his adoptive home town. His right is raised in blessing. We cross the draw-bridge and count ourselves blessed to be here again.

Through the Renaissance archway we pass into a high windowless space, a ramped courtyard, stone-flagged and stone-walled but open to the blue, swallow-swept sky above. Still only on the threshold of the old city, it is as if we are in some kind of time-lock, held in an ante-chamber to the past. Against the stone, a crowded staircase dog-legs to the left dropping to a second archway in the inner wall, older and smaller. Through this lower, cramped defile a relentless stream of people ebbs and flows. Escaping the crush, a few turn away from the stair preferring instead a slower stroll over the paved inclines of the ramp. But we go with the flow, caught up as always in careless tumbling anticipation. And, as always, we are not disappointed.

We reach the foot of the stairs, turn right under the Gothic arch of the inner gate and there it is. Placa. The Stradun.

This is one of the great city streets of the world, instantaneous in its impact, all the more so for its sudden revelation. And it is *a street*. It does not aspire to grandeur. There is neither the metropolitan scale nor the Parisian elegance of the Champs Elysées, none of the boulevard bustle of Václavské náměstí in Prague, still less the absurd bombast of Buenos Aires' Avenida de 9 Julio. Here, on the contrary, there is both modesty and intimacy. Yet this reserve is unequivocally urban and urbane. No architectural grandiloquence, no traffic, not a single tree, only the ubiquitous, grey-golden stone of Dalmatia, much of it from the quarries on Korčula. Stone and more stone; the marble pavements shining like golden ice. Almost everything is the work of the late seventeenth century when, after the catastrophic earthquake of 1667, the city set about rebuilding itself with pragmatic dignity. That it was built for men and women to live and work in hardly seems possible. Now and throughout the day it is crowded with strangers who will walk its length bewitched, pause for a glass of cool white wine at one of the streetside cafés, then leave to rendezvous with their air-conditioned coach for the trip back to their hotel at Lapad or Babin Kuk. Only early in the morning when the street-cleaners are finishing their work and shopkeepers begin to open their doors and these same tourists are wondering whether to turn over and miss breakfast, or later at four or five in the afternoon when school is out and floods of teenagers, noisy, a little intimidating and (both sexes) extraordinarily beautiful, make their arm-linked way home, or again, later still, at eight in the evening as the *korzo* absorbs *Dubrovčani* and *stranci* alike, only then does the city reclaim its rights to this amazing promenade.

The street is straight but not long. Not three hundred metres. At its widest, perhaps twenty; at its narrowest, about ten. Its symmetries are many and simple, yet at the same time they are subtly inflected. Blocks of three- and four-storey houses are repeated and mirrored down the length of the street, eaves lines run in parallel, shadowed lanes cut into the street wall at regular intervals; every flat-fronted façade is ordered identically, its shutters green, its shopfronts formed to the same Renaissance standard, window and door under a single round-headed arch. *Or so it seems*. But though patterns recur, the houses are not all the same; gabletted dormers animate the roofscape with arbitrary frequency, here and there the eaves line jumps, all but imperceptibly the sequence and spacing of windows varies. The city's network of narrow streets and lanes, so immediately apparent, so seemingly regular, deceives the eye's desire for order, for the intersections are not all equally spaced, the alignment of the grid not always rectilineal. And at each end of the street are buildings breaking the coherence and continuity of the otherwise unassuming residential scale. On the north side, close to the inner gate at Pile is the votive Church of the Holy Saviour (Sveti Spas), said to have survived the earthquake of 1667 because its builders mixed the breast milk of Dubrovnik mothers in their mortar. Beside its vaguely Venetian façade, the long gaunt wall of the Franciscan Church stretches east, relieved only – but wonderfully – by a pilastered portal surmounted by a moving Pietà carved by the Petrović brothers in the fifteenth century. At the far end of the street is the Baroque Church of the city's patron St Blaise (Sveti Vlaho) and across from it the Sponza Palace pushing its five-bay portico into the throng. Of all Dubrovnik's buildings none is more Venetian-Gothic in character than the Sponza – but only at first floor where two traceried, ogee-arched openings flank a large tripartite window carved with trefoils and quatrefoils. After the earthquake, this, the early sixteenth-century work of Ragusa's municipal architect and engineer, Pasko Miličević, was restored along with the storey above and the portico below, both of which are, in fact, classical in style. At each end of the street too there is a tower, the one similar to the other, yet different: in the west, the fifteenth century *campanile* of the Franciscan Monastery; in the east, the more minaret-like city bell-tower, also of the fifteenth century, though completely rebuilt in 1929. And at each end of the street there is breathing space. Below Pile, a square opens around the brick-domed drum of the Large Onofrian Fountain, while opposite the Sponza Palace a second, more elongated public space, Luža, spills south to the Rector's Palace and the Cathedral.

We pause with the teenagers and backpackers to drink at the Fountain. Cool in its curving shadow we watch the parade on the Stradun; tourists in the sunlight, locals making more purposeful progress along the shaded southern side of the street. High above us on the walls the parapet walk is busy with people setting out on their elevated circuit of the city. Others are struggling up the frighteningly steep staircase that climbs to the wallhead. There is an access point here at Pile, one of only three, and in the wedge-shaped inshot between the walls and Sveti Spas the queues have started. I look across at the little church, its quaint, far from scholarly façade dwarfed between the Franciscan Monastery and the still higher city walls. I look and I remember how it was in 1992 less than nine months after the city's fiercest bombardment. Boarded up in heavy protective timbers, only the segmental pediment and flanking quadrants at the top of the gable betrayed it as a place of worship. And hung across the hidden façade, a white banner with the city's plea to the world painted in achingly polite English – NO WAR ANY MORE PLEASE.

That year we had come to Dubrovnik by ship. Not by choice – though there is no better way to arrive in the city than to sail into Gruž harbour – but out of necessity. It was September then too. The worst of the city's war was over; had it not been we should never have made the trip from the island safety of Korčula. Even so, the front line was only a few kilometres to the south. On the northern side of the city, the land route from Ston at the head of the Pelješac peninsula, where only nine months earlier the plundering advance of the Yugoslav army forces had been halted, was open but still mined and under military control. The only way in was by sea. If we took the mid-day boat south we could see the stricken city and return to Korčula when it sailed north again on the following morning. We suppressed our *voyeur*'s shame.

At Gruž the *Slavija* docked in front of the shattered port. The military were in control. In the half-destroyed port offices we had to explain ourselves and show our passports, although we had not, of course, crossed any border. Then we were in.

Along the quayside motor boats and yachts lay partially submerged, many peppered with bullet holes, some sunk, all abandoned as an irrelevance in the face of more pressing concerns. Left at the roadside, burnt-out cars had suffered the same fate. There was little traffic; a municipal bus with its poignant *Libertas* livery, some lorries, the occasional private vehicle. People on the streets were just as rare. There were no tourists and no old ladies with rooms to rent. Had we known Mrs Kralj at that time we should have felt less helpless. As it was, we were suddenly alone.

Unsure whether a bus would come, despair threatening, we started to walk towards the Old Town. Amazingly, a taxi passed, drew to a halt and offered to take us to Pile. No doubt we paid too much. I can't recall. What does remain is the memory of a wounded Dubrovnik, a half-deserted city in silent pain. The afternoon heat was as normal. As always palm trees and pittasporum greened the streets. But much was an affront. Pock-marked stone, scarred stucco, scorched timber, buildings that had collapsed in a tangled confusion of concrete, steel and tumbled orange roofing tiles. At the main intersections, sandbagged check-points. Groups of soldiers. The absence of crowds. Even at Pile there were few people about. The same on the Stradun.

Whenever we could, we asked if there were rooms to be had. Nothing. Taking pity on us, two women dressed in black – whether old or recent widows, we could only guess – suggested a hotel. But which hotel? Only one was doing business, the Hotel Argentina. We knew it to be expensive – and some distance uphill well beyond the Ploče Gate.

As we walked the length of the Stradun, the street seemed barely alive, eerie in its desolation and silence. A few figures hurried by or crossed from the darkness of one lane to another; no-one strolled.

At Luža, where the street ends, the façades of both the Sponza Palace and the Church of St Blaise had disappeared, still boarded up to protect their ornament and detail. Part of the balustrading of the low terrace fronting the church was in ruins. Between the two, Orlando's Column, the symbol of Ragusan freedom, had been boxed in timber as if the very idea of liberty, personified in the hidden statue of the hero of Roncesvalles, had been crated ready for despatch to safe-keeping should Dubrovnik yet fall. We walked on, through the pointed archway below the clock tower and up between the Dominican Monastery and the city walls to reach the Ploče Gate. Once out beyond the walls the sense of claustrophobia which had gripped

211

us in Stari Grad eased. Through the courtyards of the old Lazaretto we could see the sea and offshore the green island of Lokrum. The air seemed fresher.

But still there was destruction. The Excelsior Hotel, though it had escaped the kind of bombardment from the sea that had left the Libertas Hotel on the other side of the Old Town no more than a charred tier of concrete slabs, was out of commission, its own layer cake of continuously windowed storeys comprehensively shattered by shell blasts. Finally, further up the hill, we came to the Argentina.

'Are you reporters? Which agency?'

'No. No, we're… tourists', I replied, unable to say the word without imagining inverted commas.

The receptionist gaped. He found it hard to believe us. Almost ashamed, we managed a smile and launched into an explanation of where we had come from and why. It would only be for a night. He told us that almost the entire hotel had been given over to refugees and that only one floor of the hotel was functioning normally. But he found us a room.

I don't remember much about our stay. There was little to do but pass the time in our room where the only alternative to the view from the window or balcony was some Italian TV, snowy and incomprehensible. We ate, of course. The restaurant in use was small, the dining room of the rather select Villa Ursula attached to the hotel. There we spent much of the evening observing our fellow diners, correspondents and photographers covering the ongoing war for various agencies and newspapers. We recognized none of them but consoled ourselves with the thought that since we were now on our second bottle of Postup they might take us for their own kind and wonder just exactly who *we* might be. Perhaps they did, perhaps not. As we drank more of the wine it ceased to matter.

Later that night we were awakened by an explosion. We had no idea what or where it was. We ran out onto the balcony but were none the wiser. Back in bed we lay closer together. At breakfast no one volunteered an explanation and we made a point of not inquiring.

That morning we retraced our steps, took photographs and strove to fix images of the abused city in our mind's eye. Things looked better in the early sunlight but not enough to make us want to stay. It was a long walk to Gruž but we reached the quayside in good time. It was as well, for the *Slavija* was crowded with travellers. Many were refugees from the city or from the devastated area of Konavle to the south; some sailing north to stay with friends or relations until it was wise to return, others leaving for good. We had friends who had already chosen to start a new life on Korčula so traumatised were they by three months spent intermittently in caves while the city was under fire from land or sea or both. It was a strange journey: we, no better than prurient tourists, in the company of hundreds whose lives were one way or another in crisis, and all of us steaming through Adriatic scenery whose untouched beauty set against the ravaging events of the past year seemed as much an indictment as an irrelevance.

Back in Lumbarda that night we sat round the Batistić table as we so often did. We had a story to tell. It seemed odd that we should be describing the state of the city, yet it was we who had been there. We recounted everything. When it came to the midnight explosion, Nebojša smiled wryly. 'Ah! Dubrovnik nights', he said.

The memory of that 1992 visit haunts our every re-acquaintance with Dubrovnik. Not morbidly, no negative response triggered by personal pain or loss or even the bittersweet sight of reconstructed stone; passing through the Pile Gate, we do not fall prey to malign depression. Unlike many *Dubrovčani* whose months under siege have left them with deeper and more permanent scars than those inflicted on the roofs and walls around them, for us that brief experience of the desolate city, seen in selfish safety – even the mysterious explosion heard at distant remove from the months-long ordeal of bombardment suffered by the inhabitants – seems to have intensified our pleasure in its restored life. Walking with the crowds on the Stradun, we are again aware of that joy. The scale of the street, the modesty of its architecture, the continuities of stone and style, all seem attuned to the most civilized urban culture. It is as if the original builders, chastened by the destructive forces of nature so manifest in the earthquake of

1667 and compelled to economies, had eschewed all pomp and pretension, choosing instead to shape the fabric of the rebuilt city with simple measured reserve. That the streets and lanes of this recreated Ragusa should more than three hundred years later survive the assault of spiteful barbarism makes it a place doubly precious. Do we sense this? I look at the people passing, at the busy café tables, and wonder. Perhaps we do, perhaps they and we would not be here were it not that, however unsuspecting, we respond to the city's calculated magic, its inbuilt respect for civic life and human dignity. I feel a little humbled at this thought, embarrassed even that the city should think so well of us. Like taking coffee with Mrs Kralj.

It's difficult not to linger, the temptation to spend the day in one café after another watching the world go by all but irresistible. The city is seductive. Truth to tell, that is what brings us back every year, it's why we're here again now, to fall under the spell of sun-polished stone and feel ourselves again, if only briefly, citizens of this most beautiful of city states.

So we find ourselves under the striped awnings on the terrace of the *Gradska Kavana* feigning patrician *savoir vivre*. It helps that the terrace is raised a few steps above street level, that the low stone balustrade implies a certain social distinction between us and the passing crowd, that the waiters go about their business with practised deference, and that those who sit at the tables around us are in the main *Dubrovčani* of a certain age. A white-haired gentleman, whose stick lies across the chair beside him, puts down his copy of *Vjesnik* to allow a waiter to serve him with a glass of what looks like Prošek. Alone too, a woman, perhaps in her fifties, lights up a cigarette; with studied pretension she preens the fall of her long black hair, holding her cigarette at arm's length between elegant red-nailed fingers. Catching my eye, she crosses her legs. I look away, turning my attention to the older ladies seated at the back of the terrace. I count nine of them: smartly dressed, *bürgerlich*, evidently regulars, they drink their coffee or tea with lemon, nibble at their *schlag*-topped cakes, with an unhurried proprietorial confidence. I have the feeling that they, perhaps more than anyone, certainly more than the tribes of tourists who pass by shepherded in 'follow-my-leader' flocks, are at ease with their surroundings. They belong. Comfortable, convivial, civilized, they are the very personification of the city

It occurs to me that just as each morning the old ladies take their places on the terrace of the *Gradska Kavana* with casual regularity, so our day in Dubrovnik takes its course, regular too – and as enjoyably desultory. We have our routine but, lazily pursued, it has none of the peremptory purposiveness of the sightseer. Long ago we ceased to be tourists. We have walked the walls. We have 'done' all the churches: been intrigued by the plan of St Blaise with its nine-square symmetry, disappointed by the airy but dull Baroque of the Cathedral, humbled in the high stark silence of the Dominican Church. We have paused for breath on the Jesuit steps that spill in convex waves down into the market from the dusty square below the great Baroque façade of Pozzo's Church of St Ignatius. We have seen the Sephardic synagogue, little more than an upper room but still enriched with its original seventeenth-century furnishings. We have smelt incense and sadness in the Orthodox church. We have lingered in the cloistered courtyard of the Franciscan monastery enjoying its leafy shade. We have marvelled at the intricacy of the carved capitals on the arcaded portico to the Rector's Palace, stood under blue skies in the *cortile* of the Sponza. We have heard Mozart from the boxed balcony of the Marin Držić theatre, listened to the Sorkočević quartet – piano, flute, violin and bass – in the candle-lit interior of Sveti Spas. We have stumbled through the submarine gloom of the aquarium, counted the models of Clyde-built ships in the maritime museum, and, headachey with sun and tiredness, we have bought our paracetamols at the oldest pharmacy in Europe. Yet after all this, our guide-book agenda exhausted, we are still coming – again and again – not to identify the trees but simply to walk in the wood. And we have learned to walk slowly, to savour the city with all the idle assurance of the *flâneur*, going nowhere, enjoying everywhere.

There is, of course, some sort of sequence to our day. Breakfast *en plein air* at Pile. The slow meandering stroll along the Stradun. Coffee on the terrace of the *Gradska Kavana*, still in the morning shade. Perhaps there is an exhibition to see. Then

215

there is lunch, not much but wine enough to ease us into siesta sleep back at Mrs Kralj's. A late afternoon swim. A shower. And then, with the low evening sun behind us, we are back on the Stradun, caught up in the warmth of the *korzo*. A glass of Pošip, streetside. Dinner. Bed.

Today's exhibition is in the Sponza Palace. Leaving the old ladies with a smile and an involuntary inclination of the head that elicit in response what I fancy to be a mildly flirtatious raising of eyebrows, I find I have taken Jasna's hand as if with this simple act of fidelity we might win the passing affection of the city's matronly muses. Content in our intimacy, we walk back across Luža straight towards the palace's arcaded portico.

Not for the first time, I feel ill-at-ease with this full-frontal approach. Something is not quite right. It is not that the façade manages to hold both Gothic and Renaissance forms in harmony; this in itself is a familiar enough stylistic idiosyncrasy of Dalmatian architecture. There is something more, something disturbing in the relationship of the five-bay vaulted loggia (significantly it was added to the main building before the end of the sixteenth century) and the symmetry of Miličević's earlier Gothic-Renaissance façade rising above. In fact, the five bays of the portico are not all the same. The spacing of the columns does not coincide with the balanced symmetry of the upper floors since the second bay from the east has been made slightly wider than the others, this in order to respond to the position of the entrance portal and the inner axis of the palace plan. Yet this subtle visual infraction seems to sharpen the perception. Once in the elongated *cortile* all is harmonious. There is a stillness and a severity in the geometry. Left and right, arcuated bay echoes arcuated bay. A hint of nave-and-aisles seems to sanctify the space, though the oblong nave is open to the sky. And while the building has never had a religious function – it was first a warehouse and customs house, incorporated a mint and an armoury, later served as a school and is now the home of the city's rich archive – around the extrados of the single wide arch that closes the far end of the atrium is carved the admonitory motto, *fallere nostra vetant et falli pondera; meque pondero cum merces ponderat ipse deus*, 'our weights neither deceive nor are deceived. When I weigh merchandise, God also weighs me'.

The Sponza holds many of Dubrovnik's archival treasures, some so valuable that only the specialist scholar may hope to see them but others that from time to time are put on public display. Today, as Mrs Kralj was so keen to tell us, a collection of architectural drawings is on show. These are the work of Lorenzo Vitelleschi, *ingegnere di seconda classe*, who came to Dalmatia with the French in 1811 and for the next twenty years left his mark on the buildings and infrastructure of the whole coastal region. As municipal architect of Dubrovnik he did much to ensure the conservation of the city's built heritage including being responsible for directing the restoration of the Rector's Palace. The framed drawings, hung on the walls of the *cortile* and in one or two of the rooms ranged along the 'side aisles', are varied in nature, some technical, some more atmospheric. I find it an interesting exhibition but I doubt if Jasna does. And in this she is evidently not alone for, of those who like us have wandered in from the Stradun, barely a handful of people are intent on examining the drawings on the walls while the others, clustered in the centre of the atrium, are admiring the building around them. As always, beside architecture itself, architectural drawings seem a 'stale, flat, and unprofitable' alternative.

But there is in the Sponza a smaller, now permanent exhibition that few visitors fail to find moving. In a pair of linked rooms opening off the courtyard row upon row of portrait photographs line the walls. These are the faces of the men and boys who died in the defence of Dubrovnik during the nineties war. Each portrait is identical in size. Each is named and dated. A few remain poignantly blank. People pass through in silence. We do too.

This memory of the city's trauma stays with us as we step out from the shadows of the Sponza portico back into the mid-day bustle of the Stradun. The brightness is blinding; the reflux of irony bittersweet. A sudden surge of saddened respect makes me call to mind the scarred city we saw in 1992. But as hard as it is to recapture the experience of that brief but sombre visit made in the safe aftermath of destruction, it is so much harder to

217

conceive the terrifying reality of war, to imagine what it must have been like to be under fire in this beautiful street. Yet there, alongside the rows of portraits in those quiet Sponza rooms, were the photographs to prove it had all happened, not the least affecting the amazing last images shot by Pavo Urban: the walls hit by shelling, the old harbour ablaze, the Stradun a misty canyon choking with dust and smoke. There is no forgetting. Yet how different it all is now, the city full of sunlight and life. I think of Mrs Kralj, the tokens of the past around her, opening her home to us and speaking like the resurrected city not of yesterday but of today and tomorrow.

Remembrance fulfilled, we drift back into the present, retracing our steps through the throng. Ahead of us the sun is high over the Cathedral dome. There are tourists everywhere. They come in droves, down from the Ploče Gate or along the Stradun from Pile. They file into and out from St Blaise's Church, they crowd in front of the Rector's Palace. They have colonized the streetside cafés and on the terrace of the Gradska Kavana the waiters are effortlessly multi-lingual. The old ladies have gone.

In search of lunch we turn into the market square, Gundulićeva poljana, one of the few open spaces within the city walls. The business of the morning market – fruit, vegetables, flowers, cheese, eggs, etc. – is more or less over and most of the stall holders have already packed up. Along the edge of the square, however, the sellers of dried figs, *rakija*, lavender water and embroidery are still hoping to catch custom from the tourists. Elsewhere tables are being folded and stacked, left-over produce re-crated. A high pressure hose, turned on the square to wash away the dust and refuse of the morning, scatters the local cats leaving crowds of scavenging pigeons free to splash in the shallows. Careless of the spray, since for us, too, the light rain of water is cooling, we cross the square on the diagonal making for *Kamenice*.

There are perhaps twenty tables ranged in rows of four or five on the western side of the square. All but one or two at the edges are shaded from the sun by a canopy of brightly coloured umbrellas. The restaurant is already busy with locals and tourists, but we find a table.

'*Dobar dan. Izvolite.*' The waitress, a robust buxom woman in her fifties or sixties whose gruff manner might to some be intimidating but to us is always perversely welcoming, slaps the menus on the table and rushes on.

We need hardly look. It's a brief list with the emphasis as the name of the restaurant implies (*Kamenice* means 'oysters') on sea-food. And that's why we have come – that and the fact that many *Dubrovčani* choose to lunch here.

'*Imate male ribe?*' We ask the question as our waitress, laden with a steaming tureen of mussels, hurries past.

'*Ima*,' she cries back over her shoulder.

So we order *male ribe*, literally 'small fish', whitebait deep fried in the merest coating of flour, and with it a mixed salad, a half litre of white wine and a half litre of mineral water. The platter is heaped high and though the fish are hot from the kitchen we find it easier and altogether more satisfying to eat with our fingers every so often licking the oil and salt from our skin. The wine goes well – and quickly – so that after the first glass we change to *bevanda*, diluting our glasses with the mineral water. Even so, we order a second carafe. As they say here, 'Fish must swim'.

And so must we. But not until we have slept off the drowsy contentment of lunch back at Mrs Kralj's. It's almost three when we climb the winding stair in the little house on Od Tabakarija. The shutters are drawn and the sheets cool. I lie on the bed gazing at the ceiling listening to Jasna's breathing ebb and flow into sleep like the slow soft surge of the sea on Pržina shore. Soon I am adrift, swept out far beyond the beach. Gulls swoop above me in the sunlight. I feel the fleeting touch of invisible fish.

It is past four when I wake, saliva on the pillow, the faintest headache lingering behind my eyes. Jasna is reading, waiting, already changed into her swimsuit. Her costume is new; black and one-piece. An older woman's choice? I wonder. And then, as she turns away from me revealing a low-cut back, I'm caught up in the erotic web of thin straps that criss-cross her tanned skin. I trail my finger-tips down her spine. She stiffens slightly. I do too. She turns again and laughs.

'Time for that swim,' she says, getting up from the bed.

No more than a few metres uphill on the other side of the stepped stone street from Mrs Kralj's doorway a small arched gateway opens through the wall. It's an unprepossessing entrance; it looks private and where it leads is unclear. You might easily pass by. But, in fact, a twist and turn on the other side of the wall takes anyone inquisitive enough to explore down to a shingle beach hidden at the head of a small precipitously flanked cove. On one side Fort Lovrijenac towers above the sea; on the other, the promontory of Danče on the summit of which our car is baking.

The tiny beach is already half in shade but the sun is still warming the rocks below Lovrijenac. A dozen or so people, almost certainly all locals familiar with this secret place, are enjoying the late afternoon heat. We lay our towels on the narrow concrete terrace that at some time in the past has been crudely but conveniently laid to provide a level ledge at the foot of the cliff and then, treading gingerly on the gritty surface, make for the metal ladder that drops down into the deepening water. It's rusty and no longer fully anchored in the rock below but it holds firm as one after the other we push off towards the open sea. While Jasna swims out far enough to catch a glimpse of the walled town around the headland, I stay closer to shore, my modest breast-stroke not up to the challenge of the swell but confident enough within the calmer, to-and-fro confines of the cove. In any case, I tell myself, this is about relaxation. That languid pleasure to be had from the aimless perambulation of the city streets is as nothing compared to the exquisite freedom of the sea. I swim right and left, from sunlight to shadow, from shade to sun, tread water, dive, lie on my back, float, watch gulls and swallows, dream. Quite suddenly I am tired. A delicious fatigue sweeps over me so much so that it takes an assertion of will rather than any muscular effort to haul me up the loose ladder and out of the water. Still wet, I fall onto the towel and into sleep.

Only when I wake some twenty minutes later do I begin to take note of those around us. Croatian is the only language to be heard. Not, it's true, from the two grey-haired men who are playing chess but from almost everyone else. Engaged in their own more mysterious games, some young children, not yet school age, are shouting to one another as they run from terrace to shore and back again or leap into the water. The rest are women, well able, it seems, to keep an eye on their young charges while at the same time knitting and chatting with equal enthusiasm. A mother or two, but the majority, middle-aged or elderly, more likely grandmothers. Old ladies again! All are in swimming costumes or in some interim stage of *déshabillée*. It is all very unfashionable, entirely everyday and natural. Why should there be any reason to be at prudish pains to conceal the fact that flesh, bulging or sagging, is anything other than flesh? I am smiled at gently and I wonder if perhaps these unabashed ladies may have taken coffee earlier today on the terrace of the *Gradska Kavana*.

Three hours later in the candle-lit dusk we are eating dinner, as we often do, at *Rosarij*, a small place with half a dozen tables tucked into the lanes behind the Sponza Palace. I'm still wondering. Not so much now about the elderly bathers; that smile and a certain self-possessed dignity in their nakedness were enough to persuade me that, if these late-in-the-day swimmers were not in *fact* the same smartly-suited, respectable matrons who had earlier sipped their coffee at the *Gradska Kavana*, then let them be so in *fancy*. Yet the puzzle remains. Why do the old ladies of Dubrovnik tease me? And why is it, I wonder, that for me the muses of this beautiful city are so advanced in years?

'It's because *you*'re old.' Jasna smiling, raising her glass and mocking the sententious conversation I have forced on her throughout most of the meal.

'Old?'

'Well, aren't you? Me too. We both are.'

'Not that old,' I protest, without much conviction.

'Old enough.'

'Old enough for what?'

'Well, to want re-assurance. Some sense that age has its compensations. Dignity maybe. A kind of worn beauty. You know the clichés – the lived-in face; many a good tune on an old fiddle; all that. Dubrovnik's old. Korčula's old. We're old. You're a man, you see the city you love as a woman – *ergo*!'

Jasna pours herself another glass of wine.

I say nothing but for a long time think about what she has said.

'Maybe,' – I hesitate – 'maybe I see the city like that because I'm in love with an older woman. Reflections in a mirrored mirror.'

'Ha! Maybe.' Jasna's response is dismissive. But she fills my glass with the last of the Postup.

ENVOI

'Who among us, if he has been fortunate enough ever to have enjoyed it, does not remember with delight and longing such a simplified interval of time?'

Freya Stark
1956

Back in Lumbarda, bags packed for tomorrow's departure, I am lying dreaming on the sand at Tatinja bay. It's past four o'clock in the afternoon and the October sun is still warm. I'm alone and, but for the distant whine of a powered saw in someone's workshop, the beach is quiet. The summer visitors have gone, taking their sunshades, loungers, and bikinis with them. Like the day, the year is growing old. And so, I suppose – though I find it hard to believe – am I. It's a realization that seems now to come with every autumn, not so much a sobering thought as one inviting instant if mild inebriation. But *Feral*, the little waterfront bistro not fifty metres from where I am lying, has closed for the season. There is no chance of a carafe of *Grk* to drown my sorrows.

I'm saved from morbidity by the sound of a car coming round the point from the village. An old blue Renault is crawling along the tarmac track that rounds the bay tight to the sea's edge. Pulling in close to the houses built hard on the landward side of the road, it comes to a halt near me. With some difficulty an elderly lady dressed in a voluminous robe of turquoise blue towelling emerges from the driver's seat. I recognize Lady Veronica Maclean, widow of Sir Fitzroy and *doyenne* of the old ladies of Korčula. She is white-haired, a little stooped and somewhat hampered in her movements by what seems to be a poor hip, but her face has retained the great beauty of her youth. Stabilising herself with her walking stick, she manages to draw a succession of items from the back seat of the car – a folded sun umbrella, blow-up mattress, already inflated, towels, a wide-brimmed sun-hat, and that indispensable requisite of all ladies of a certain age, a large leather handbag. I get up to see if I can be of assistance but already she is throwing these accoutrements (all except the handbag) down onto the sand. She herself, however, does need some help and I offer her my hand to make it easier for her to cope with the few irregular stone steps that negotiate the half-metre drop from road to beach. She is grateful, gracious even, as only older women can be, and we exchange some polite pleasantries. We have spoken before, of course, meeting in Korčula on Plokata or Rampada or in the square before the Cathedral near the house where she and Fitzroy passed many summers and to which she still comes; but I have the feeling she has not come to Tatinja for company and so, having helped her raise the parasol against the late afternoon sun, I keep a respectful distance.

For some time she is content to sit in the shade with her back propped against the low wall below the roadway. She is reading a Penguin paperback, one of those green-white-and-green-covered thrillers – I can see that the pages are browning at the edges and I imagine that the book is at least fifty years old, probably a first edition. But after fifteen minutes or so even the shade has become a little too hot for comfort. With the help of her stick she gets up and, unbuttoning a few buttons, allows her robe to fall gently on to the sand. She has come prepared; she is wearing a swimsuit, modestly cut, a darkish grey in colour, though not so dark as to exaggerate the contrast with her only slightly tanned skin. For a woman of all but eighty years, clearly beset by osteoporosis, she still retains a certain aristocratic poise. Only the walking stick betrays her arthritic limitations. She needs it to reach the water – and beyond. But once through the shallows, she turns to the shore and with some bravura throws the stick back to dry land. Then she is off, swimming elegantly out into the bay, her white head no longer bowed by age.

As I watch Lady Veronica make her stately progress out into the still waters of the bay, I realise again how late in the season it is. Late for Lumbarda and late for us. We are alone, she and I; no-one else on the beach, no-one else swimming, the tiny harbour for the moment asleep, the old houses quiet. Across the channel out beyond the tree-clad back of Vrnik, sun-cast folds of shadow fall over Sveti Ilija. A pleasant solitariness intensifies the senses. It is not just the bittersweet pain that comes with age that I feel, not that despairing zest for a present ebbing away as relentlessly as the day dims, not that only, but something more, something beyond the personal, something of the spirit of the place. This – and perhaps the dawn that only the lone fisherman sees – this is when the Adriatic is at its most beautiful; the sea and the land left to be themselves, the sky suffused with a long low light, lingering and transcendent. It is as if for this hour we have been allowed to intrude; she gently stirring the flat mirroring sea, I wandering in reverie.

The stillness is warm and anodyne. With closed eyes I listen to the silence, at one with this magical place. And slowly, as the darkness burning under my eyelids clears, Korčula casts her spell. I see a sail over Knežić, hung on a wide coathanger sprit pivoting at the mast-head, the white cloth limp in the heavy air. There is no wind, yet mast and sail pass steadily toward the west. Across the water I catch the murmur of a low rhythmic beat and then, in sinister dignity, mast, sail and hidden hull emerge from behind the island. I hear the plash of oars pulling through the sea; bireme or trireme, the vessel is too distant to tell. But I see the horned prow, its painted eye watching on the water-line. I see the high upswept stern menacing like a scorpion's strike. Strangers. Antenor and his fugitive Trojans, searching for sanctuary on unknown seas? Greeks from Ionian Knidos, their gaze strained with emigrant longing? Imperial Augustus bent on destruction? Perhaps. Perhaps.

Lance-like, the ship drives on. Her eye does not blink and the tiered oars, drummed to measured power, plunge deep, dragging their white wake across the bay. Each cut marks the seconds – ten... fifteen... twenty, no more – until, under a burnished sky, she slips below Koludrt and is swallowed up in the island darkness. The western light is on fire, the sea steel, the island black.

This is how it has always been in Illyria. The islands under the mountains, the sea a highway for invader and settler, raider and refugee. Greeks and Romans, Goths and Byzantines, Venetians and Turks; they have all passed this way. But the Croats have remained, content, for more than a thousand years, to keep faith with the spirit of the place, tending the vineyards and the olive groves and fishing the sea. From stony villages hidden high in the hills they have watched the dark ships come – and they have watched them go.

The chimes of the church bell on Glavica wake me. Six o'clock. Lady Veronica has gone. So too the dream. But now the village is coming to life again. Behind me on Mala Glavica, where all summer they have been building new houses and renovating old, a cement mixer has resumed its gutteral chant. I can hear the saw again, some intermittent hammering, over all a strimmer's rasping descant. Near the slipway beyond *Feral,* someone is caulking or painting an upturned hull; another summer-long scene. Up on the terraces where the olives have begun to ripen, a family has returned to finish the day's picking; I can hear their laughter and smell the sweet smoke drifting from the fire of pruned branches. At work on the jetty, a husband and wife, a father and son, are preparing nets and lines for the night's fishing, while rounding the breakwater the first of the Tatinja boats is already heading out into the channel, the putt-putt beat of its outboard bouncing back across the water. It's time for me to go too.

I walk home up through the shadows on Mala Glavica. It's a narrow path winding uphill between high walls. Underfoot, a carpet of autumn leaves and a few of the gnarled locust nuts that have long ago fallen from the carob trees. Through gateways and gaps there are glimpses of the old and the new. Overgrown gardens staked out with the stone columns of abandoned pergolas, melancholy in the early evening light. Green-shuttered old houses, hard-edged and simple like children's drawings. New villas too: one built by Bebić's daughter Maruška and her merchant seaman husband Robert; another, with its sumptuous two-level swimming pool, on which our neighbour Marjan has laboured all summer for a rich Zagreb client. A little out of breath I reach the crest then head down again by the vineyards. The going is easier now but I take my time and, pleasantly content with my own company, decide to avoid the village centre and take the path that leads up past the Batistić house. There's no-one in Katica's garden but from behind the high wooden gate that screens the yard comes Jagoda's voice remonstrating, less than seriously I fancy, with Ante's mischief. For a moment I wonder what he might be up to – a gecko in the ironing basket, a drop of vinegar in Nikša's wine, soap in the mouthpiece of Frano's trumpet – but, loath to allow even Ante's fun to intrude on the singular contentment that has me in its spell, I walk on up the sharply steepening slope to Vela Postrana. There the lane twists and turns between the houses, rising and falling along the contour. A flight of wide-treaded steps leads down to the road that runs west to Račišće bay and on to Korčula and in a moment or two I'm home. But not quite. Beside the pomegranate tree that grows by Sveti Bartul I pause to look down over the church and the village roofs out across Prvi Žal to the sea. The flanks of Sveti Ilija are dark now but the channel below Pelješac is streaked with evening light.

It's a familiar view. Beautiful and forever enchanting and yet, in the past, for those up here on the hillside watchful and wary of strangers, a prospect sometimes tempered with dread. Roman triremes. Venetian galleys. Even now, no more than a handful of years ago when the sound of the guns at Ston carried over the water, it became again a view to die for. We see it and savour it every time we arrive by car. It's what we try to fix as a last memory each time we leave. But that's for tomorrow – and tomorrow.

A BRIEF NOTE ON
PRONUNCIATION

Although to the English speaker Croatian, with its unfamiliar words often liberally sprinkled with diacriticals, may seem baffling and daunting, in one respect at least it is relatively straightforward. Despite being a highly inflected language, it does, unlike English, follow rules as far as pronunciation is concerned. Each letter always has its sound. Learn the sounds, enunciate each, and it is possible to read more or less everything – without, of course, understanding anything.

The sounds of each letter are the same as in English with the following important exceptions –

    c   as 'ts' in English 'cats'

    č   as 'ch' in English 'church'

    ć   strictly as 'ty' in English 'future' but often indistinguishable from 'ch'

    đ   as 'dy' in English 'endure'

    h   as 'h' in English 'hot' but shading to Scots 'ch' in 'loch' before a consonant

    i   as 'i' in 'machine'

    j   as 'y' in English 'yawn'

    o   between 'aw' in English 'paw' and 'oa' in 'boat'

    r   always rolled as in Scots 'r'

    s   as 'ss' in English 'ass', i.e. always soft.

    š   as 'sh' in English 'shut'

    u   as 'oo' in English 'foot'

    ž   as 's' in English 'measure'

BIBLIOGRAPHY

This bibliography is necessarily brief and is intended to guide the reader who might want to pursue some topics further. It does not, however, include any references to the extensive literature addressing the events and issues of the 1990s war which led to the disintegration of Yugoslavia.

Ball O.	*Dalmatia*, London, 1932
Barber A.	*Visible Cities, Dubrovnik*, Budapest, 2001
Belamarić J.	*Osnutak Grada Korčule*, Zagreb, 2005
Bošnjak M. ed.	*Biseri Jadrana, Otok Korčula*, Zagreb, 2004
Brown H.F.	*Dalmatia,* London, 1925
Carter F.W.	*Dubrovnik (Ragusa), A Classic City-State*, London/New York, 1972
Denham H.M.	*The Adriatic, A Sea Guide to its Coasts and Islands*, London, 1967
Edwards L.F.	*Introducing Yugoslavia*, London, 1988
Evans A.J.	*Illyrian Letters...*, London, 1878
Foretić V.	*Otok Korčula u srednjem vjeku do 1420*, Zagreb, 1940
Freeman E.A.	*Sketches from the Subject and Neighbour Lands of Venice*, London, 1881
	Godišnjak Grada Korčule No.1, 1996 No.7, 2002

Harris R.   *Dubrovnik, A History*, London, 2003

Irving C.   *Essentially Yugoslavia*, London, 1988

Ivančević N. and Filippi Ž.

                     A Guidebook of Korčula, Split, 1984

Jackson H.   *The Shores of the Adriatic – Austrian Side*, London, 1908

Jackson T.G.   *Dalmatia, The Quarnero and Istria*, Oxford, 1887 (3 vols.)

Kalogjera B.   *Korčula, Portret Jednog Grada Istočnim Jadranu*, Korčula, 1995

Maclean F.   *Eastern Approaches*, London, 1949

Mohorovičić A.   *Architecture in Croatia*, Zagreb, 1994

Oliver J.   *Croatia* (Lonely Planet guide), Melbourne Oakland/London/Paris, 1999

Paton A.A.   *Researches on the Danube and the Adriatic...* Leipzig, 1861 (2 vols.)

Protić I.   *Župa Blato*, Blato, 1998

Violich F.   *The Bridge to Dalmatia*, Baltimore/ London, 1998

West R.   *Black Lamb and Grey Falcon*, London, 1942

Wilkinson Sir J.G. *Dalmatia and Montenegro...,*London, 1848

Korčula maintains two excellent web-sites and anyone interested in finding out more about travel to the island, accommodation, activities and events, current news, history, etc. should access.

www.korcula.net
www.ikorcula.net

The author is grateful for information gleaned from

Baničević, B., "The Cathedral and the Episcopal Treasury of St Mark",

http://www.korcula.net/history/dbozo/dbozo_katedrala.htm

Batistich, N.S., "Building and Development of Lumbarda",

http://korcula.net/history/lumbarda/history.htm